SEURAT'S CIRCUS SIDESHOW

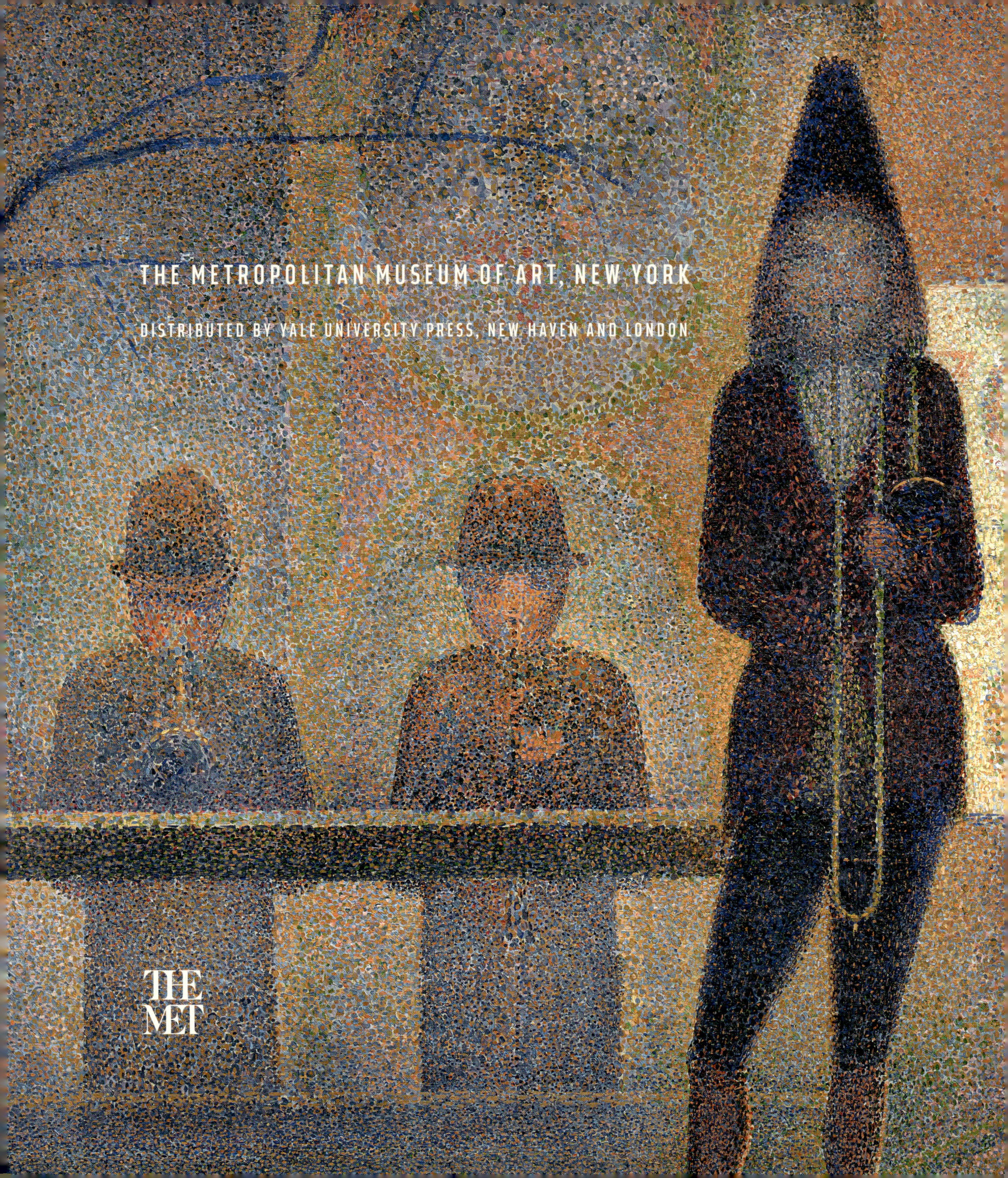
THE METROPOLITAN MUSEUM OF ART, NEW YORK
DISTRIBUTED BY YALE UNIVERSITY PRESS, NEW HAVEN AND LONDON
THE MET

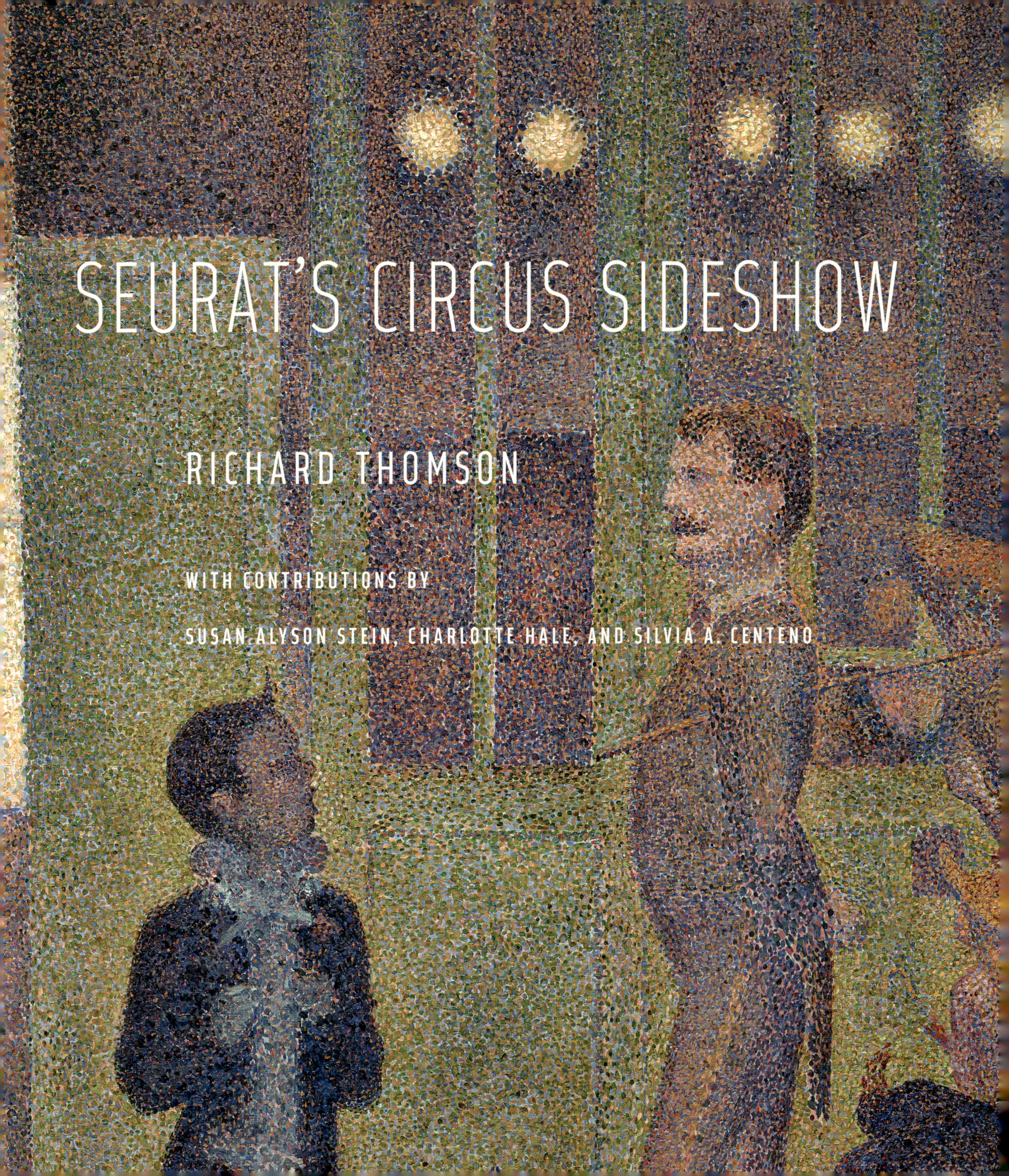

SEURAT'S CIRCUS SIDESHOW

RICHARD THOMSON

WITH CONTRIBUTIONS BY

SUSAN ALYSON STEIN, CHARLOTTE HALE, AND SILVIA A. CENTENO

This catalogue is published in conjunction with "Seurat's Circus Sideshow," on view at The Metropolitan Museum of Art, New York, from February 17 through May 29, 2017.

The exhibition is made possible by the Janice H. Levin Fund, the Gail and Parker Gilbert Fund, and an Anonymous Foundation.

This publication is made possible by the Janice H. Levin Fund.

Published by The Metropolitan Museum of Art, New York
Mark Polizzotti, Publisher and Editor in Chief
Gwen Roginsky, Associate Publisher and General Manager
 of Publications
Peter Antony, Chief Production Manager
Michael Sittenfeld, Senior Managing Editor

Edited by Livia Tenzer
Designed by Susan Marsh
Production by Sally VanDevanter
Bibliography edited by Amelia Kutschbach

Photographs of works in The Metropolitan Museum of Art's collection are by the Imaging Department, The Metropolitan Museum of Art, unless otherwise noted.

Additional photography credits appear on page 144.

Typeset in Walbaum 2010 Pro, Good News Sans, and Meta Pro
 by Matt Mayerchak
Printed on 150 gsm MagnoVol
Separations by Professional Graphics, Inc., Rockford, Illinois
Printing and binding coordinated by Ediciones El Viso, S.A.,
 Madrid, Spain

Jacket illustrations: (front and back) Details of *Circus Sideshow*
 (*Parade de cirque*), fig. 1
Frontispiece, pp. 2–3: Details of *Circus Sideshow*
 (*Parade de cirque*), fig. 1
Frontispiece, p. 6: Detail of *At the Concert Européen*, fig. 78
Frontispiece, p. 8: Detail of *Trombonist*, fig. 57
Frontispiece, p. 10: Detail of *At the Concert Parisien*, fig. 79
Frontispiece, p. 14: Detail of *Circus Sideshow*
 (*Parade de cirque*), fig. 1
Frontispiece, p. 106: Detail of *Circus Sideshow* (*Parade de cirque*), fig. 1

The Metropolitan Museum of Art
1000 Fifth Avenue
New York, New York 10028
metmuseum.org

Distributed by
Yale University Press, New Haven and London
yalebooks.com/art
yalebooks.co.uk

Library of Congress Cataloging-in-Publication Data

Names: Thomson, Richard, 1953- author. | Stein, Susan
 Alyson, writer of added text. | Hale, Charlotte, 1959- writer
 of added text. | Centeno, Silvia A., writer of added text.
 | Seurat, Georges, 1859-1891. Paintings. Selections. |
 Metropolitan Museum of Art (New York, N.Y.), host
 institution, issuing body.
Title: Seurat's Circus sideshow / Richard Thomson ; with
 contributions by Susan Alyson Stein, Charlotte Hale,
 and Silvia A. Centeno.
Description: New York : The Metropolitan Museum of Art,
 [2017] | "This catalogue is published in conjunction with
 "Seurat's Circus Sideshow," on view at The Metropolitan
 Museum of Art, New York, from February 17 through May
 29, 2017." | Includes bibliographical references and index.
Identifiers: LCCN 2016047954 | ISBN 9781588396150 (pbk.)
Subjects: LCSH: Seurat, Georges, 1859-1891. Circus
 sideshow--Exhibitions.
Classification: LCC ND553.S5 A655 2017 | DDC 759.4--dc23
LC record available at https://lccn.loc.gov/2016047954
ISBN 978-1-58839-615-0

CONTENTS

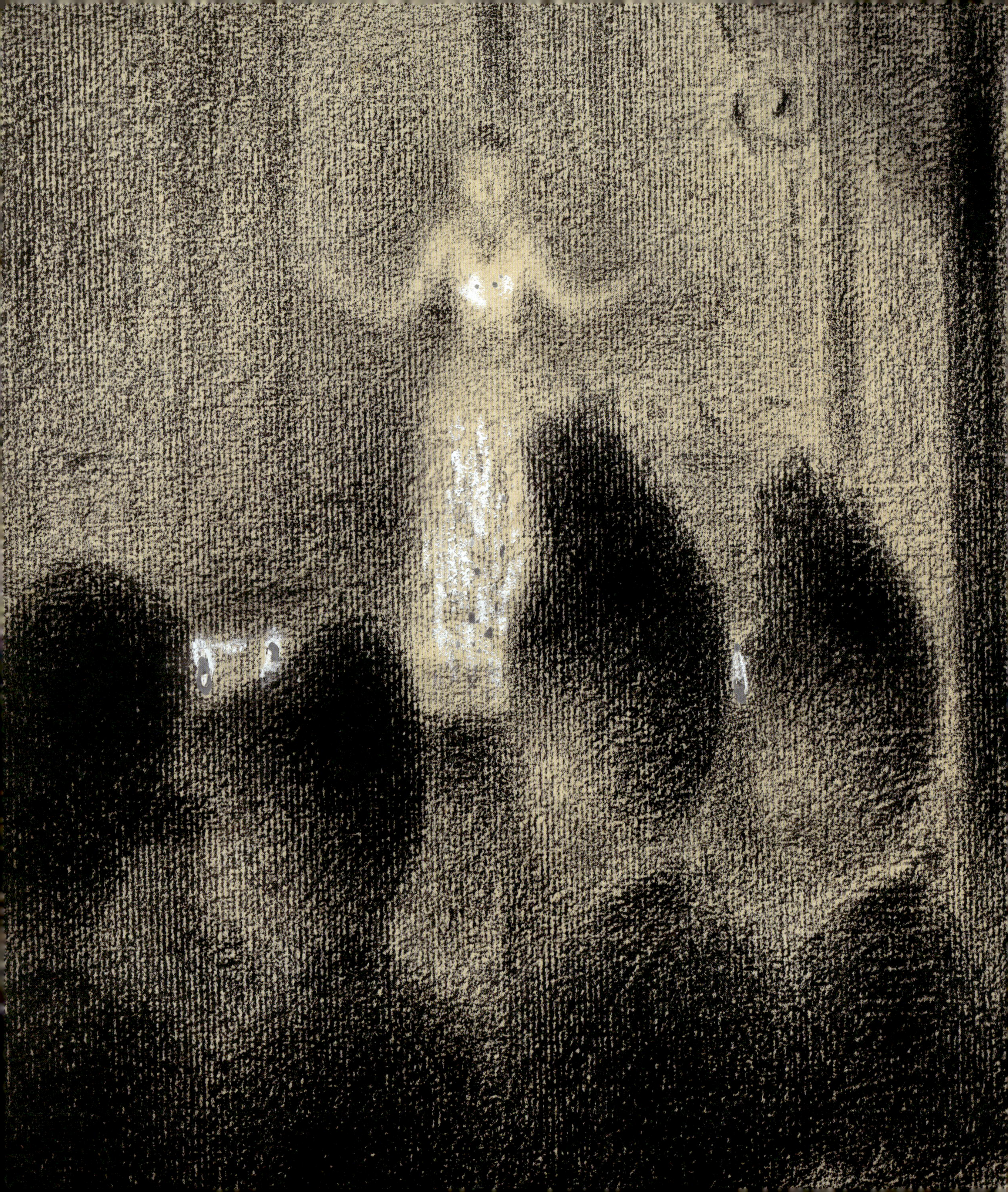

DIRECTOR'S FOREWORD

JUST OVER A QUARTER OF A CENTURY has passed since The Metropolitan Museum of Art mounted a retrospective devoted to the Neo-Impressionist painter Georges Seurat. In contrast to that expansive survey, held in 1991 to mark the centenary of his death, this occasion affords a close look at a single commanding work, *Circus Sideshow (Parade de cirque)*, which came to The Met as part of the bequest of Stephen C. Clark in 1960 and has since enjoyed a defining role in the Museum's galleries.

One of only a half dozen major figure compositions that date to the artist's short career, *Circus Sideshow* stands apart not only as Seurat's first nocturnal painting, and the first he devoted to popular entertainment, but also for its mysterious allure. From the time it debuted at the Salon des Indépendants in 1888, this nighttime scene of itinerant performers, set under the glow of nine twinkling gaslights, has intrigued critics and viewers alike. However, its heritage and legacy have yet to be fully appreciated.

The present publication accompanies an exhibition conceived by Richard Thomson, Watson Gordon Professor of Fine Art at the University of Edinburgh, and organized at The Met by Susan Alyson Stein, Engelhard Curator of Nineteenth-Century European Painting. Together they have envisioned a provocative display dependent on a carefully honed selection of works, designed to highlight—indeed, pinpoint—the genesis of Seurat's picture and the key visual sources and parallels for his invention.

Anchored by Seurat's *Circus Sideshow*, its preliminary studies, and other drawings related to its conception, the presentation explores the lineage of the *parade* subject—which depicts the sample entertainment staged outside the circus tent to entice ticket buyers—tracing the significance the theme held for artists ranging from Honoré Daumier in the mid-nineteenth century to Pablo Picasso at the fin de siècle. This rich visual narrative is supplemented by documentary material to provide a vivid sense of the seasonal fairs and traveling circuses of the day. As principal author of the accompanying catalogue, Professor Thomson has amplified telling relationships that strike a recurrent echo, bringing a wealth of knowledge and insight to the scholarship on Seurat's picture. Shorter essays by Susan Stein and by Conservator Charlotte Hale and Research Scientist Silvia A. Centeno offer two behind-the-scenes investigations of the painting: one from a historical and the other from a technical perspective. The project may be seen as a natural successor to exhibitions about other major paintings by the artist: "Seurat and *The Bathers*" in 1997 at the National Gallery, London (co-organized by Richard Thomson), and "Seurat and the Making of *La Grande Jatte*" in 2004 at the Art Institute of Chicago. The scale and scope of The Met's exhibition has been tailored to illuminate a painting that is smaller in size and evocative in subject.

Seurat's Circus Sideshow represents a concerted undertaking of many individuals, engaging the talents of various members of The Met's professional and support staff. Above all, it has enjoyed the superb cooperation of nearly fifty public and private collections (see page 11) as well as generous financial support. I would like to specially thank the Janice H. Levin Fund for making both the exhibition and this beautiful catalogue possible; the Gail and Parker Gilbert Fund and an Anonymous Foundation for their support of the show; and The Georges Lurcy Charitable and Educational Trust for its instrumental funding of educational programs.

THOMAS P. CAMPBELL
Director, The Metropolitan Museum of Art

ACKNOWLEDGMENTS

Seurat's Circus Sideshow has come to fruition thanks to the dedication and generosity of a number of individuals. In the first instance, we gratefully acknowledge the lenders to the project (see page 11), several of whom made special allowances so that key works could be shown in this unique context. Other friends and colleagues have lent their support, offering pivotal help in securing loans of interest and sharing the benefit of their knowledge, resources, and expertise. We extend our thanks to: Molly Ott Ambler, Elise Bauduin, Cristina Bausero, Marie-Sophie Boulard, Julius Bryant, Cynthia Burlingham, Emmelyn Butterfield-Rosen, Hugo Chapman, Christophe Cherix, Cyanne Chutkow, Jay Clarke, Isabelle Collet, Susan Davidson, Anne Distel, Shinichi Doi, Christophe Duvivier, Pascal Faracci, Marina Ferretti-Bocquillon, James Ganz, Christine Giviskos, Vivien Greene, Gloria Groom, Jodi Hauptman, Ruth Hibbard, Diana Howard, Jan Howard, Atsuko Kanazawa, Marjorie Klein, Dorothy Kosinski, Scott Krafft, Elizabeth Kujawski, Bernardo Laniado-Romero, Heather Lemonedes, Christophe Leribault, Raphaële Martin-Pigalle, Geraldine Masson, Edward McGee, Jocelyn Monchamp, Marina Monti, Marie-Hélène Montout-Richard, Maureen O'Brien, Mary Ann Prior, Marie Robert, Fleur Roos Rosa de Carvalho, Polly Sartori, Manuel Schmit, Innis Shoemaker, Miriam Simon, David Simonneau, Jérôme Sirdey, Kathi L. Stanley, Jonas Storsve, Valérie Sueur-Hermel, Catherine Tambrun, Belinda Thomson, Oliver Tostmann, Jocelyne Van Deputte, Marie-Paule Vial, and Catherine Whistler.

The realization of this project depended greatly on key members of The Met's staff. We are especially grateful to Research Assistant Laura Corey, who was intimately involved in all aspects of the planning of the exhibition and catalogue. Her tireless dedication and superb research, administrative, and organizational skills were an enormous asset. Conservator Charlotte Hale and Research Scientist Silvia A. Centeno contributed mightily to our technical understanding of the picture. The catalogue was produced under the direction of Mark Polizzotti and Michael Sittenfeld, sensitively edited by Livia Tenzer, and beautifully designed by Susan Marsh. We would like to acknowledge as well Gwen Roginsky, Peter Antony, Sally VanDevanter, Amelia Kutschbach, Jane S. Tai, and Anne Rebecca Blood for their indispensable work on this publication. The handsome design of the installation and its graphics are the work of Daniel Kershaw and Ria Roberts of the Design Department.

Other colleagues at The Met made valuable contributions: Keith Christiansen, John Pope-Hennessy Chairman, Rebecca Ben-Atar, Jane Becker, and Patrice Mattia of the Department of European Paintings; Michael Gallagher, Sherman Fairchild Conservator in Charge, Paintings Conservation; Marjorie Shelley, Sherman Fairchild Conservator in Charge, Paper Conservation; Nadine M. Orenstein, Drue Heinz Curator in Charge, Ashley Dunn, and Elizabeth Zanis, Department of Drawings and Prints; Dita Amory, Robert Lehman Collection; John Carpenter, Mary Griggs Burke Curator of Japanese Art, Department of Asian Art; J. Kenneth Moore, Frederick P. Rose Curator in Charge, and E. Bradley Strauchen-Scherer, Department of Musical Instruments; Kenneth Soehner, Arthur K. Watson Chief Librarian, Holly Phillips, and Mindell Dubansky, Thomas J. Watson Library; Jason Herrick, Development Department; Reagan Duplisea, Registrar; Jennifer Russell, Quincy Houghton, Martha Deese, and Linda Sylling, Exhibitions; Barbara J. Bridgers, Imaging Department; Jennifer Mock, Education Department; and Christopher A. Noey, Digital Department.

SUSAN ALYSON STEIN
RICHARD THOMSON

LENDERS TO THE EXHIBITION

PUBLIC COLLECTIONS

United States
Albany, New York State Library
Chicago, The Art Institute of Chicago
Cleveland Museum of Art
Evanston, Charles Deering McCormick Library of
    Special Collections, Northwestern University
    Libraries
Hartford, Wadsworth Atheneum Museum of Art
Los Angeles, Hammer Museum
New Brunswick, Zimmerli Art Museum
    at Rutgers University
New York, The Metropolitan Museum of Art
New York, The Morgan Library and Museum
New York, The Museum of Modern Art
New York, Solomon R. Guggenheim Museum
Philadelphia Museum of Art
Providence, Museum of Art, Rhode Island School
    of Design
San Francisco, Fine Arts Museums of San Francisco
Washington, D.C., The Phillips Collection
Williamstown, Sterling and Francine Clark
    Art Institute

France
Lyon, Bibliothèque Municipale de Lyon
Marseille, Musée Grobet-Labadié
Paris, Bibliothèque Nationale de France
Paris, Musée Carnavalet
Paris, Petit Palais, Musée des Beaux-Arts de la
    Ville de Paris
Paris, Centre Pompidou, Musée National d'Art
    Moderne/Centre de Création Industrielle
Poitiers, Musées de Poitiers
Pontoise, Musée Camille Pissarro

Japan
Kasama Nichido Museum of Art

Mexico
Mexico City, Museo Soumaya. Fundación Carlos Slim

The Netherlands
Amsterdam, Van Gogh Museum

Spain
Barcelona, Museu Picasso

Switzerland
Geneva, Association des Amis du Petit Palais

United Kingdom
London, The British Museum
London, Victoria and Albert Museum
Oxford, The Ashmolean Museum

Uruguay
Montevideo, Museo de Bellas Artes
    Juan Manuel Blanes

PRIVATE COLLECTIONS

Max N. Berry
Allan Charles, Baltimore
Mr. and Mrs. Barron U. Kidd
Scott and Nicole Mather
Mr. and Mrs. Jack Rennert, New York
Private collection, courtesy Luc Bellier
Private collection, New York
Anonymous (8)

SEURAT'S CIRCUS SIDESHOW

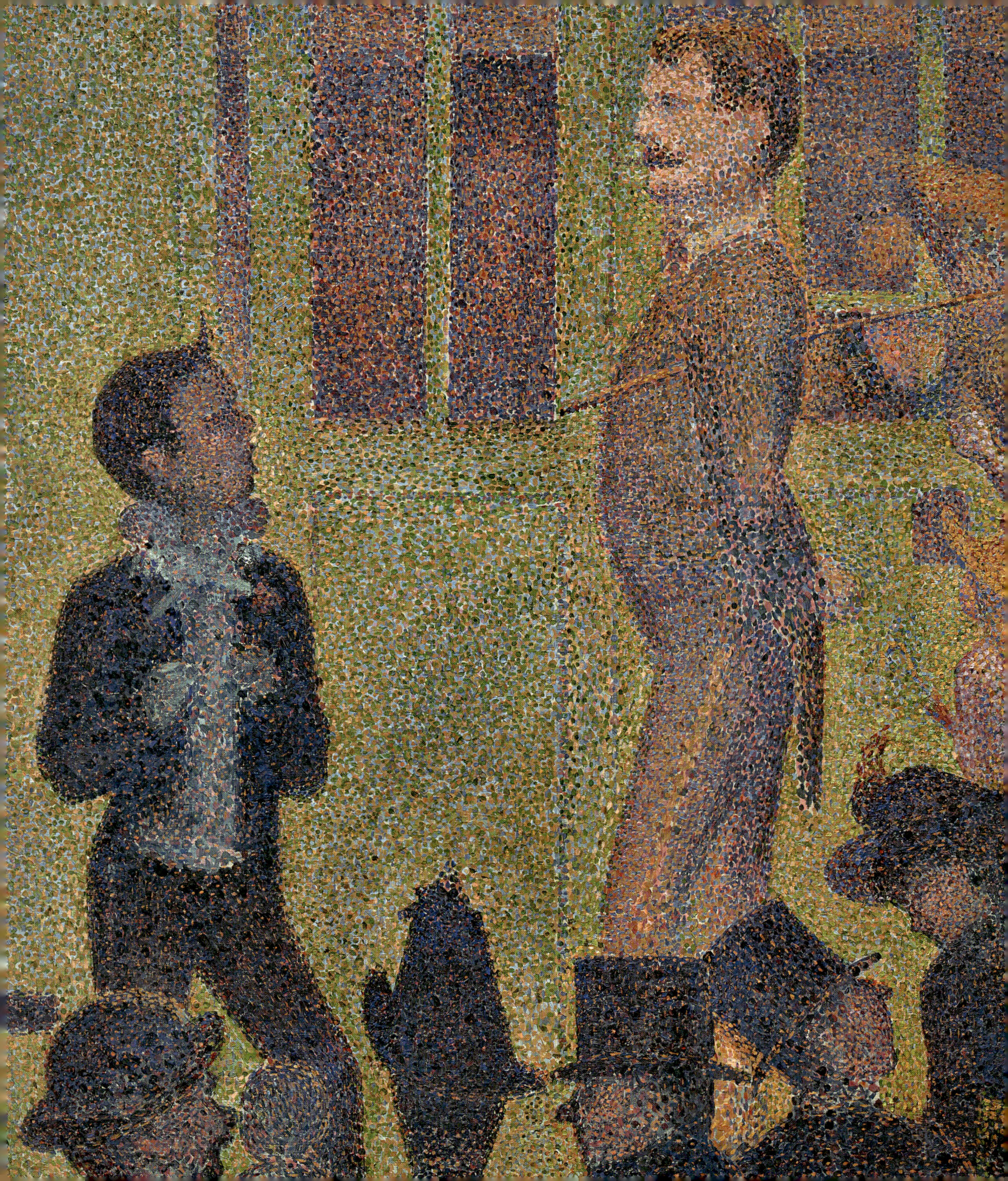

SEURAT'S CIRCUS SIDESHOW: A PARADE OF PARADOXES

RICHARD THOMSON

GEORGES SEURAT'S *Circus Sideshow* (*Parade de cirque*) is the most haunting and enigmatic painting of this major artist's short career (fig. 1). Fascinating to look at, perplexing to understand, the canvas belongs within a rich heritage of imagery and social history and yet remains as challenging for us to read today as it was for Seurat's avant-garde contemporaries when it was first exhibited in 1888. The task here, as we examine the painting closely and survey the traditions it emerged from, is to cast light on the enigma, to illuminate Seurat's mysterious nocturnal subject.

At the center of Seurat's painting a trombonist stands poised on a pedestal, mouthpiece to his lips and right leg slightly angled to steady his weight. Behind him to the left are four fellow musicians wearing bowler hats and blowing their brass and woodwind instruments under the bare branches of a scrawny tree. To the other side of the central figure is a short fellow with his hair combed upward and an elaborate bow at his neck — some kind of buffoon perhaps — and farther to the right we see the proud profile of a proprietorial man, assertively moustached, chest puffed out, cane under the arm, hands clasped above the tails of his jacket. The spectacle of these performers is watched from below by thirteen onlookers — men and women and a baby — seen only from the shoulders upward, some in profile and others from directly behind. Their forms are relatively dark, as they are in the gloom of night, but their faces catch the light cast from the show before them. To the far right a mother and her small daughter are more strongly illuminated; they have climbed the steps behind the proprietor to reach the ticket window and entered the zone of light radiating from the line of gas jets that runs above the stage and from the globes behind the cashier. For what Seurat represents in his painting is a partial

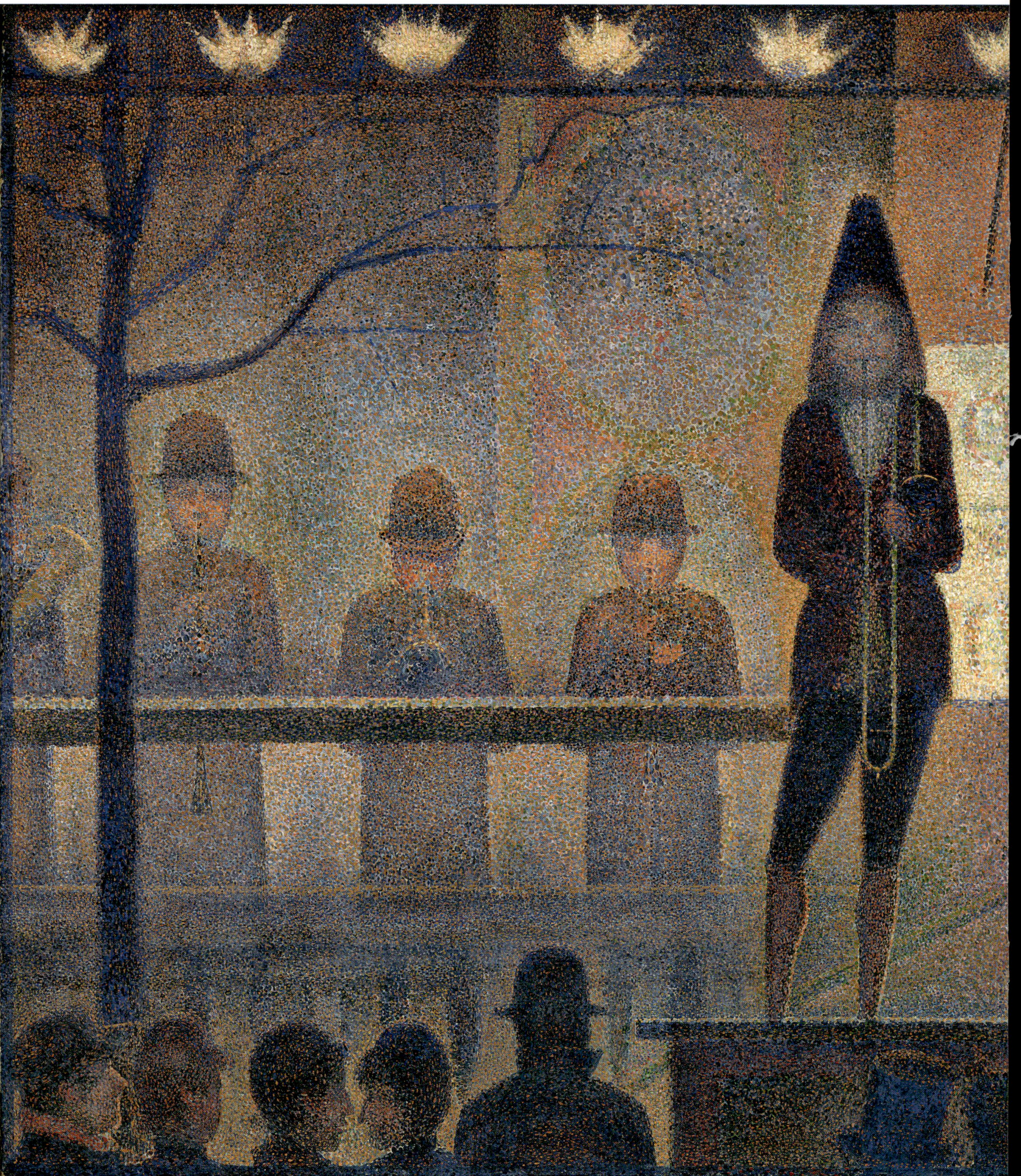

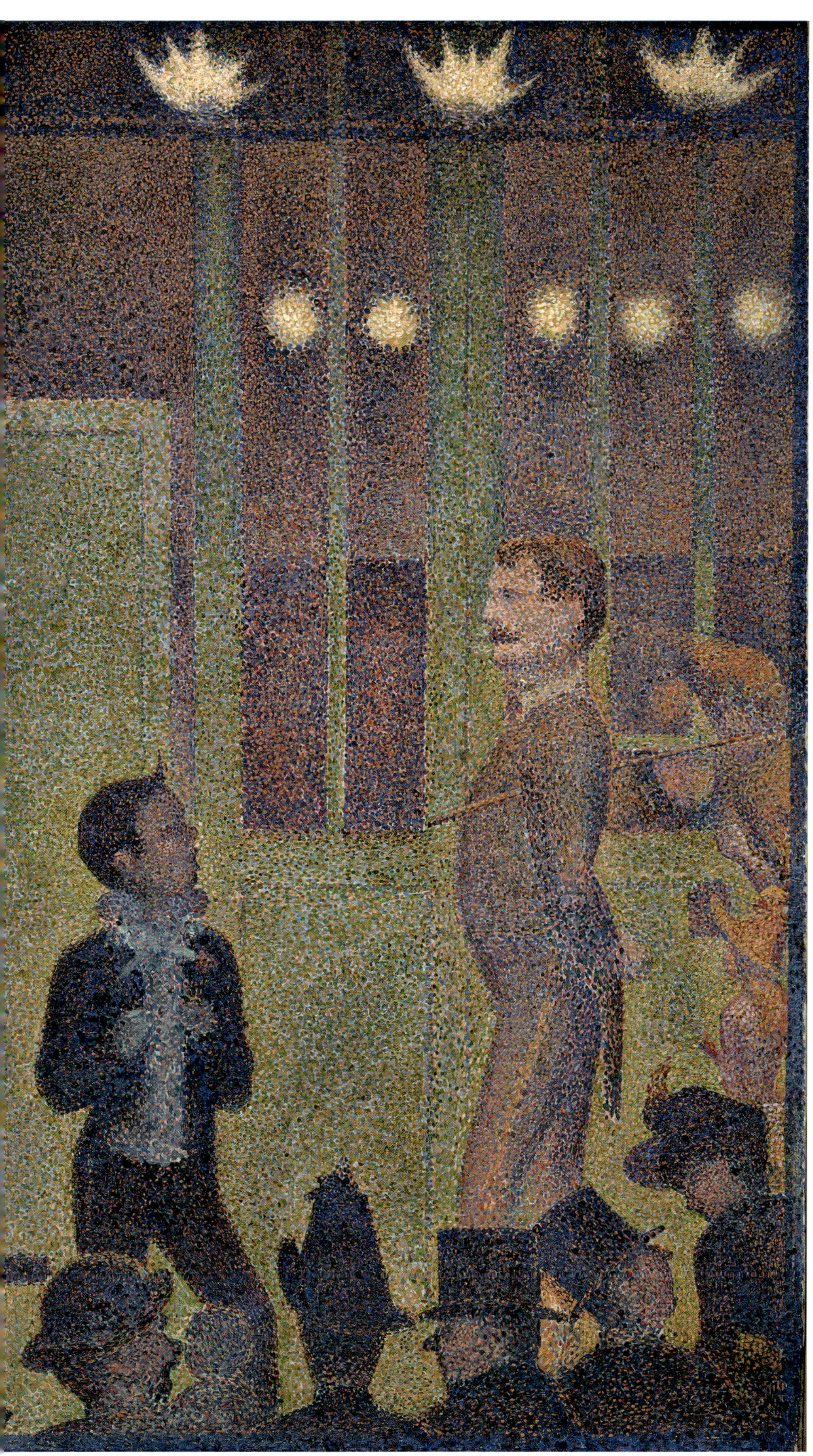

FIG. 1. Georges Seurat, *Circus Sideshow (Parade de cirque)*, 1887–88. Oil on canvas, 39 ¼ x 59 in. (99.7 x 149.9 cm). The Metropolitan Museum of Art, New York, Bequest of Stephen C. Clark, 1960 (61.101.17)

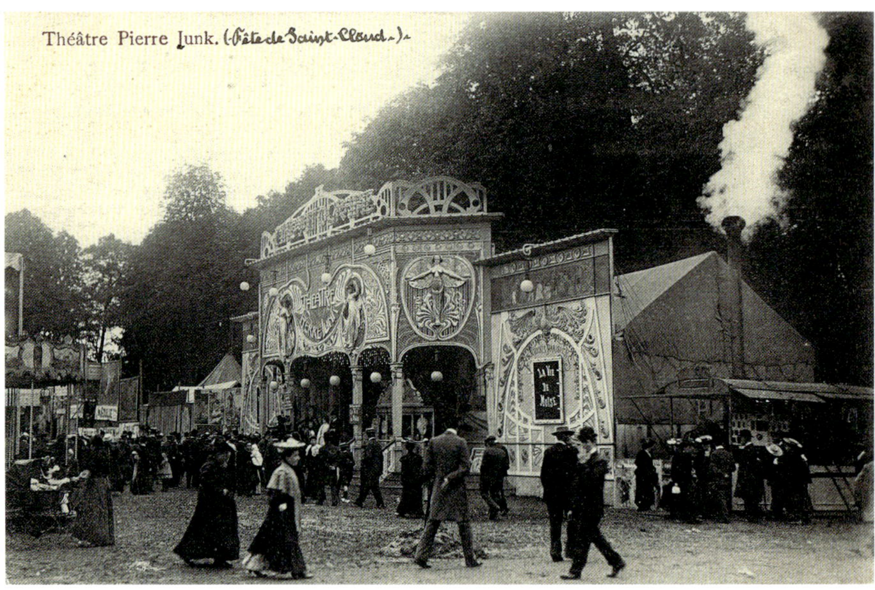

FIG. 2. Main tent behind booth facade, Théâtre Pierre Junk, Saint-Cloud Fair, ca. 1905. Postcard. Musée des Civilisations de l'Europe et de la Méditerranée, Marseille

view of the entrance to a temporary structure erected for a traveling circus, with some of the company's personnel standing on raised platforms trying to attract the custom of the crowd milling around outside.

The structure itself is difficult to interpret, as our field of vision does not reach its extremities. The pedestal on which the trombonist stands would have been matched on the opposite side of the steps at the painting's far right, which the mother and child have ascended, followed by a woman who turns to her male escort. These form the structure's central stairway, with the regular green woodwork of the windows and door at the top marking the entrance to the big top. A side stair, indicated by its slanted banister, runs behind the trombonist's dais. The four other musicians, who play the ophicleide or saxhorn, cornet, and clarinets, stand between a horizontal rail, which may hold their scores, and a canvas backdrop, which masks the main tent and is painted with scenes from the circus within (see fig. 2).[1] But the haze of light emanating from inside the big top and from the gas jets blurs the musicians and creates a certain ambiguity between the posts of the painted balustrade in front of them and the shadows cast by their legs from behind it. The scene is bathed in warm light, with dark violets and greens — the last colors the human eye distinguishes at twilight — heated and heightened by the roseate glow from behind the musicians, while the stronger illumination by the entrance gives an orange timbre to the proprietor and the clients behind him, and filaments of light fleck the edges of the foreground figures, whether the calves of the trombonist or the profiles of the gathering public. The overall effect of the painting is at once

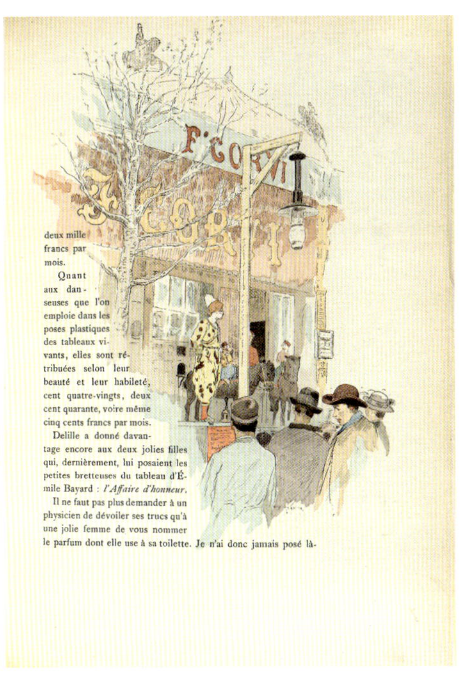

FIG. 3. Jules Garnier, *Corvi Circus*, from Hugues Le Roux, *Les Jeux du cirque et la vie foraine* (Paris, 1889), p. 71. The Metropolitan Museum of Art, New York, Irene Lewisohn Costume Reference Library, Gift of the New York City Ballet from the Library of Barbara Karinska

subtle and ambiguous, on the one hand warm and indistinct, on the other ordered and hieratic. For out of the ordinariness of his fellow citizens at a fairground Seurat conjured a night scene of exquisitely measured mystery.

Seurat's painting is rife with paradoxes, most noticeably relating to its subject and mood. It represents a scene at a *fête foraine*, a kind of seasonal fair that would typically be a place of racket and bustle, with crowds enjoying carnivalesque entertainments, but Seurat completely downplays animation or noise. He focuses on a traveling circus, but instead of the dazzling acts in the big top itself, depicts the sideshow — known in French as the *parade* — which was free entertainment put on outside to lure the passing crowd to purchase tickets and go in. Such a *parade* was designed to promote a particular show, to vaunt it over competitors' offerings; it necessitated directness, display, drama, but Seurat's painting is strangely restrained, the music somehow silent. The musicians play their instruments, and some of the public turn to each other, but there are no demonstrative gestures, no expressions of appeal or excitement. The painting presents a night scene that is strongly lit, yet few shadows are cast. And while it may exude a welcoming aura, we are faced with a rank of excluding backs.

It is not just how the painting looks, however, but also what it responded to, that is paradoxical. Although Seurat does not draw attention to it, *Circus Sideshow* represents a particular circus — the Cirque Corvi (Corvi Circus) — which regularly visited Paris in his day. His friend Gustave Kahn made the identification in an 1888 review, and Robert L. Herbert first noted the contemporary illustrations of this troupe by Jules Garnier and Oswald Heidbrinck (figs. 3, 4).[2] The tent and facade erected by such traveling shows might well have had an inescapably ad hoc quality of sagging canvas and skewed signs.[3] Seurat, however, represented it all taut and ordered, with perfectly pitched ovals and rectangles, adapting what we see in a 1906 postcard that coincidentally shows almost exactly the same left-hand-side view of the Corvi Circus as his painting (fig. 5). Circus structures were normally emblazoned with images of the featured acts — indeed, half of Seurat's picture is "a painting of a painting," as the warm zones behind the five musicians reproduce these scenes.[4] But in rendering them lit from both front and back, Seurat made the scenes blurred and indecipherable, thus all but effacing the authentic imagery of the very popular culture to which his subject of the *parade* responds.[5] The composition he chose — viewing a performance of some kind over or around the heads of the watching public — was both long-standing in caricature and up-to-the-minute in contemporary naturalist painting, as we shall see. Yet Seurat's handling of it is neither obviously satirical nor frankly descriptive.

The response of others to *Circus Sideshow* presents a further paradox. The work was painted during a period of dynamic avant-garde momentum

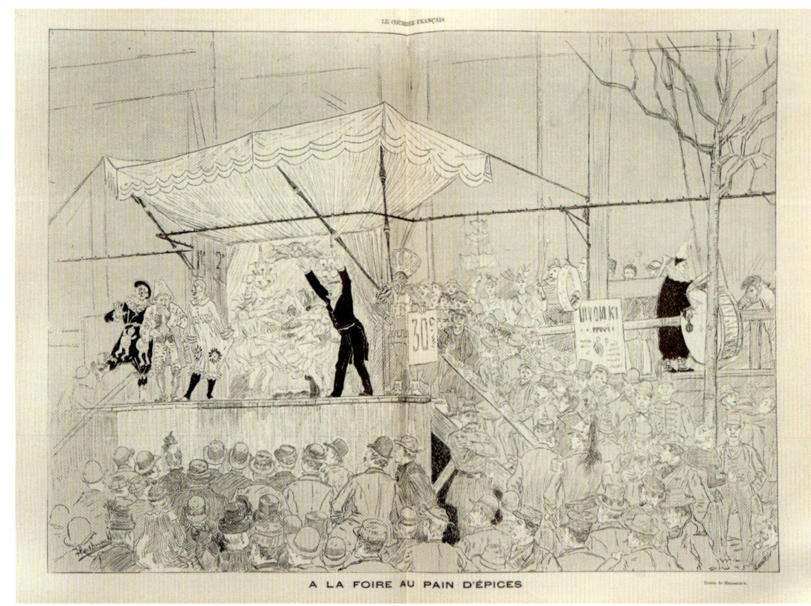

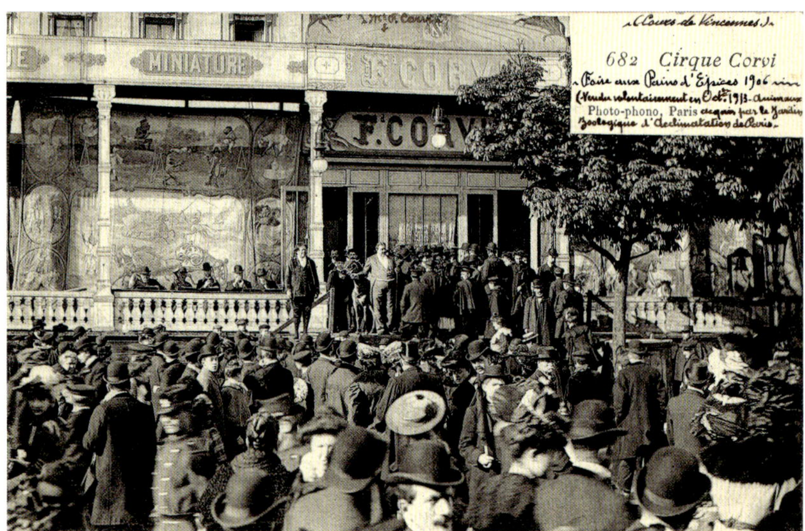

in Paris, with radical new departures in painting, literature, and music being generated by exciting young talents, among whom Seurat had been acknowledged as perhaps the most challenging visual artist since the display of his *A Sunday on La Grande Jatte (1884)* (*Un Dimanche à la Grande Jatte [1884]*) at the final Impressionist exhibition in 1886 (see fig. 47). This monumental painting, which introduced his novel divisionist (or pointillist) technique — using a dotted touch to combine both local and complementary color — to render an outdoor sunlit scene, was the second of only six major

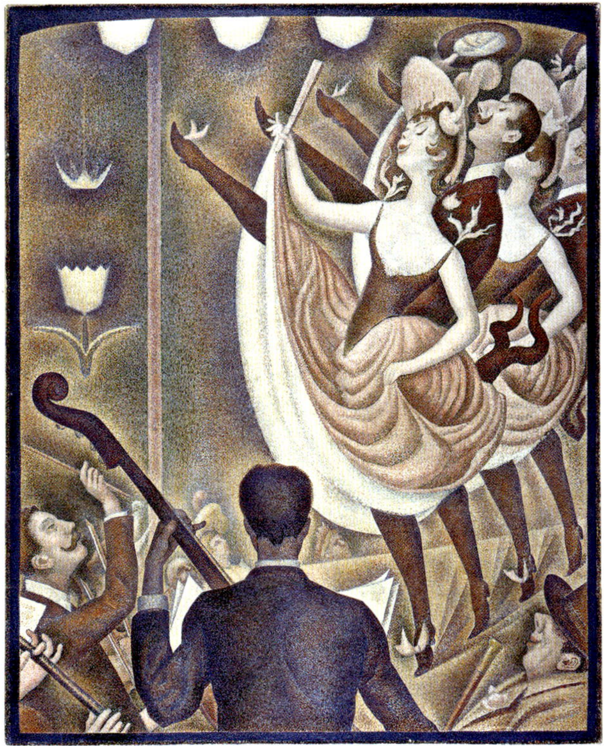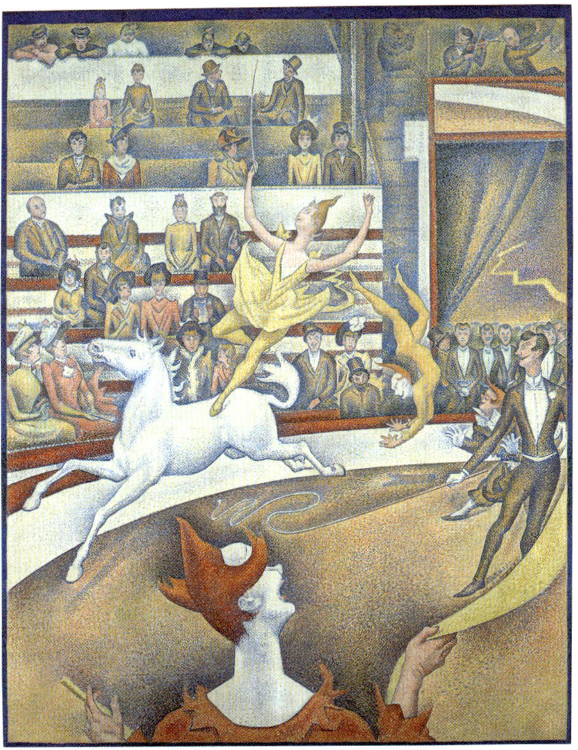

figure compositions he made during his short career. *Circus Sideshow*, a singular experiment in painting outdoor nocturnal illumination, came fourth, initiating a final trio of works that focus on aspects of popular entertainment, rounded out by *Chahut* (named for a raucous version of the can-can) and *Circus* (*Cirque*) (figs. 6, 7). The artist's fascination with the juxtaposition of performer and audience was reinforced by the starkly evocative drawings of Parisian music halls (*cafés-concerts*) that he exhibited alongside *Circus Sideshow* at the 1888 Salon des Indépendants (see figs. 75–78).[6] Yet for all the innovative authority of the painting, it was barely acknowledged in reviews of the show, even those by his avant-garde friends.

Redolent as it is with mystery and contradictions, *Circus Sideshow* has attracted many interpretations. It has been seen, to give some instances, as an image of the vanity of human pleasures, and read in terms of sadness and alienation; it has been thought to evoke the social divisions inherent in modern consumerism, specifically in whether or not to buy what is on offer; and it has been related to the reordering of perception and attention in the nineteenth century, the so-called "industrialization of contemplation."[7] Such diverse readings suggest that we do well to approach the picture from multiple perspectives, seeking no simple solutions. The paradoxes of *Circus Sideshow* lie in what it shows and doesn't show, in how its color works, in its nocturnal setting, in its fragmented figures, none of which is depicted entirely whole, and in its symmetry and hieraticism. Moreover, Seurat himself offers no explanations; like his painting, the artist was noted for his silence. Twice in 1888, the year *Circus Sideshow* was first shown, people who knew him referred to this: in February Camille Pissarro wrote to fellow painter Paul Signac, "he's mute," and that April the critic Paul Alexis noted "the speechlessness of Seurat" in his article on the new avant-garde periodical *La Revue indépendante*.[8] While Seurat would later exhibit drawings at this journal's offices, and his work was praised in its pages, he did not contribute vociferously to its debates on aesthetic matters.[9]

As we seek to unlock the mute mysteries of *Circus Sideshow* we will need to go beyond the painting itself. Throughout the nineteenth century the *parade* had been a stock motif in popular print culture and notably in caricature, where it was particularly useful for political targets. During the 1880s it was a regular subject in the descriptive naturalist paintings shown at the annual Paris Salon, which exemplified the documentary aesthetic that Seurat and his avant-garde colleagues were striving to replace with more suggestive and synthetic styles. We will ask how Seurat absorbed, adapted, or rivaled these distinctive and quite different visual languages. And we will need to bring into play both the social history of the subject Seurat chose and the associations that it carried. For the world of the traveling fairs and circus entertainers that fascinated Seurat was complex and shifting. Before considering his great painting in further detail, a passage through the imagery, art, and popular culture of this marginal world will introduce us to the rich range of references from which Seurat drew.

Saltimbanques and the *Parade*: Stock Images of Caricature

Circus Sideshow represents performers and their potential public at an open-air fair, or *fête foraine*, in Paris. This form of popular festival, dating back to the Middle Ages in France, was traditionally tied to saints' days or public holidays and often featured traveling players and a marketplace.[10] By the late eighteenth century the visitors to such fairs embraced all sections of society, from the lower and middle classes to the aristocracy, who sometimes hired the players to perform in their homes.[11] These performers were called *saltimbanques*, a word derived from the Italian *saltimbanco*: someone who jumps on a bench. In the Middle Ages they were known collectively as *la banque*, and hence *banquistes* became another term for acrobats and actors, comics and animal tamers, musicians and magicians.[12] On arrival in a town or village, having set up their tent or stage, the costumed *saltimbanques* would play instruments and demonstrate fragments of their performances to entice the local public to pay to see the whole show; this acted-out advertisement was the *parade*, and the promotional patter that went with it was the *bagatelle de la porte*.[13]

Rootless because they were constantly on the road, eternally dependent on the fickle whims of the public, *saltimbanques* had by Seurat's day long been associated with melancholy and alienation.[14] In a series of articles on the *fêtes foraines* published in the journal *Gil Blas* in 1882 and aimed at its bourgeois readership, the ex-Communard Jules Vallès made clear that, for all their show of gaiety on stage, *saltimbanques* suffered a daily existence of exclusion. Similarly, in 1884 at age fourteen, the adolescent future artist Maurice Denis noted in his journal that while a *fête foraine* offered fascinating subjects, he always came away "with somber ideas about what I've seen."[15] The paradox of the sad clown — gaily performing, internally suffering — had established a quasi-mythic place in both the common and the political imagination.

Indeed, the subject of *saltimbanques* had attracted the great caricaturist Honoré Daumier, who made a significant number of works on the theme toward the end of his career in the late 1860s.[16] This is when he produced a group of well-finished watercolor drawings that together add up to an informal sequence, a potential narrative of arrival, appeal, desperation, and disappointed departure. For example, one shows a family of performers setting up at a fairground, the father banging a drum to attract attention while his family looks with discouragement toward the crowd gathered at a nearby attraction (fig. 8). A second depicts a grim-faced drummer posed in front of a banner advertising a fat lady, beside which an unnaturally thin clown presents himself as foil, while behind them a *parade* draws the crowd to another booth (fig. 9). A third, represented here by a study, gives us a *parade* with different performers frantically shouting and gesticulating from a raised platform as they urge the unseen public to see their entertainment (fig. 10). Finally, a fourth shows a small family of *saltimbanques* leaving a town dispirited, as they carry away their meager props (fig. 11). The mood of all these drawings is indeed somber; they are moving images of anxiety and dashed hopes.[17]

Daumier also depicted the *parade* subject in small oil paintings during this period. While these show diverse aspects of the *parade* — yelling out the feats of the circus strong man, banging on the big bass drum — they are consistent in presenting their figures' appeal for attention, whether by cries or music, and in their size of approximately ten by thirteen inches, as if Daumier envisaged them as potential companion pieces (see figs. 12, 13). These little panels were of a scale on which it was easy to complete and sell work; so the artist was as aware as the *saltimbanques* he represented of the need to market one's product.

FIG. 8. Honoré Daumier, *Saltimbanques*, ca. 1866–67. Charcoal, pen and ink, wash, watercolor, and conté crayon on paper, 13 ¼ x 15 ⅝ in. (33.7 x 39.7 cm). Victoria and Albert Museum, London, Bequeathed by C. A. Ionides

FIG. 9. Honoré Daumier, *The Sideshow (La Parade)*, ca. 1865–66. Charcoal, pen and ink, gray wash, watercolor, gouache, and conté crayon on paper, 17 ¼ x 13 ¼ in. (43.8 x 33.7 cm). Private collection

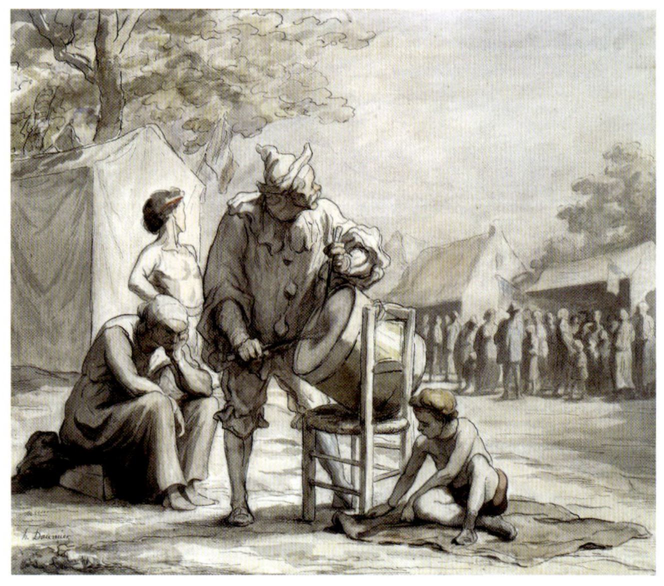

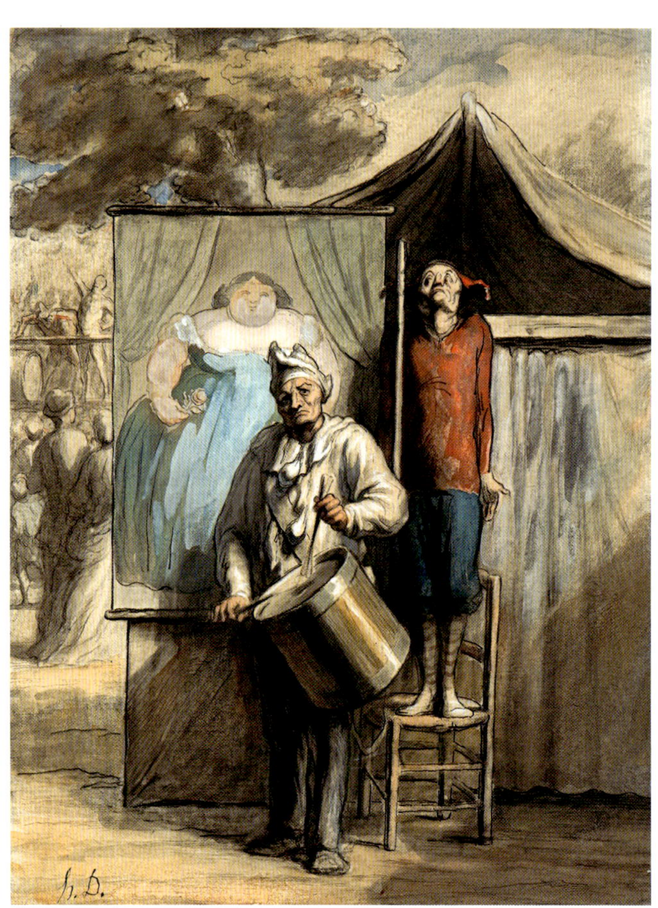

FIG. 10. Honoré Daumier, *The Sideshow (La Parade de saltimbanques)*, ca. 1865. Watercolor, charcoal, pen and ink, and chalk on paper, 10 ¼ x 13 ⅝ in. (26 x 34.6 cm). Hammer Museum, Los Angeles, The Armand Hammer Daumier and Contemporaries Collection, Gift of the Armand Hammer Foundation

FIG. 11. Honoré Daumier, *The Saltimbanques Changing Place*, ca. 1866–67. Charcoal, gray wash, watercolor, and conté crayon on paper, 15 ⅞ x 12 ½ in. (40.3 x 31.9 cm). Wadsworth Atheneum Museum of Art, Hartford, Connecticut, The Ella Gallup Sumner and Mary Catlin Sumner Collection Fund

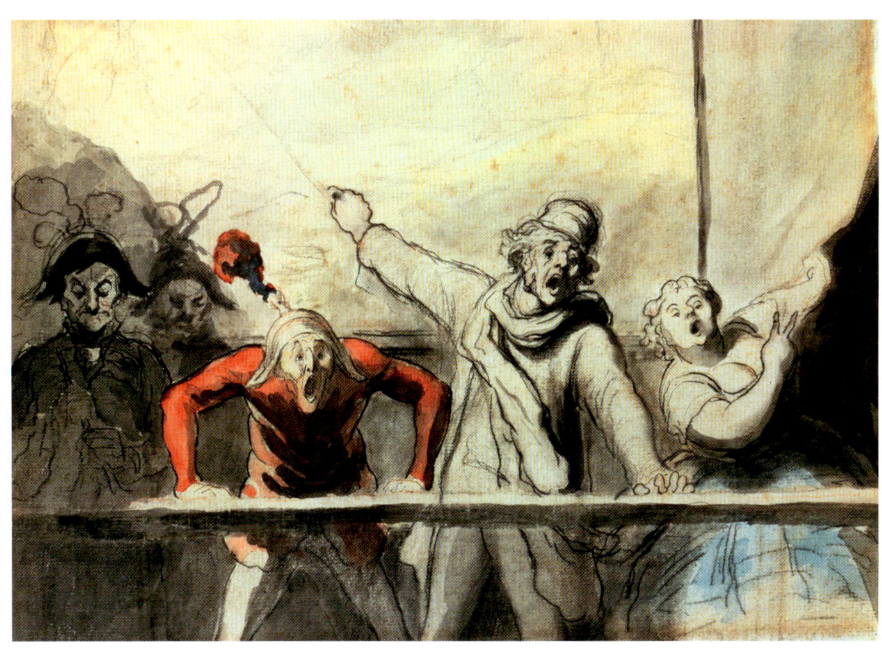

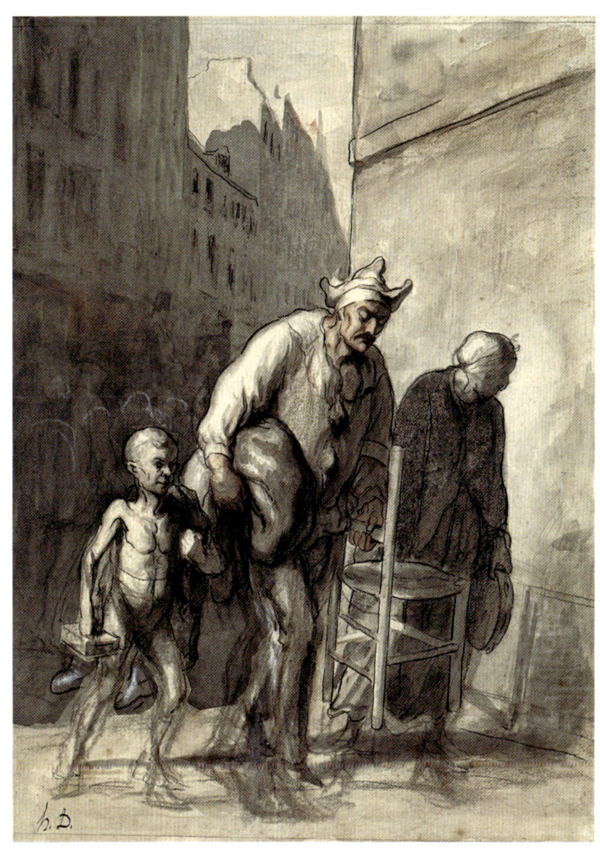

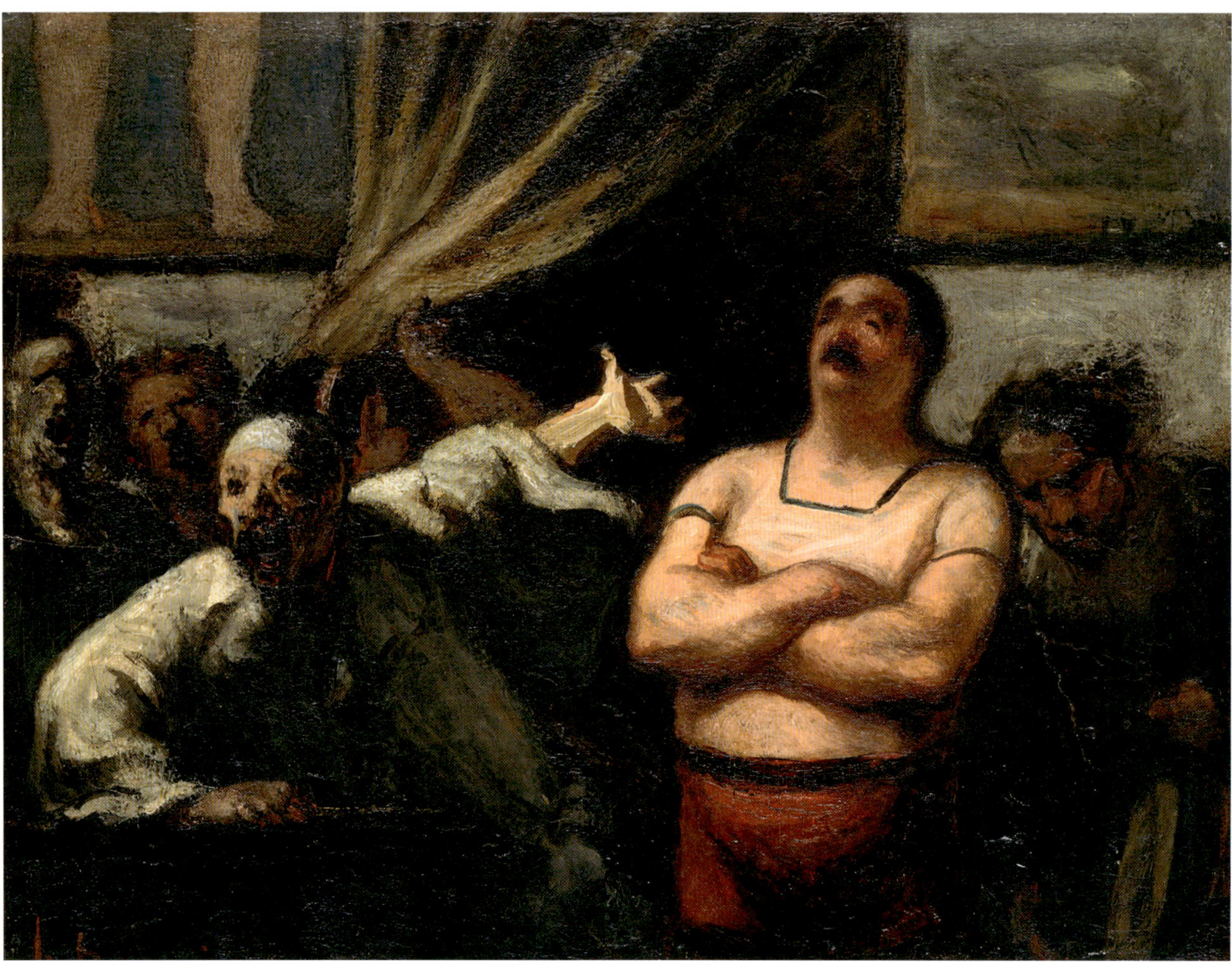

Daumier's final years coincided with the period when Seurat was a student at the Ecole des Beaux-Art in Paris. In April 1878, less than a year before the older artist's death, a committee of his friends rented the Durand-Ruel gallery to stage an exhibition of his paintings, drawings, and caricatures. The watercolors of the *saltimbanques* were well represented.[18] Although attendance and sales were poor at the retrospective, Daumier's reputation burgeoned posthumously. He was consistently praised in critical writing for his representation of body language and gesture; Edmond Duranty's review of the 1878 exhibition, for instance, admired his "incomparable examples of what one can express with poses of the human figure."[19] When the painting of the strong man (fig. 12) appeared on the Paris art market in December 1887, it was bought and sold within days by the art dealer Theo van Gogh, brother of the artist, at the gallery Boussod et Valadon.[20]

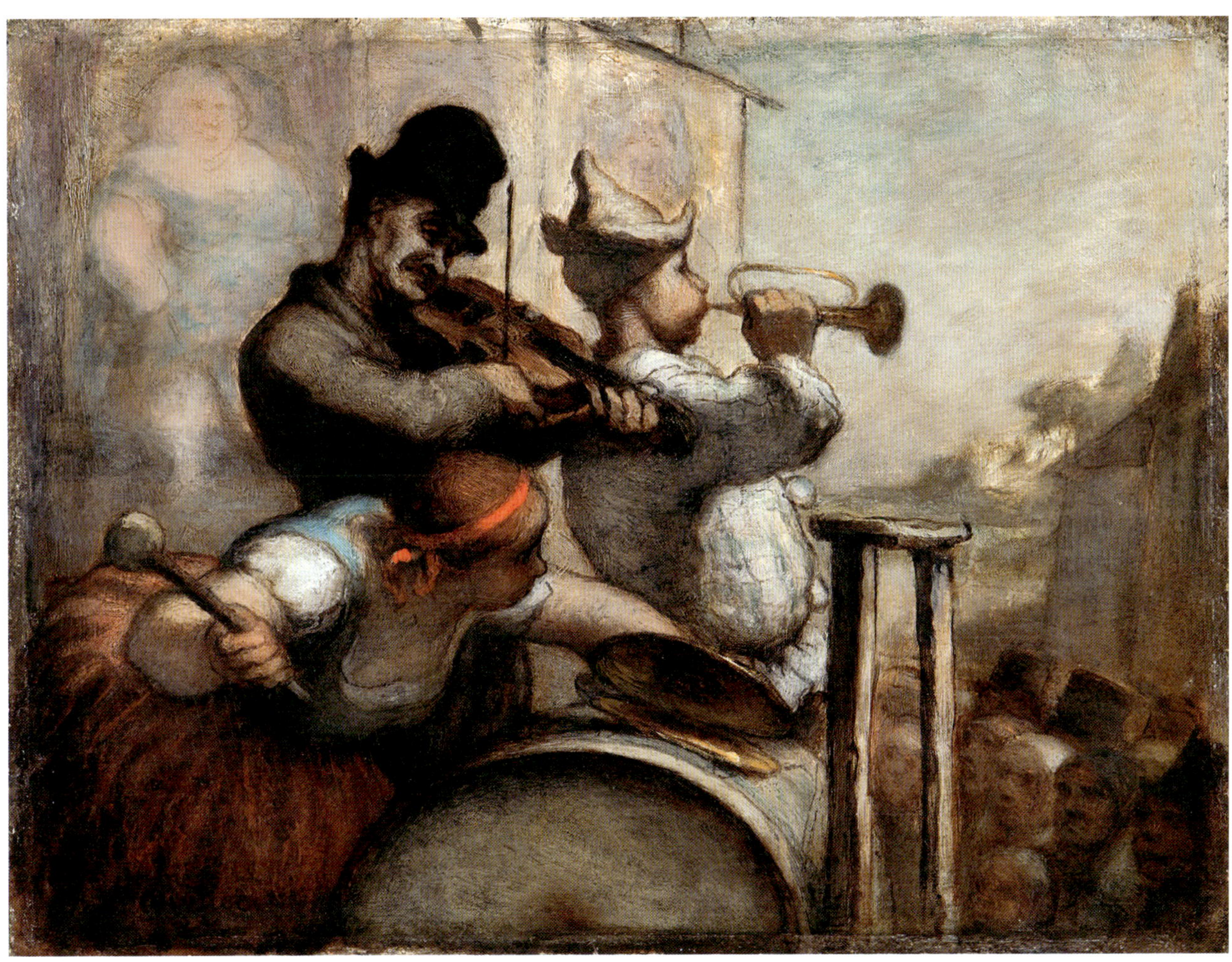

 Honoré Daumier, *Sideshow*
(*Parade de saltimbanques*),
ca. 1860–64. Oil on wood, 9 ⅞ x 13 in.
(25 x 33 cm). Private collection

Appreciation of Daumier's legacy reached a high point in 1888, the year Seurat exhibited *Circus Sideshow*, its subject echoing the themes of the great caricaturist. That year Arsène Alexandre published an extensive and well-illustrated monograph on Daumier, whose work was a substantial feature in a major exhibition on the history of French caricature staged at the Ecole des Beaux-Arts.[21] In particular, Daumier was much admired in Seurat's circle. The young critic Félix Fénéon, with his eye for subversive innovation, praised him for his "drawing that is logically expressive even when carried to hyperbole."[22] Painters of Seurat's generation were collecting his lithographic caricatures, which they admired as much for their economical draftsmanship as for their antibourgeois attitudes, Louis Hayet tipping off Lucien Pissarro in September 1886 that one could buy Daumier prints for twenty centimes near the Pont Saint-Michel.[23]

The exhibition at the Ecole des Beaux-Arts and books such as John

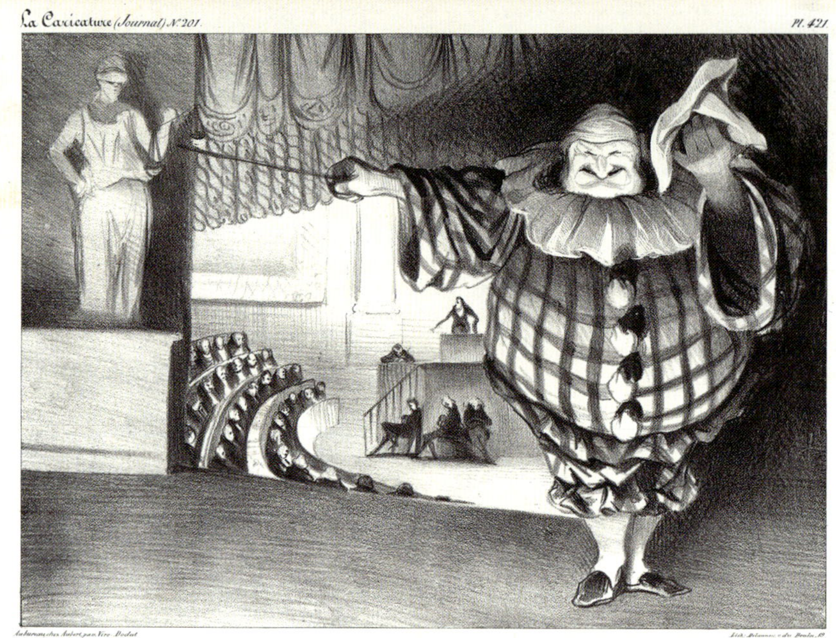

Grand-Carteret's *Les Moeurs et la caricature en France* (Customs and Caricature in France), also published in 1888, demonstrate how conscious contemporary French culture was of its caricatural heritage. During the nineteenth century, with the development of ever cheaper and more efficient printing technologies, speedier circulation, and burgeoning literacy, caricature had become central to daily experience. If the appetite for it was consensual, its targets were divisive. *Parade* imagery had long been recognized as an acute device for parodying politicians, who—like *saltimbanques*—are trying to sell something. A standard French dictionary followed its definition of a *parade* as the promotional gambit at a traveling fair with the additional allusion "*Parade politique*, political behavior that is no more than a joke,"[24] while Grand-Carteret's book drew attention to an album of ten political caricatures, *Les Parades* (1826), each image successively parodying the political regimes in France since the Revolution of 1789.[25] The same tropes were used to skewer the mandarins of literature and the arts. Indeed the combination of *parade* and *saltimbanque* imagery with caricatural means of expression pitted two kinds of "low" art—the circus and the popular cartoon—against "high" culture and politics in a current consistent throughout the century.

Daumier repeatedly used *parade* imagery in his caricatures. His great lithograph *Bring Down the Curtain; the Farce Is Over*, printed in *La Caricature* in 1834, has a grotesquely fat Louis-Philippe—sovereign of the

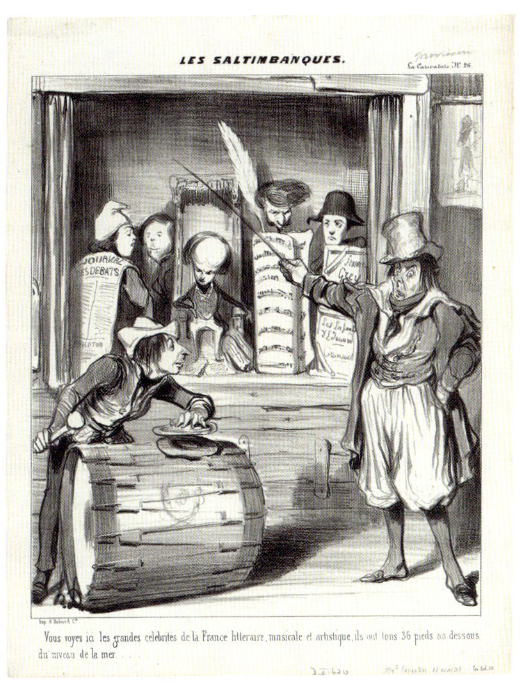

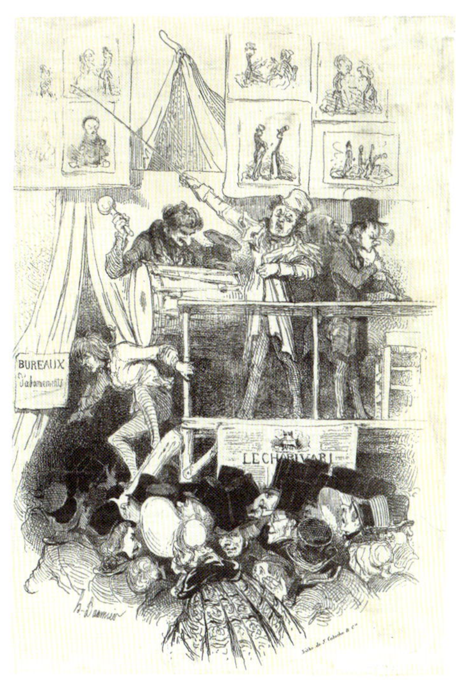

July Monarchy (1830–48) — wearing greasepaint and a Pierrot costume while he lowers the curtain on the French Parliament (fig. 14). The caption, the reputed last words of the sixteenth-century French comic writer François Rabelais, deploys a historic witticism to make a sardonic attack on modern political cynicism. A lithograph from *La Caricature* of 1839, which takes aim at high art (fig. 15), ridicules the novelist Victor Hugo, the composer Hector Berlioz, the painter Paul Delaroche, and other cultural grandees by presenting them as freaks at a *fête foraine*, with their characteristics — Hugo's high forehead, Berlioz's extravagant coiffure — much exaggerated. The lengthy caption — "Here you see the great celebrities of literary, musical, and artistic France; they are thirty-six feet tall, measured below sea level" — itself takes on the bombastic patter of the fairground barker. Daumier could turn the same imagery on himself and his colleagues. Another lithograph, printed in *Le Charivari* the same year, depicts its publisher Charles Philipon ostentatiously promoting the journal at a *parade*, with Daumier on the steps of the platform (fig. 16).[26]

While there were plenty of canvases of *saltimbanques* in the early and middle decades of the century that innocuously represented their traveling existence, on occasion a painting could take on caricature's cutting edge. This was the case with Octave Penguilly L'Haridon's *Sideshow (Parade): Pierrot Presents His Companions Harlequin and Polichinelle to the Crowd* (fig. 17). It sets up a crafty interplay between artifice and reality, the

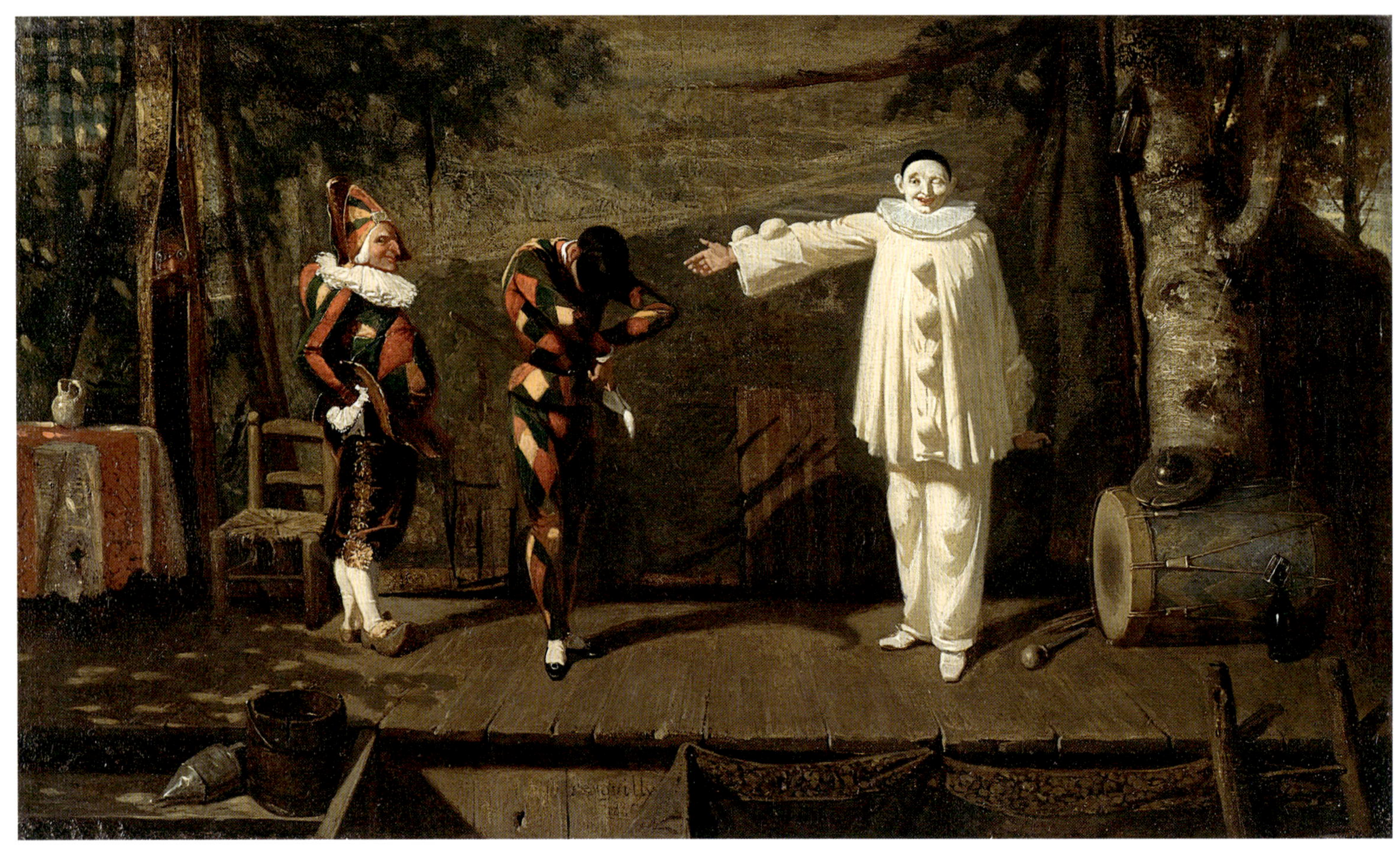

FIG. 17. Octave Penguilly-L'Haridon, *Sideshow (Parade): Pierrot Presents His Companions Harlequin and Polichinelle to the Crowd*, 1846. Oil on wood, 10 ⅝ x 18 in. (27 x 45.8 cm). Musées de Poitiers

costumed figures disporting themselves in front of a landscape painted on a backdrop, itself tied to a "real" tree. Exhibited at the Salon of 1846, its sparse composition attracted the attention of the poet Charles Baudelaire, who particularly admired the Polichinelle with his "slightly vinous head, fatuous glance, poor little feet in heavy clogs."[27] Baudelaire captures the mood of the painting, for what seems like a typically cheerful *parade* is on closer inspection rather sinister. As Pierrot presents the ironically bowing Harlequin he winks knowingly at the spectator, while behind the curtains to the left lurks a furtive masked and bespectacled figure. Pierrot's gesture recalls the outstretched arm in Daumier's *Bring Down the Curtain* of a decade earlier, suggesting a fruitful exchange between caricature and painting. Indeed, at the end of the nineteenth century Penguilly-L'Haridon's painting was owned by the important collector Etienne Moreau-Nélaton, a great aficionado of Daumier.[28]

The imagery of the *parade* was widely shared among Daumier's contemporaries in the world of illustration and cartoons. Auguste Raffet

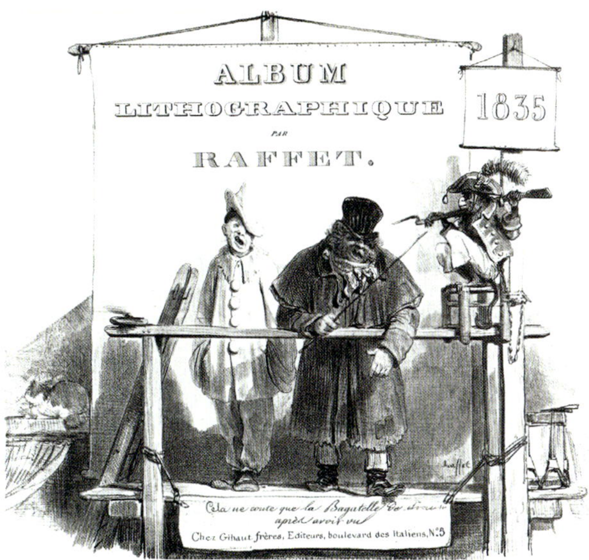
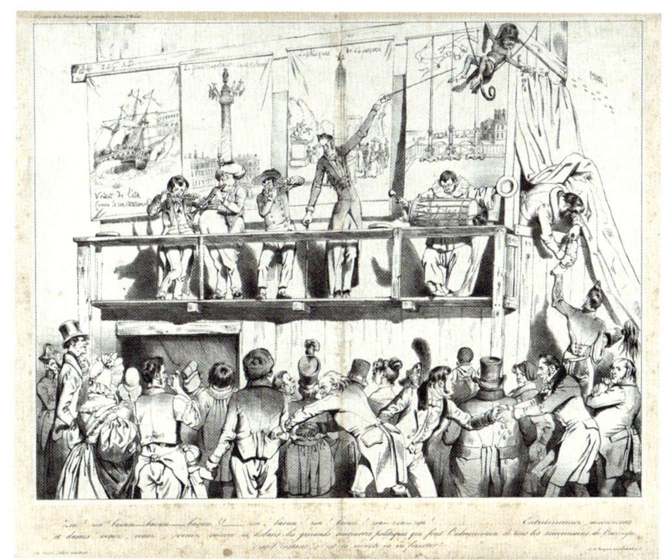

 Auguste Raffet, title page, *Album lithographique*, 1835. Lithograph, 10 ¾ x 15 ⅛ in. (27.3 x 38.5 cm). The Metropolitan Museum of Art, New York, Gift of Mrs. Edwin De T. Bechtel, 1961 (61.538.2)

 J. J. Grandville and Auguste Desperret, *Zing! Zing! Boom_Boom_Boom!!! The Show of the Grrrreat Political Tumblers*, from *L'Association mensuelle*, August 1833. Lithograph, 14 ¼ x 21 ⅝ in. (36.2 x 54.9 cm). The Metropolitan Museum of Art, New York, Bequest of Edwin De T. Bechtel, 1957 (57.650.623[14])

produced an annual *Album lithographique* between 1830 and 1837, each with twelve images of Napoleonic subjects such as battles and war veterans. The 1835 cover depicts a *parade*, with a scrawny Pierrot accompanied on the platform by a thuggish figure with a whip and a monkey in uniform clutching a musket, suggestive, perhaps, of the depths to which Bonaparte's loyal troops had fallen twenty years after the Battle of Waterloo (fig. 18). The onomatopoeic title of J. J. Grandville and Auguste Desperret's 1833 *Zing! Zing! Boom_Boom_Boom!!! The Show of the Grrrreat Political Tumblers* comes from the bass drum beaten while the king hands out bags of money and his ministers pickpocket members of the crowd (fig. 19).[29]

Parade imagery's associations of political chicanery remained consistent throughout Louis-Philippe's reign, the short-lived Second Republic, and Second Empire (1852–70) that followed. A wood engraving by the artist known as Bertall (Charles-Albert Arnoux) initially appeared in the multi-authored and lavishly illustrated *Le Diable à Paris* (The Devil in Paris), a lampoon of the city's morals published in 1846, and was widely recycled, even in a New York publication (fig. 20).[30] While the image presents simple grotesques, Edouard Ourliac's accompanying text on *saltimbanques* accentuated the parallels between *parades* and politics.[31] When revolution toppled the monarchy in 1848, Bertall parodied political radicals in *Le Journal pour rire*, showing leftists such as the republican Louis Blanc, the Fourierist Victor Considerant, and the anarchist Pierre-Joseph Proudhon peddling their ideologies alongside the fictional Robert Macaire, archetype of the huckster who promotes property and finance schemes (fig. 21). And under the Second Empire in the 1850s and 1860s the *parade* theme

FIG. 20. Charles-Albert Arnoux Bertall, *Saltimbanques*, from *Le Diable à Paris*, vol. II (Paris, 1846), p. 161. Wood engraving. The Metropolitan Museum of Art, New York, Gift of Mrs. Edwin De T. Bechtel, 1961 (61.538.4.2)

FIG. 21. Charles-Albert Arnoux Bertall, *The Fair of Ideas*, from *Le Journal pour rire*, October 14, 1848. Lithograph. The Morgan Library and Museum, New York, Purchased on the Gordon N. Ray Fund, 2007

FIG. 22. Attributed to Paul Hadol, *The Sideshow (La Parade: Théâtre Badinguet)*, 1871. Hand-colored lithograph, 22 ⅛ x 31 ⅛ in. (56.1 x 79.1 cm). Musée Carnavalet — Histoire de Paris

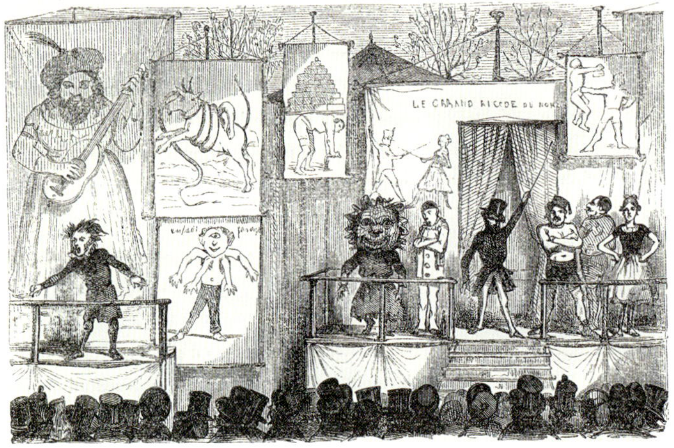

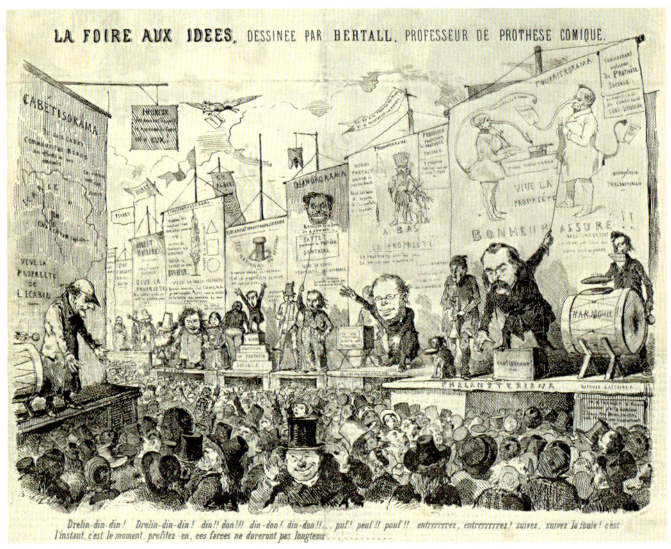

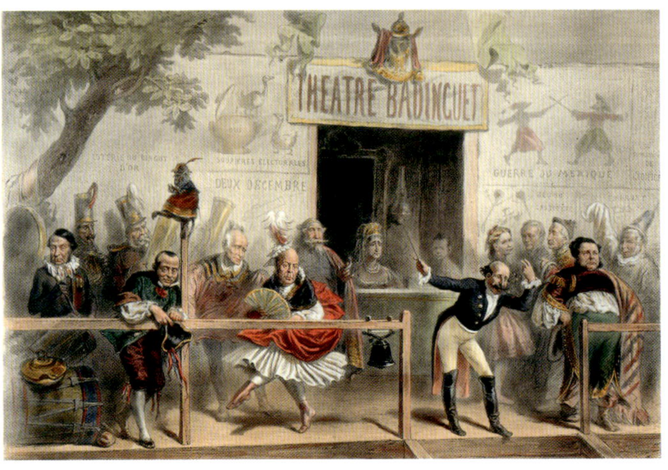

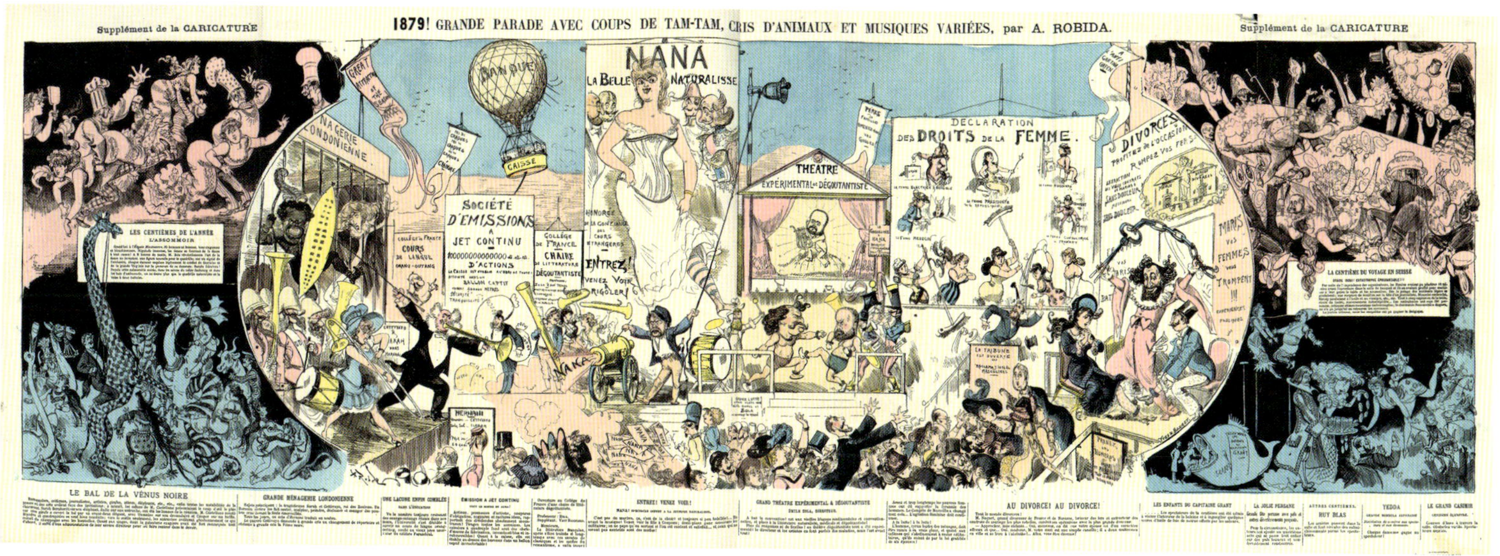

FIG. 23. Albert Robida, *1879! Grand Sideshow with Beating Tom-Toms, Animals' Screeches, and Various Music*, supplement to *La Caricature*, January 3, 1880. Color lithograph, 12 x 44 ⅜ in. (30.3 x 112.5 cm). Charles Deering McCormick Library of Special Collections, Northwestern University Libraries

continued to have powerful currency as political satire. A lithograph attributed to Paul Hadol represents a *parade* at the "Théâtre Badinguet," a play on the nickname for the emperor, Napoleon III, who sits sleepily smoking in the background beside a stony Empress Eugénie while his half-brother, Charles, the duc de Morny, attempts to draw an audience for the dubious attractions of the regime's ministers and cronies (fig. 22).[32]

Seurat's own working life took place under the Third Republic, which had come to power in September 1870 with the fall of Napoleon III in the Franco-Prussian War. Initially conservative, it became more genuinely republican from the late 1870s, introducing reforms such as the liberalizing Law on the Freedom of the Press of July 29, 1881. The practice of parodying politicians flourished at the *fêtes foraines* as well as in print. The radical Jules Vallès expressed glee that under the Republic's first president, the portly Adolphe Thiers, fat dwarves were common and under his successor, the ex-soldier Patrice de Mac Mahon, clowns often sported moustaches like his.[33] Alfred Robida launched his new comic weekly *La Caricature* in January 1880, with a large colored foldout mocking the previous year, *1879! Grand Sideshow with Beating Tom-Toms, Animals' Screeches, and Various Music* (fig. 23). Like Daumier, he pilloried cultural targets (Emile Zola's naturalist novel about the prostitute Nana) and also incorporated contemporary political issues (Alfred Naquet's campaign to legalize divorce), as well as up-to-the-minute international issues, with King Cetshwayo kaMpande of the Zulus, who had recently defeated the British at Isandlwana, performing Victor Hugo's play *Hernani*. And in 1888, over half a century after Daumier and Grandville and the very year Seurat's *Circus Sideshow* was exhibited,

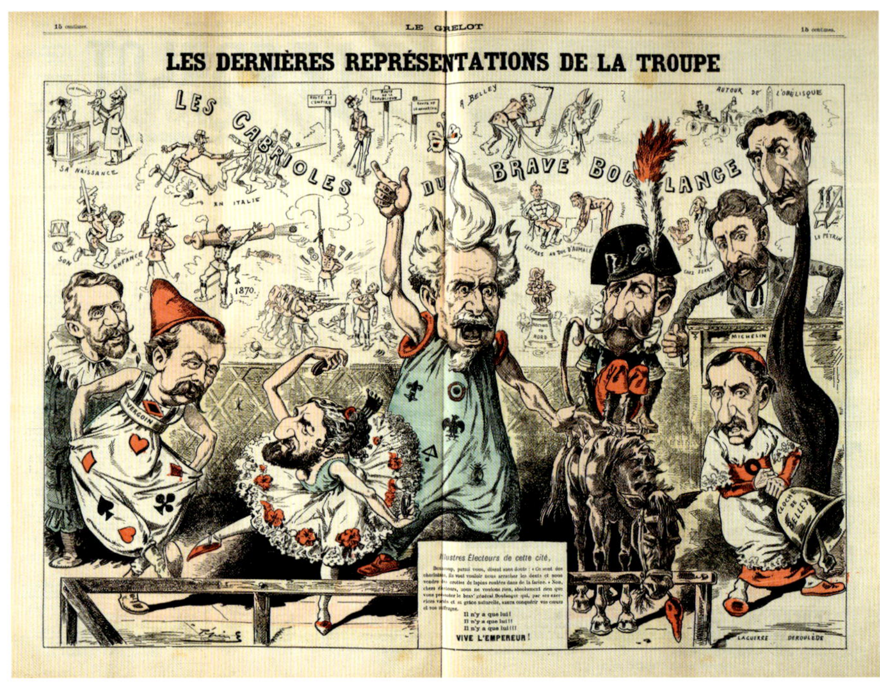

FIG. 24. Edouard Pépin (pseudonym of Claude Guillaumin), *The Troupe's Last Shows*, from *Le Grelot*, August 19, 1888. Color lithograph, 19⅛ x 25¾ in. (48.5 x 65.5 cm). New York State Library, Albany

the caricaturist Edouard Pépin (a pseudonym), used the *parade* to mock the populist general Georges Boulanger and his supporters, ridiculing the former's vain ambitions to restore one-man rule (fig. 24).

Naturalist Painting and the *Parade*

The *parade* theme was common not just in caricature but also in contemporary naturalist painting. Emerging in France in the 1860s, naturalism was concerned with creating a precise *document* of social reality, whether in the novels of Zola, Edmond and Jules de Goncourt, and Guy de Maupassant or in the paintings that filled the annual Paris Salon, the nation's leading art exhibition. This emphasis on registering everyday events in works of art that could be understood by all suited the egalitarian ideals of the Third Republic, and by the mid-1880s naturalism was entrenched as the dominant aesthetic.[34] Reviewing the 1884 Salon, the aristocratic art critic Louis de Fourcaud noted the proliferation—which he attributed to "democratic mania"—of subjects drawn from mundane modern experience: "a railway station, a gang of urchins hanging around a gate, the *parade* of wrestlers at the Foire de Neuilly."[35]

Indeed, the *parade* made a perfect subject for the naturalists. It offered artists a spectacle to which viewers were accustomed to being drawn when

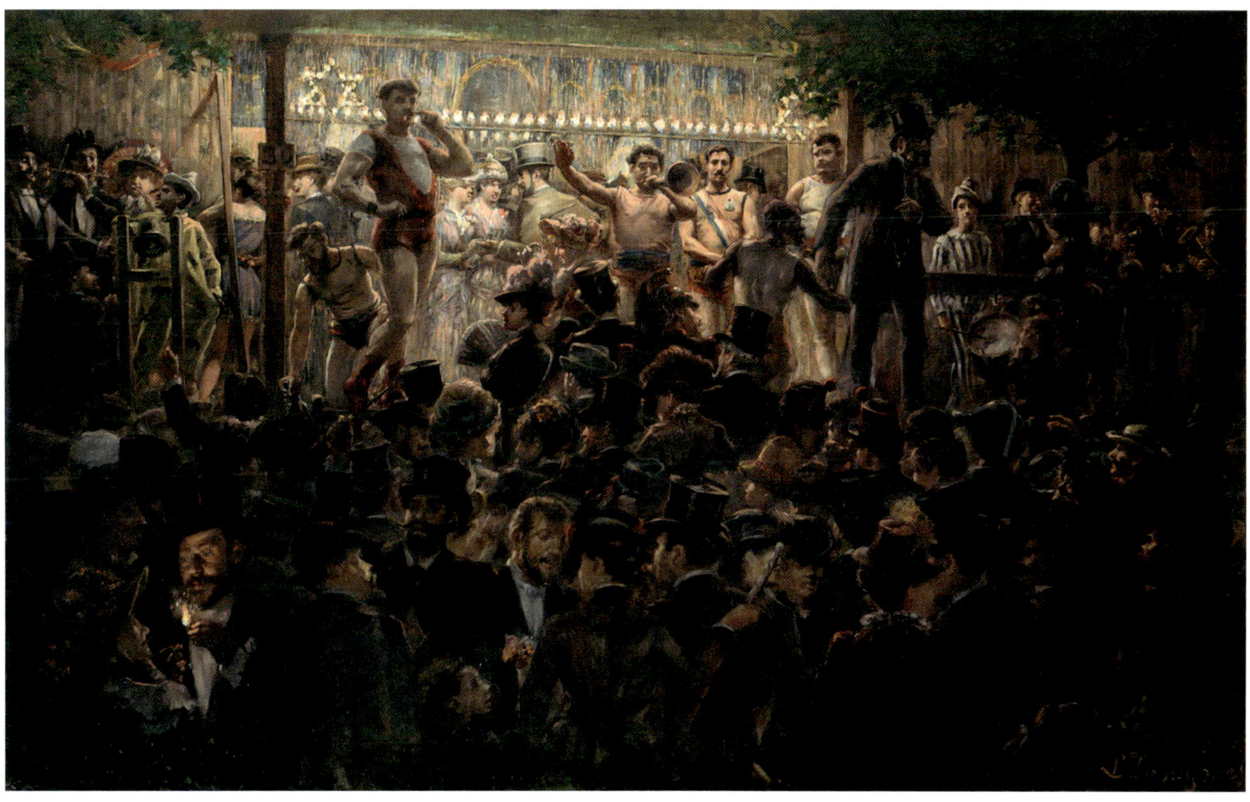

visiting the fairground, as well as an opportunity to show the reality of circus life and the mixture of social classes attending the fairs. It also challenged the painter to replicate the physical experience of the crowd, to suggest the contact of the jostling bustle, the need to see the performers through or over the heads of fellow spectators. Compositional devices for rendering crowds watching performers that had been pioneered in caricature had by the 1880s become commonplace in naturalist pictures, heightened by close observation. This is the kind of painting that Seurat would have known; it had to come into account, if only to react against it.

The painting to which Fourcaud alluded in 1884 was probably Léon Dehesghues's *The Fair at Neuilly — "Let's go and see Marseille"* (*"Allons chez Marseille"*) (fig. 25). This vivid picture encapsulates the expectations of naturalism. Its title not only establishes a specific fair, held in June at Neuilly, a western suburb of Paris, but also the performers, as the conversational subtitle refers to the Marseille brothers, well-known wrestlers long established on the circuit.[36] By naming them Dehesghues made the Salon visitor complicit in this knowledge, a virtual participant in the fair. His crowd is a dark mass animated by momentary likelihoods — the man's face illuminated as he lights a cigarette, the girl trying to sell flowers to a

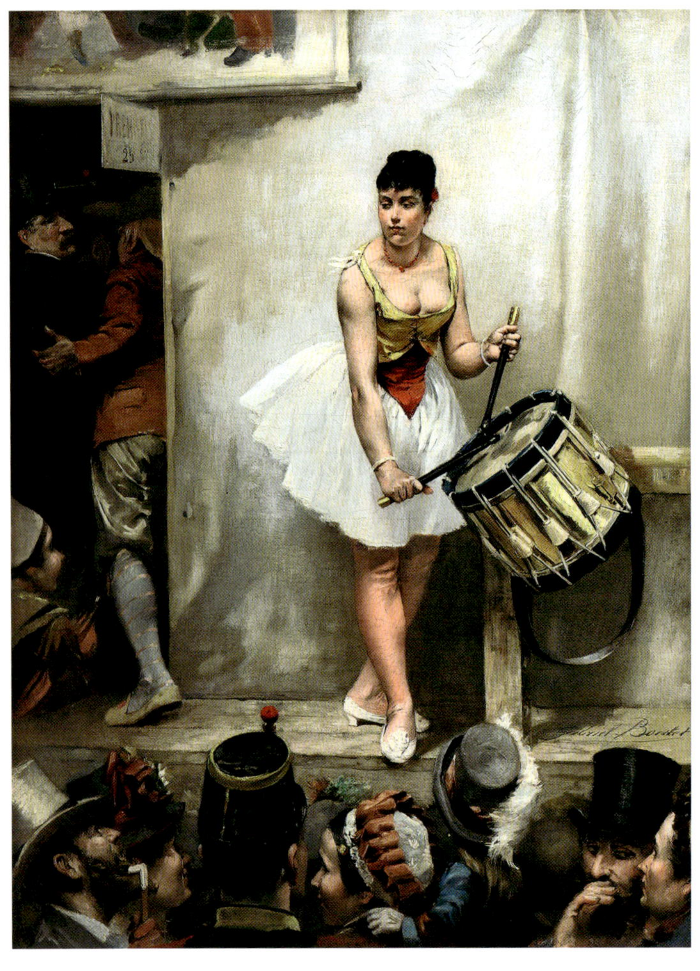

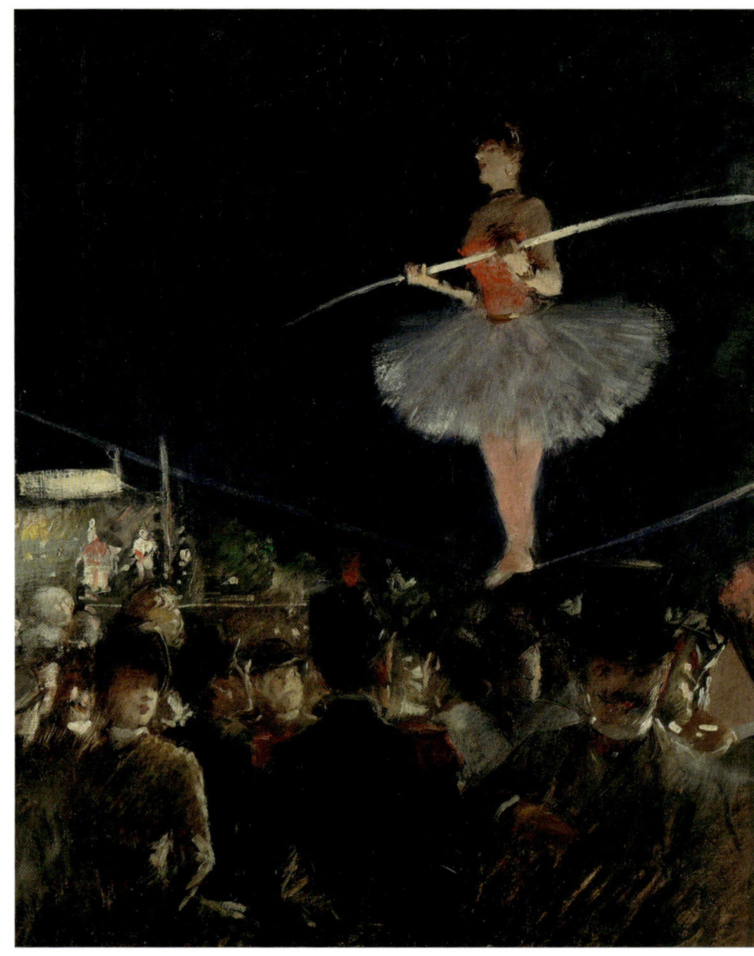

FIG. 26. Gabriel Boutet, *The Fair at Montrouge*, 1885. Oil on canvas, 31½ x 23¾ in. (80 x 60.3 cm). Scott and Nicole Mather

FIG. 27. Jean-Louis Forain, *Tight-Rope Walker*, ca. 1885. Oil on canvas, 18⅛ x 15 in. (46.2 x 38.2 cm). The Art Institute of Chicago, Gift of Mrs. Emily Crane Chadbourne

lady—while the wrestlers emerge under a line of stage lights. In several respects Dehesghues's depiction of a *parade* shares common ground with Seurat's: the roughly tripartite configuration, musicians to the left, customers climbing up steps beside a dais with a prominent performer, the mix of social classes, even the observation of artificial light at night, so that the tricolor on the central wrestler is tinged with green, while the top of the African wrestler's head is touched with pink. *The Fair at Montrouge,* which Gabriel Boutet exhibited at the Salon the following year, illustrates how differently a naturalist painter might conceive the same subject (fig. 26). Again the occasion is specific, set here in a southern suburb, but Boutet elected to focus on a fetching female drummer, while showing only the heads and shoulders of the crowd beneath her platform, yet enough to establish by their various headgear an appropriate class mixture—the bourgeois in top hats, a red-ribboned wet nurse, and a member of the military in his kepi.

Seurat's Circus Sideshow

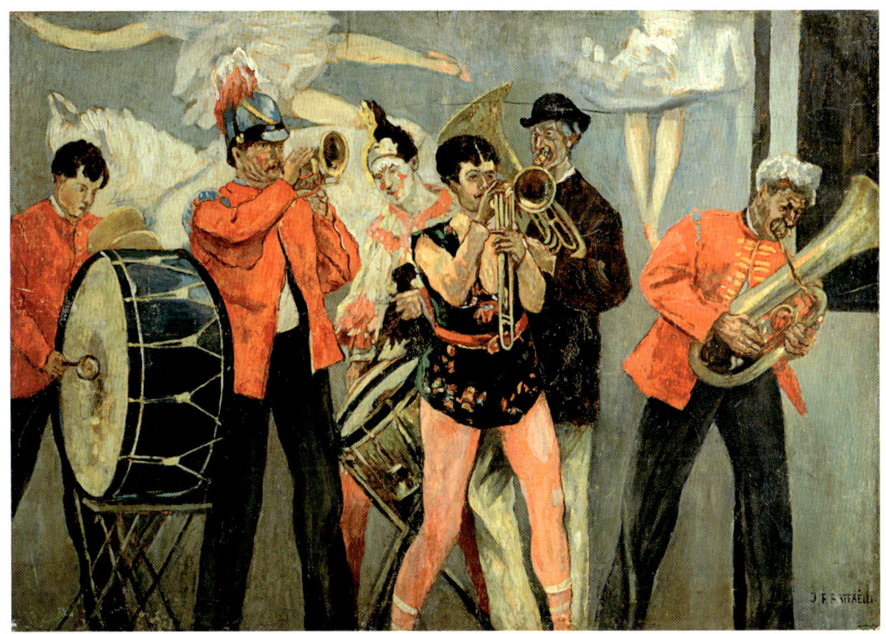

To the left customers are being ushered into the big top. Critics read such pictures in terms of actuality, of noise and anecdote, one imagining the drummer's exhortation: "Come in! Come in! Follow the crowd!"[37]

More independent artists, such as Jean-Louis Forain and Jean-François Raffaëlli, both of whom had exhibited at the Impressionist group shows, also treated *parade* subjects in a naturalist mode. Forain's *Tight-Rope Walker* (fig. 27), made in the mid-1880s, shares Dehesghues's transitory nocturnal light effects, with the performer illuminated from below and the red mark beneath the moustache of the man in the foreground at right showing he is smoking. Forain contrived the picture so that our gaze from within the crowd oscillates between the people at our shoulder, the acrobat silhouetted above us, and the distant *parade* to the left. In *Saltimbanques — The Sideshow Orchestra* (fig. 28), one of two *parade* subjects Raffaëlli exhibited in his 1884 one-man show, the musicians are less lively than the horse rider and dancer painted on the canvas behind them, but their red jackets stand out vividly against the blue and white backdrop.[38] Later that year the painting was reproduced in color in the wide-circulation *Paris illustré*, an aptly popular choice given its raucous fairground subject and implicitly patriotic hues.[39]

In 1887 *Paris illustré* carried another chromotypogravure, *The Sideshow (La Parade)* by Eugènc Grasset (fig. 29), which not only demonstrates the ubiquity of the subject but also how naturalist devices — the vigorous action of the dancer in midkick, an angle of view which defines the spectator as close up to the stage—had become commonplace in popular illustration. The exuberant body language of such images was something Seurat would dismiss, though he adopted a close-up viewpoint in some of his depictions of performers (see fig. 76). Another popular image, Heidbrinck's *The Three Fat Men* (*Les Trois Gras*) from *Le Courrier français* of 1888 (fig. 30), presents a view over the backs of a crowd, much as in the examples by Dehesghues and Forain. While this drawing may have been made for the illustrated press and rely on a pun on the Three Graces, it is closer in composition and actuality to naturalist Salon painting than to caricature. It thus manifests the easy translation between the two genres, high and low. Together they formed a body of descriptive images of and for the ordinary citizens, bourgeois and working class who shared the pleasures of the *fête foraine*, images that validated both republicanism and naturalism.

Not all naturalist images of *parades* in the 1880s were so positive in their outlook, however. At the Salon of 1888 Fernand Pelez exhibited *Grimaces and Misery—The Saltimbanques*, a massive composition over twenty feet in width (fig. 31). Intended to attract attention, it did so, and won a silver medal when exhibited the following year at the Exposition Universelle of 1889. Pelez had earlier contact with the fairground world; a circus wrestler had posed for him in 1879 when he painted a scene from ancient Roman history.[40] *Grimaces and Misery* presents its lifesize figures with striking actuality, from the white-faced clown who apathetically

FIG. 29. Eugène Grasset, *The Sideshow* (*La Parade*), from *Paris illustré*, February 1, 1887. Chromotypogravure, 17¼ x 12¾ in. (43.8 x 32.4 cm). The Metropolitan Museum of Art, New York, Thomas J. Watson Library, Gift of Friends of Watson Library

FIG. 30. Oswald Heidbrinck, *The Three Fat Men* (*Les Trois Gras*), from *Le Courrier français*, July 1, 1888. Photomechanical print, 16 x 11¼ in. (40.5 x 28.5 cm). Zimmerli Art Museum at Rutgers University, Museum Purchase

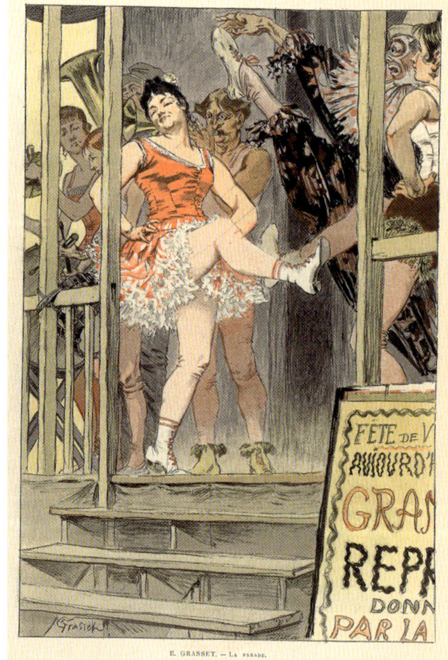

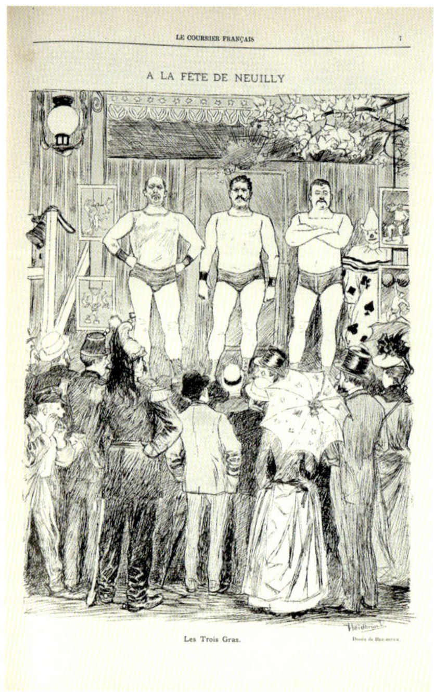

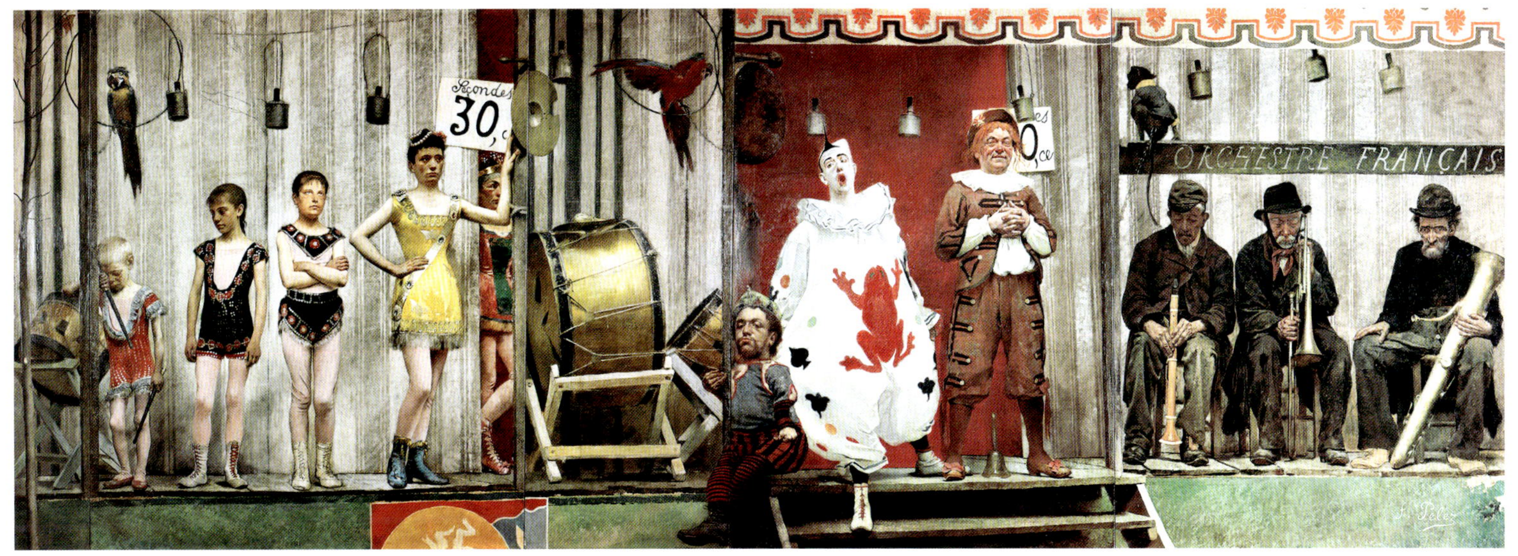

summons us while descending the steps to the sagging tights of the wan child performers lined up on the left. Only the dwarf and the performer in knee britches look toward us, ironically; the distracted children and miserable musicians exist in worlds of their own. This huge painting drew many responses from critics in 1888. For André Michel it was too much the naturalist *document* with "the dryness of an official report," while for Georges Lafenestre it could have stretched repetitively for two kilometers.[41] But *Grimaces and Misery* aroused sympathy in others. The naturalist detail inspired lengthy, concerned descriptions: the critic "Ariste" reckoned that the sniveling little boy at the left had been smacked, while Léonce Bénédite went so far as to diagnose the ailments of the musicians.[42] Still, some critics realized that the painting did more than record human suffering. Henry Houssaye observed of Pelez's cast that "their grins are without gaiety, but their misery arouses pity," Bénédite argued that *Grimaces and Misery* was "a comical and sad story that makes one think of a page by Dickens," while Gabriel Séailles compared Pelez's picture to a Russian novel, evincing "a religious feeling, the immense pity of human sadness."[43] These commentators assumed their readers' acquaintance with the notion of the sad clown, prompted by Pelez's title to acknowledge that his picture of a *parade* went beyond the direct descriptiveness of a Deheghues or a Raffaëlli to evoke deeper notions about melancholy and alienation.

The late Robert Rosenblum was the first to point out that Pelez's *Grimaces and Misery*, exhibited at the Salon of 1888, which opened on May 1, was on view almost contemporaneously with Seurat's representation of the same subject, shown at the Salon des Indépendants between March 22 and May 3.[44] The two artists, who do not seem to have been acquainted, in all likelihood selected their subjects quite independently — as we have seen, it was a common choice — and their respective paintings are very divergent in aesthetic terms. Nevertheless, there are overlaps. Séailles's long account of the Pelez described it as "a frieze formed into a triptych which divides and controls the groupings." He continued, "The painting has a center, the platform where, in the silence of the racket of drums and brass, the buffoon and the clown perform their *parade*. It's to them above all that one's gaze is drawn and remains."[45] These observations apply quite closely to Seurat's painting, too, and while *Circus Sideshow* is hardly descriptive — there are no sniveling children or saggy tights — Seurat did employ some of naturalism's eye for the likely. Just as the head of Pelez's buffoon in knee britches covers the first numeral of the notice posting the price of admission, so does the left flank of Seurat's trombonist. Most notably, Seurat opted to use the compositional formula appropriated by naturalist painters from caricature: the bunching of the heads and upper bodies of spectators into the lower foreground of his canvas. *Circus Sideshow* is far from a naturalist painting, but comparison with the descriptive pictures of the same subject by his peers in the 1880s reveals shared compositions, a mutual fascination — albeit with different solutions — with how to deal with nocturnal illumination, and a common awareness that the subject of the *saltimbanque* could carry deep associations.

The Gingerbread Fair and the Corvi Circus

Seurat's friend Gustave Kahn, the avant-garde art critic and poet, noted in his review of the 1888 Salon des Indépendants that *Circus Sideshow* represents the Corvi Circus set up at the Foire au pain d'épice (Gingerbread Fair) in Paris. Seurat would have seen the circus there in the spring of 1887, as the fair was held annually in the three weeks after Easter Sunday. It was one of the many *fêtes foraines* that crisscrossed France, mounting booths and tents at time-honored dates in a pattern that had continued for centuries. Popular awareness of this long tradition is evident in the visual culture of Seurat's day, as, for example, in the illustration of Gabriel de Saint-Aubin's 1760 painting of a *parade* in an 1888 advertisement for a book on how the French had lived on the eve of the Revolution (fig. 32).[46] Naturalist literature also described the world of the seasonal fairs: Edmond de Goncourt's 1879 novel about two acrobats in a traveling circus, *Les Frères Zemganno* (The Zemganno Brothers), which Seurat may well have read, has them visit Flanders and Alsace, the Auvergne and Provence.[47] Familiar entertainments were part of the tradition as well. The Marseillais

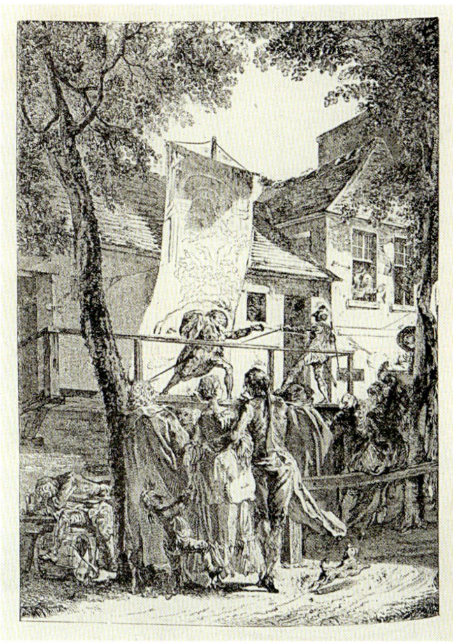

artist Adolphe Monticelli's painting of a *parade* from the late 1870s probably shows that city's monthlong Foire Saint-Lazare.[48] Executed in his distinctive rich impasto, its collection of clowns, acrobats and animals, huge *gegant* figure made out of papier-mâché, and fortune-telling cockatoos inventories the types of act on offer (fig. 33).

The Gingerbread Fair, originating in the Middle Ages, was a major event staged to the east of Paris in an area that came to be known as the Barrière du Trône after Louis XIV and Maria Theresa of Spain entered the city there in 1660 as newlyweds. The two columns erected to mark that occasion, surmounted by Saint Louis and King Philip II Augustus, are visible in the background of a drawing of the fair by Felicien Myrbach from 1884 (fig. 34). The place du Trône had been redesigned in the late 1870s as a circular hub from which boulevards and roads radiated, matching the place de l'Etoile to the west of the city (fig. 35).[49] This modernization, which involved renaming it the place de la Nation, shows how the Third Republic's authorities aimed to both embrace and control the lower-class populations of the *quartier*, for the place du Trône area had seen serious fighting in late May 1871 as the insurgent Paris Commune was finally suppressed by the French army.[50] The Gingerbread Fair stretched beyond the *place,* which was its pivot, reaching eastward along the cours de Vincennes and westward up the boulevard Voltaire.[51] The fair drew crowds of all classes from across the city: Etienne Gervais's moralizing 1866 novel *La Foire aux pains d'épice*

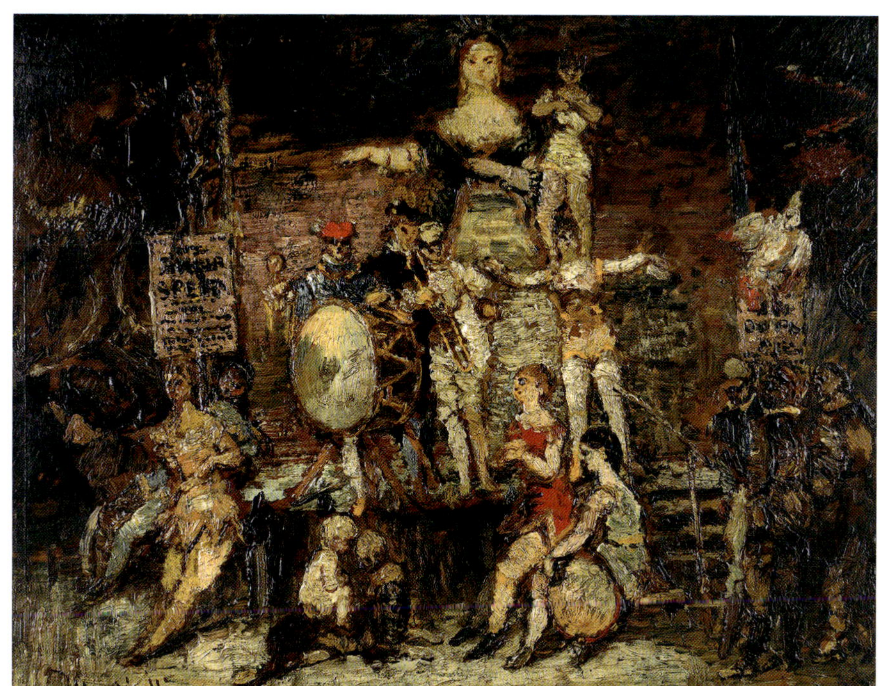

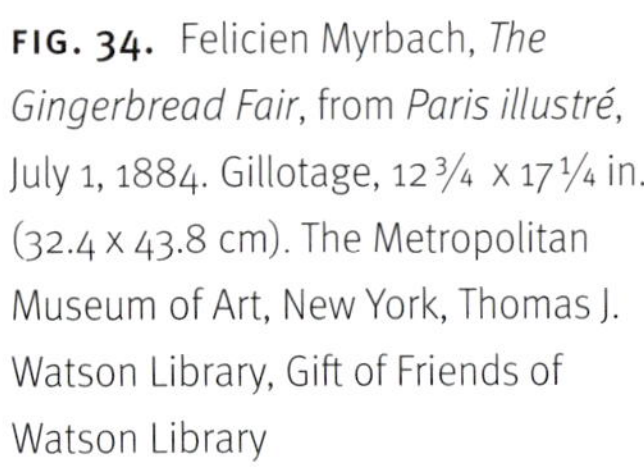

FIG. 34. Felicien Myrbach, *The Gingerbread Fair*, from *Paris illustré*, July 1, 1884. Gillotage, 12 ¾ x 17 ¼ in. (32.4 x 43.8 cm). The Metropolitan Museum of Art, New York, Thomas J. Watson Library, Gift of Friends of Watson Library

FIG. 35. Panoramic view of the place de la Nation, Paris, during the Gingerbread Fair, ca. 1900. Musée des Civilisations de l'Europe et de la Méditerranée, Marseille

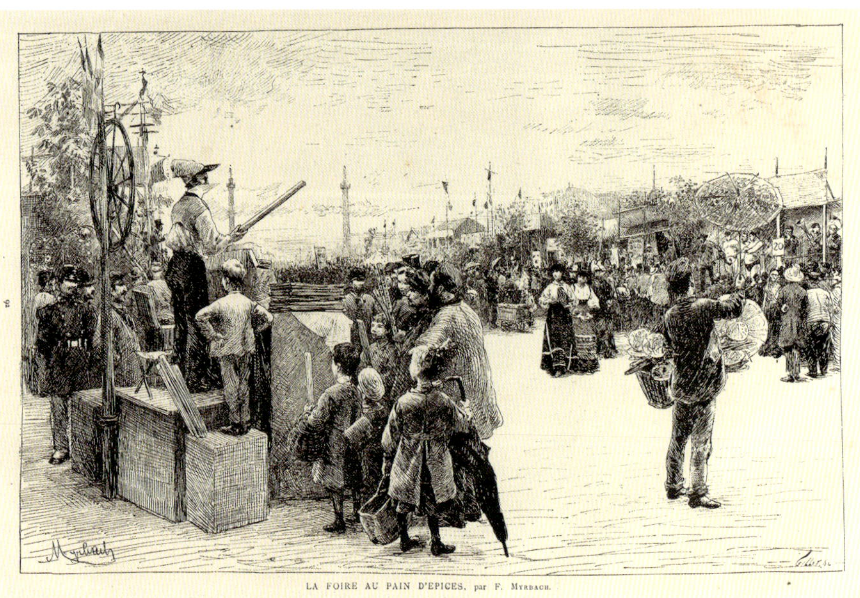

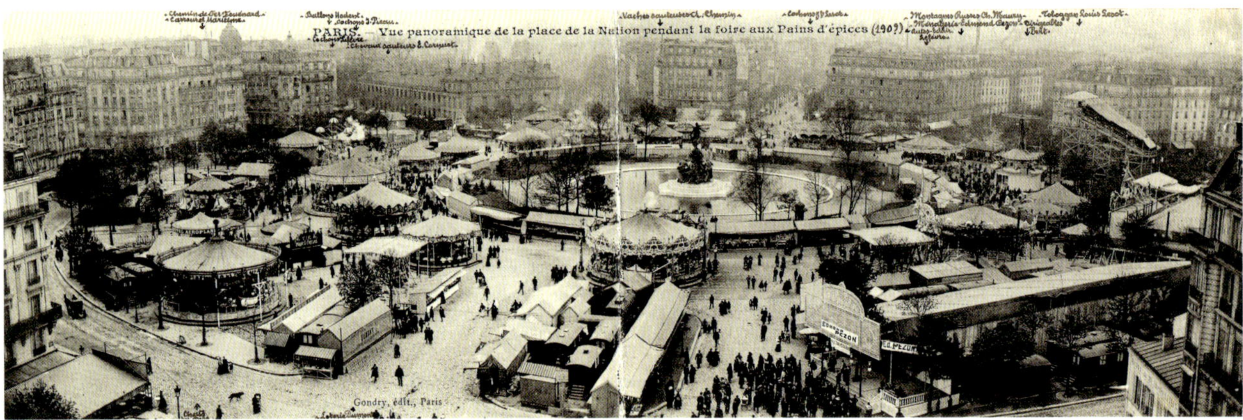

describes a varied public, arriving on foot, in omnibuses, and in their own carriages, including infants, schoolchildren, and adults.[52] Myrbach's illustration bears this out, with children to the fore and a mixture of working-class smocks and middle-class top hats visible in his crowd. The broad popularity of this and other fairs is attested also by the vast amount of ephemera—prints, magazine illustrations, song sheets, decorated crockery, and so on—that they generated (see fig. 36a–c).

Such a big fair, attracting tens of thousands each year, needed multiple popular attractions (see fig. 37). Traditionally gingerbread, *pain d'épice*, was sold in myriad fantastic and amusing forms: devils, animals normal or bizarre, Napoleon, Isis the Egyptian goddess, or huge-breasted wet nurses.[53]

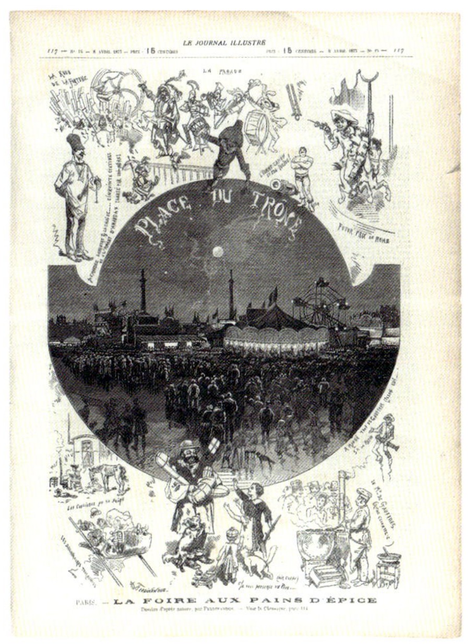 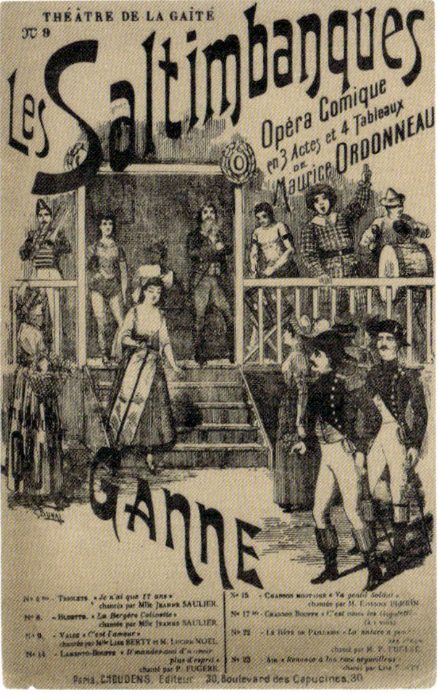 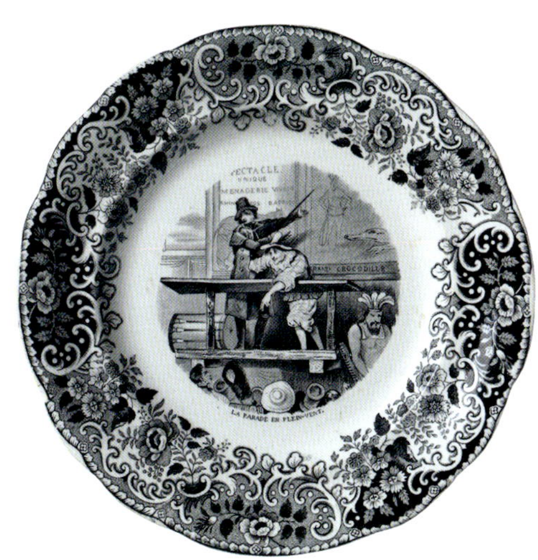

FIG. 36. (a) Alexandre Ferdinandus (pseudonym), *Paris — The Gingerbread Fair*, from *Le Journal illustré*, April 8, 1877. Wood engraving, 14 7/8 x 11 in. (37.7 x 28 cm). The Metropolitan Museum of Art, New York; (b) Ernest Buval, cover for *Les Saltimbanques: Opéra comique* (musical score), ca. 1899. The Metropolitan Museum of Art, New York; (c) Geoffroy et Cie, Gien, *The Open-Air Sideshow* (*La Parade en plein-vent*), child's plate, ca. 1850; transfer-printed earthenware, Diam. 7 7/8 in. (20 cm). The Metropolitan Museum of Art, New York, Funds from various donors, 2016 (2016.564)

The streets were lined with temporary stalls offering entertainments and diversions of an almost unimaginable range and fantasy. In the late 1870s the British journalist George Augustus Sala was unimpressed by one show with only "a broken wax figure of an Indian princess, and a lot of ramshackle old stereoscopes," but struck by Adrien Delille's booth, decorated with decent copies of Raphael's *The Triumph of Galatea* and Jacques Louis David's *The Intervention of the Sabine Women*, and featuring "a very good brass band outside, a very fair show of male and female tumblers, and, in particular, a man in the dress of a Pierrot, who whacked the big drum with the strength of a Hercules and the persistency of a Sisyphus." A wild beast show was opposite.[54] Hugues Le Roux's scrupulous study of the traveling fairs, published in 1889, explained that alongside performances at fixed times, such as plays, mini-operettas, or animal acts, there were the *entresorts*, spectacles with no beginning or end to which the public could just drop in. These included wax museums, dwarves or people who were physically deformed, tattooed ladies and performing fleas, women in contorted *poses plastiques*, "mermaids" (girls wearing seals' tails), and of course the severed head that spoke. There were performers as varied as wrestlers like the Marseille brothers and magicians such as Buatier de Kolta, who could roll a sheet of paper into a cornet and produce roses from it. Impresarios went to extraordinary lengths to stage unusual shows; a tragic case occurred in 1882 when a stunted youth, apparently only twenty-five inches in height, was trained as a "tiger tamer" to perform with six tomcats painted with stripes — which killed him.[55]

FIG. 37. Edmond-Emile Gotorbe, *Recollections of Bastille Day Fairs*, from *L'Univers illustré*, July 31, 1880. Wood engraving, 15 ¾ x 11 ⅛ in. (40 x 28.2 cm). The Metropolitan Museum of Art, New York

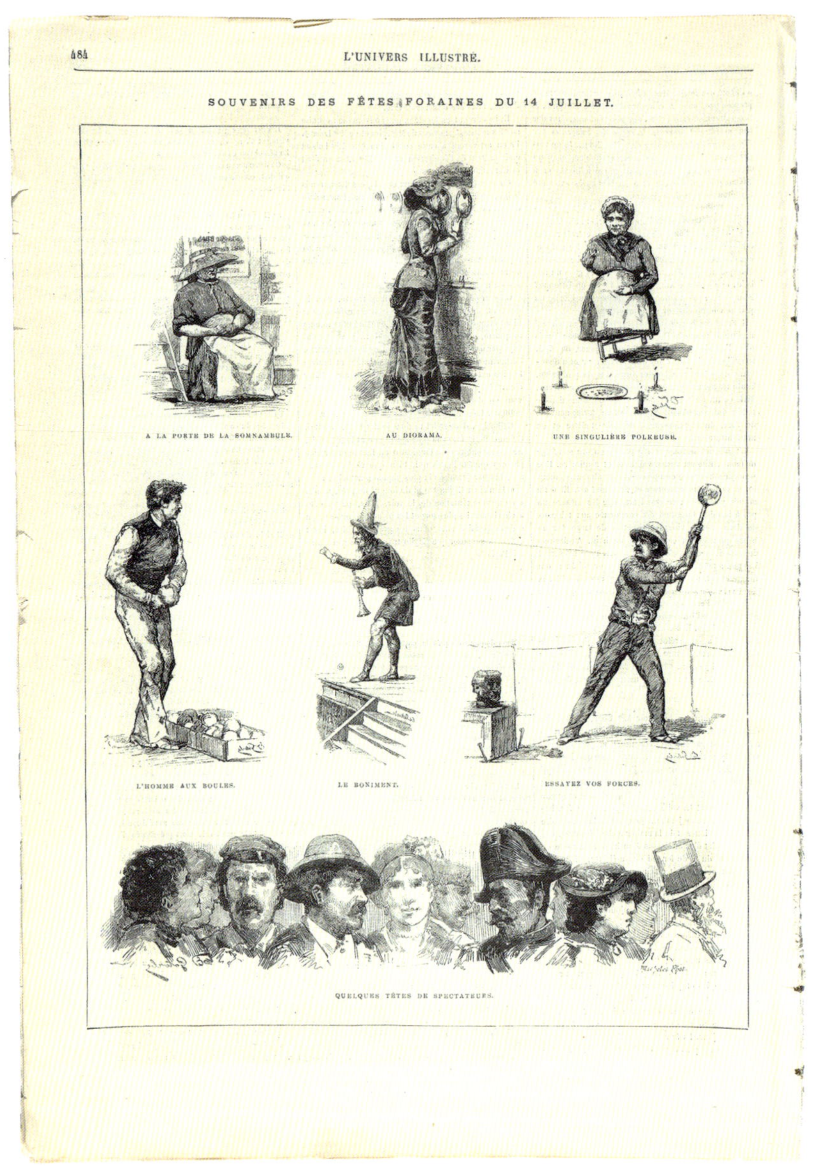

Many of these acts and spectacles were time-honored, but by the 1880s the traveling fairs were alert to the need to modernize. They presented displays such as the Grand Musée Anatomique du Docteur Spitzner with wax models that could be "dissected," masking prurience with science.[56] According to Baedeker's Paris guidebook (1881), the Gingerbread Fair had "merry-go-rounds driven by steam, miniature tramways, and bicycle courses," representing the latest in industry and transportation.[57] When Pierre Véron complained in 1888 that the fair was short on novelty, relying on the traditional American fat lady Mademoiselle Lily and *montagnes*

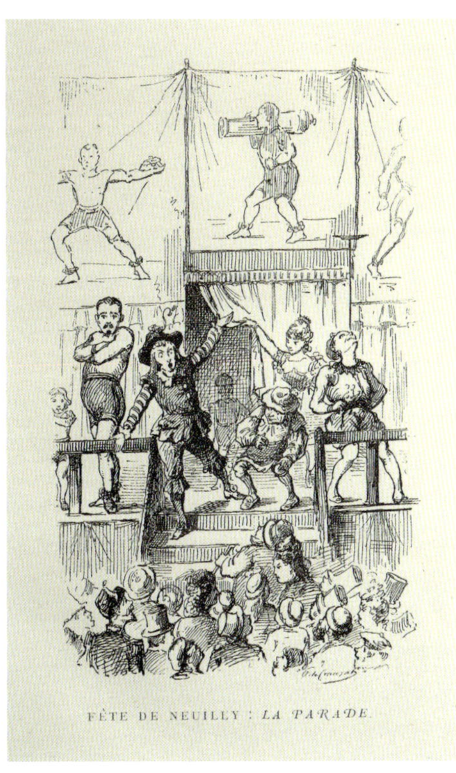

FIG. 38. Paul de Crauzat, *Fair at Neuilly: The Sideshow* (*La Parade*), from Gaston Escudier, *Les Saltimbanques: Leur Vie, leurs moeurs* (Paris, 1875), p. 19. Photomechanical print. Zimmerli Art Museum at Rutgers University, Museum Purchase, Norma B. Bartman Research Library Fund

russes (a primitive unpowered roller coaster), the following week he felt obliged to draw attention to the new *Chemin de fer de l'amour* (Railway of Love).[58] Many commentators mentioned the noise that was created by the Gingerbread Fair. An article in *La Vie moderne* in 1880 described "crazed music to the rhythm of bells and big bass drums," amid a "tumultuous sea [of people], boisterous, baying, shouting."[59] The music was not only noisy, it was repetitious, Gaston Escudier's book on *saltimbanques* admitting that the little bands at *parades* could play for a couple of hours with a single sheet of score.[60] Its illustrations capture the raucous mood (see fig. 38). The fairs were cheap, to give the chance of maximum income from the widest clientele, with entrance prices for shows ranging from twenty-five centimes to a franc.[61] But increasingly there was a sense of change about such fairs; they were no longer useful markets, as at one time in history, but places of frank expenditure on ephemeral pleasure.[62]

Between 1860 and 1890 the traveling fairs were curtailed by a new pressure—though the Gingerbread Fair would prove an exception as the only fair to be held in central Paris from 1867 to 1881.[63] Magnets for large, undifferentiated crowds, the fairs were mistrusted and so increasingly controlled by the state. During the fragile later years of the Second Empire, a series of measures limited Paris to fourteen *fêtes foraines*, permitted only in the city's outer communes, and by 1867 these too were suppressed. Not until 1874 were four fairs reinstated by the liberalizing Third Republic in peripheral arrondissements. In the ten central arrondissements, plus the Eleventh and Twelfth, which the Gingerbread Fair straddled, it was the only *fête foraine* allowed—it was simply too traditional to be tampered with. By spreading the other fairs across the outer city in the 1880s, the authorities kept at bay bourgeois anxieties about lower-class unrest, which had reached a crescendo with the bloody Paris Commune of March to May 1871. Sala, with British irony, pointed out that "every inch of the ground" on which the exuberant Gingerbread Fair was held had been fought over in one insurrection or another.[64] During the 1880s the Third Republic used public monuments to promote its claims of liberty, equality, and fraternity in the area: the maquette of Léopold Morice's statue of the Republic was unveiled in the place de la République on July 14, 1880, and Jules Dalou's model for *Le Triomphe de la République* in the place de la Nation on September 21, 1889. Thus, in *Circus Sideshow*, Seurat chose to represent a *parade* in a part of Paris known for its fractious population and demarcated by images of republican solidarity.

The traveling fairs, usually hand-to-mouth operations, faced another pressure in Paris from fixed circuses, in other words, increasing competition from capitalized ventures. Venues such as the Cirque d'Hiver, founded in 1867, the Cirque Fernando (1875), the Hippodrome de l'Alma (1877), and

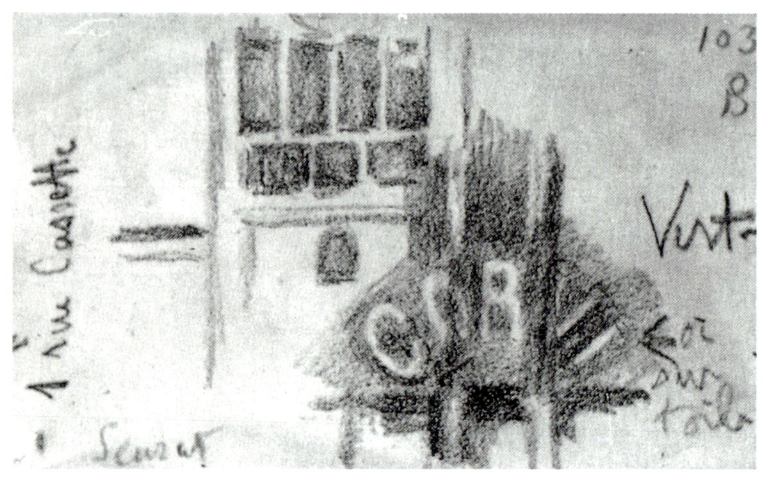

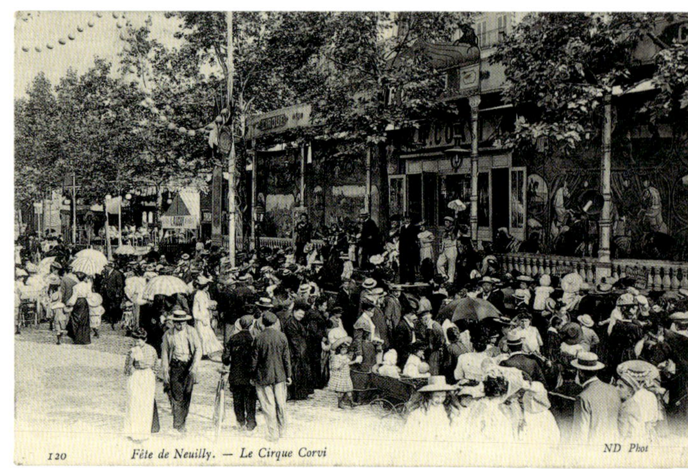

FIG. 39. Georges Seurat, *Entrance to the Corvi Circus* (page from sketchbook), 1887. Conté crayon on paper, 4 ½ x 7 ⅝ in. (11.5 x 19.5 cm). Location unknown (H382, verso of H381; see César M. de Hauke, *Seurat et son oeuvre*, vol. 1 [Paris: Gründ, 1961], p. 50)

FIG. 40. The Corvi Circus at the Fair at Neuilly, ca. 1900. Postcard. The Metropolitan Museum of Art, New York

the Nouveau Cirque (1886) were city-center businesses based in permanent buildings. They were promoted by agencies such as the one run by a certain Rosinsky, who had left the United States after a strong man at his own circus had murdered a policeman in Cincinnati.[65] The traveling fairs responded to their rivals' professionalism, setting up a trade union and a newspaper, *Le Voyageur forain*, in 1883; a new association and newspaper, *L'Union mutuelle*, was established in the spring of 1887, with Ferdinand Corvi, proprietor of the Corvi Circus, on the board.[66] From his leftist position Jules Vallès had already sensed the ramifications of these changes in his 1882 series of articles on the *fêtes foraines*. The old types of fair had been noisy but popular, providing cheap entertainment for the very poor. The personnel made a fragile living — with risks of injury, bad weather, low receipts — and their itinerant life made them outsiders. Increasing regulation, unionization, and the purchase by property developers of land outside the Paris fortifications formerly used for wintering had advantaged the richer establishments. This professionalization, Vallès argued, was disconnecting the fairs from the popular culture that spawned and sustained them.[67]

The Corvi Circus was active from the mid-nineteenth century, when it is recorded as a feature of the annual Fête de Montmartre in Paris, and it was a regular presence at the Gingerbread Fair as well.[68] We can be certain that *Circus Sideshow* represents this specific circus, even though the painting has no lettering that says so. Not only did Seurat's friend Kahn mention the connection in his 1888 review, but a small drawing by Seurat includes the letters *CORVI* alongside what Herbert first identified as a study of the ticket office window (fig. 39).[69] Ephemera such as postcards (fig. 40; see also fig. 5) and posters (see fig. 45) confirm the identification. Known as a smoothly run operation that chiefly featured animal acts, this circus also boasted some human performers, among them the famed juggler Judita

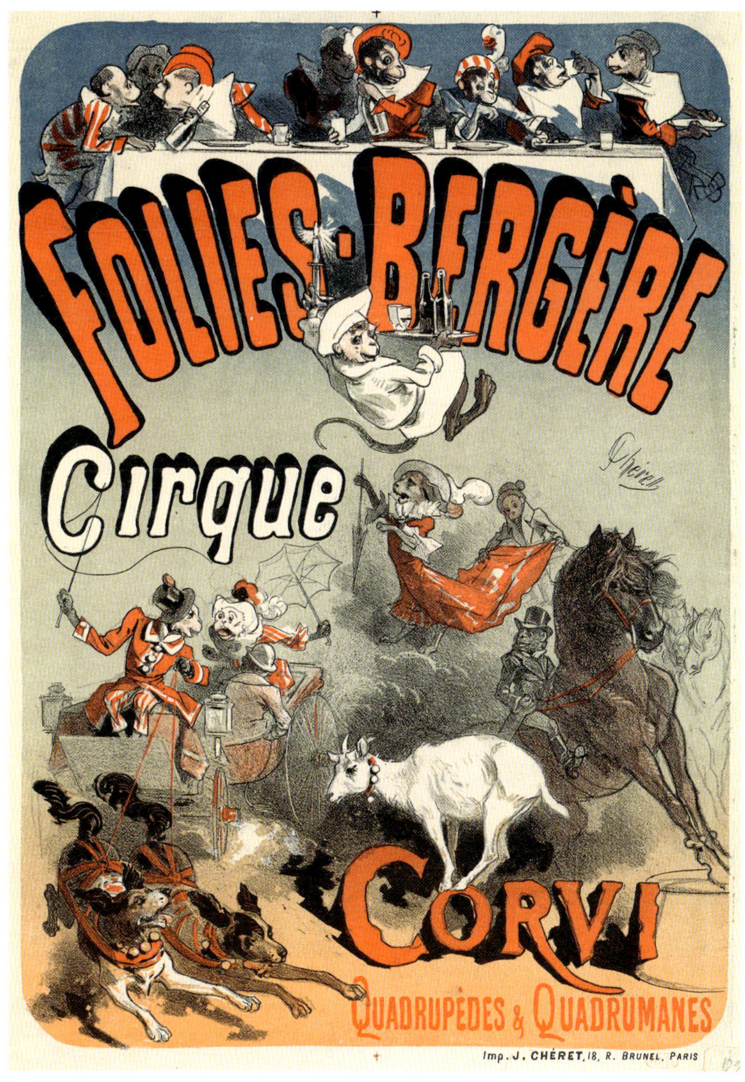

Rossi.[70] *La Vie moderne* described its *parade* in 1880: "The whole Corvi
Circus troupe joins in the *parade*: the men and women perform a respect-
able dance, during which two monkey generals, mounted on ponies, cast
a serious eye over the public."[71] While primarily a traveling troupe, the
Corvi Circus did some business with permanent institutions; for example,
in 1881 it had a season at the Folies-Bergère in central Paris. To promote
this Jules Chéret, the leading poster designer of the day, created an image
that features some of the main attractions: the monkey banquet, the pony
with simian rider, and the goat balanced on a ball (the *O* of Corvi), which
became a leitmotiv of Corvi publicity (fig. 41). The animal acts were elaborate and well drilled. The apes and monkeys had been trained to stage a

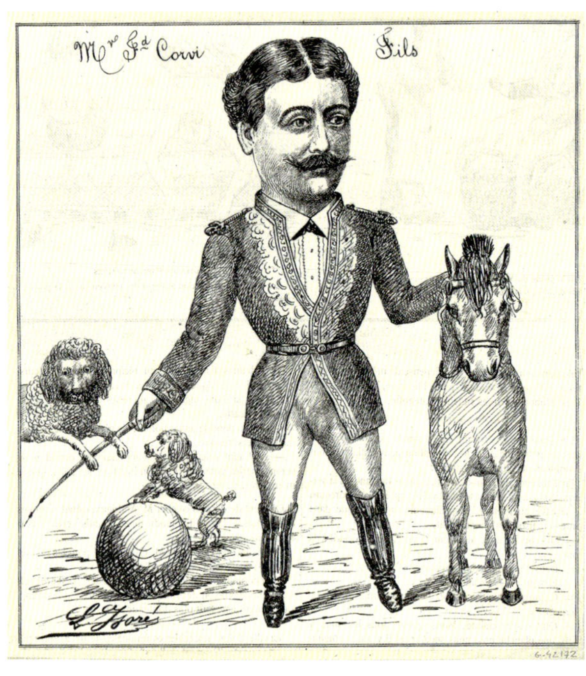

FIG. 42. L. Isoré, *Ferdinand Corvi, Jr.*, ca. 1882. Lithograph, 9⅝ x 9 in. (24.5 x 22.7 cm). Musée Carnavalet—Histoire de Paris

FIG. 43. Affiches Américaines, Charles Lévy, Paris (printer), *Fair at the Tuileries: F. Corvi's Miniature Theater-Circus*, ca. 1882–88. Color lithograph, 43⅛ x 33⅛ in. (109.5 x 84 cm). Musée Carnavalet— Histoire de Paris

FIG. 44. Affiches Américaines, Charles Lévy, Paris (printer), *Fair at the Tuileries: F. Corvi's Miniature Theater-Circus*, ca. 1882–88. Color lithograph, 22¾ x 16½ in. (57.9 x 42 cm). Musée Carnavalet— Histoire de Paris

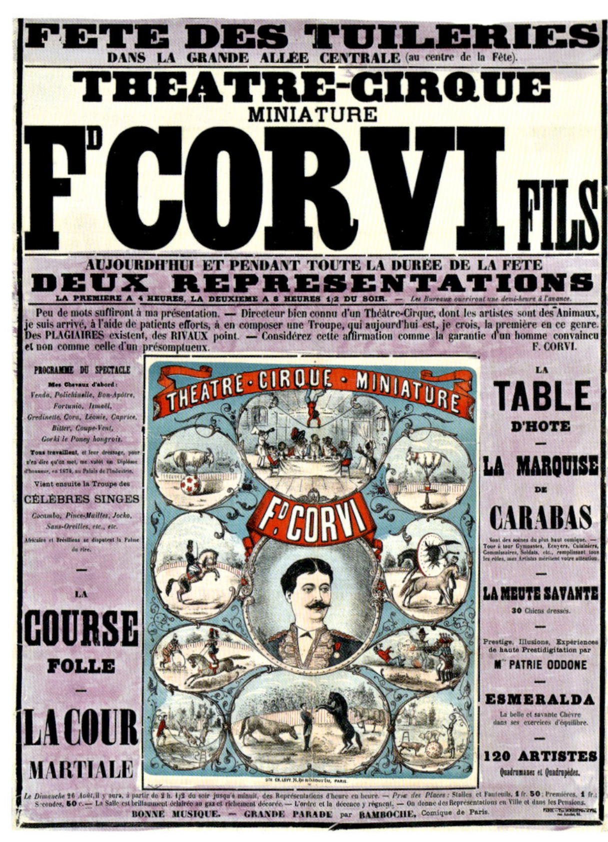

version of Thomas Couture's famous painting *Romans of the Decadence* (1846–47; Musée d'Orsay, Paris) and to perform a pantomime about a soldier executed for desertion; each "actor" had a trained replacement, their owner boasted in an interview.[72]

Ferdinand Corvi himself, sometimes called "fils," or Jr., featured prominently in the publicity of the 1880s. Indeed, a review of popular images makes a strong case for identifying the proprietorial man in *Circus Sideshow* as none other than he. A caricatural print with Corvi's head of exaggerated size, apparently dating from about 1882, shows him alongside a pony, which is posed with formalized frontality (fig. 42). Intriguingly, one of Seurat's preliminary drawings for *Circus Sideshow* adopts this device (see fig. 58); insofar as he admired naïf popular imagery, this is not surprising. Most likely Seurat was aware of other pieces depicting Corvi, as the circus promoted itself with various types of colored posters. A large poster advertising its presence at the annual Fête des Tuileries, for example, features Corvi's portrait at the center (fig. 43). He is surrounded by medallion-like motifs of the circus's chief attractions, such as the monkey on horseback and the goat on the ball. These replicate the ovals painted on the canvas that surrounded the

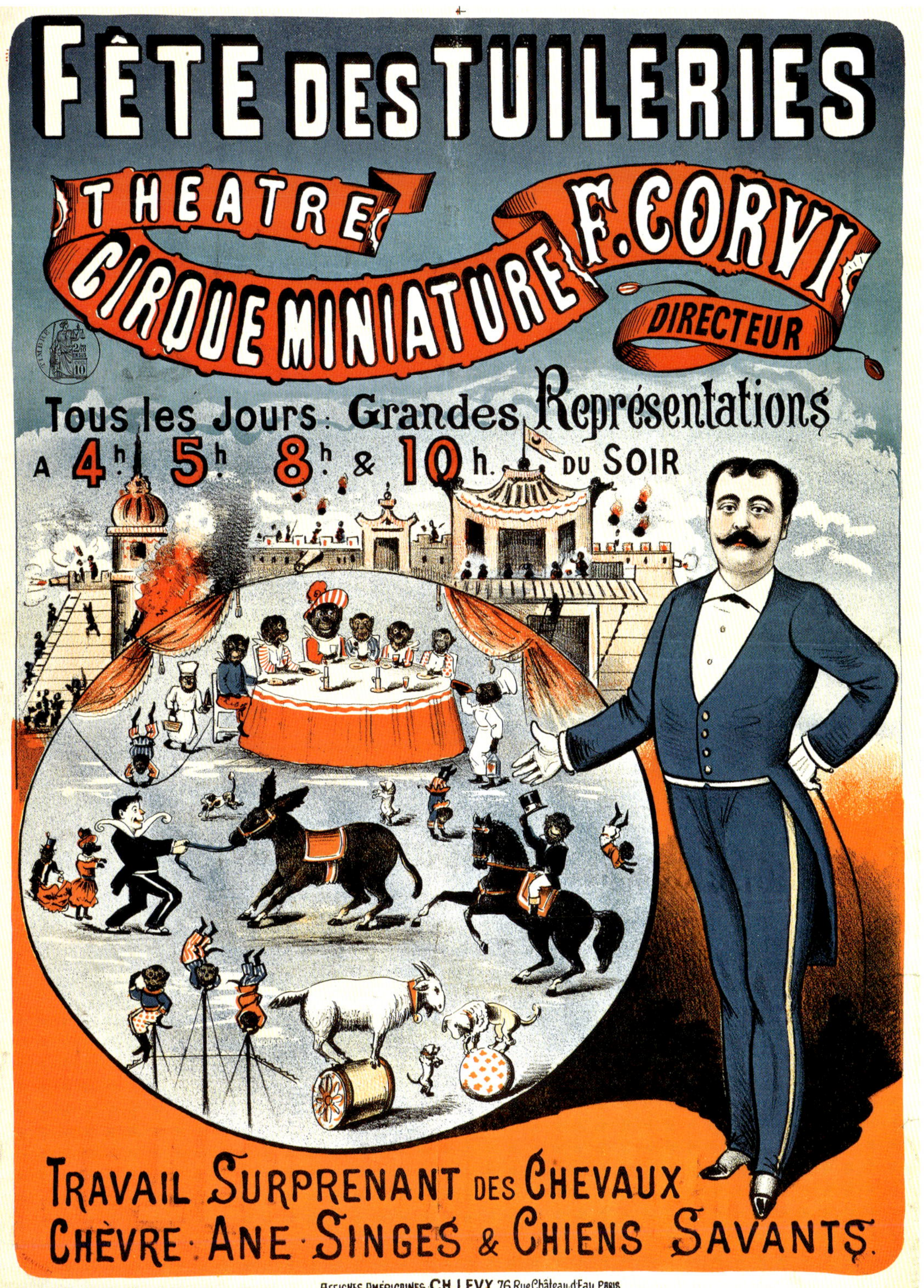
FÊTE DES TUILERIES
THEATRE
CIRQUE MINIATURE
F. CORVI
DIRECTEUR
Tous les Jours Grandes Représentations
A 4h. 5h. 8h. & 10h. DU SOIR
TRAVAIL SURPRENANT DES CHEVAUX
CHÈVRE ANE SINGES & CHIENS SAVANTS.
AFFICHES AMÉRICAINES CH. LEVY, 76, Rue Château-d'Eau, PARIS.

circus's big top to show passersby what acts were on offer; they are evoked in Seurat's painting on the backdrop behind the musicians. A smaller poster for the Fête des Tuileries shows the animal acts inside a circus ring and lists them by name at the bottom, while a towering Corvi stands at right as ringmaster presenting his spectacle (fig. 44). His erect posture, puffed-up torso, and bristling moustache are evidently typical of the dominant persona he projected. Le Roux's 1889 book on the fairs identified Corvi as one of the last to wear the old-style formal tailcoat, and this sartorial choice was featured by Seurat in his profile of proud Corvi.[73]

A third poster, interestingly similar to Seurat's painting, shows in schematic form the totality of the temporary circus structure of which his canvas depicts a fragment (fig. 45). We see the symmetrical frontage of the Corvi Circus, with a balustraded dais on each side of the central steps leading to the ticket office. The band stands to the left, and the elegant Corvi to the right, accompanied by some of his animals as well as a buffoon with his hair combed into a silly peak and wearing a ridiculously full white bow tie; above them is the long pipe with its gas jets, and behind them the painted canvas backdrop. The crowd outside is presented from the back and predominantly as bourgeois, presumably in order to play up the market. To each side of the ticket booth signs announce that the cheaper seats — second tier and galleries — are to the left and the more expensive ones — first tier and stalls — to the right, which explains the class division of the onlookers to those two sides apparent in Seurat's painting.

Although the identification of the Corvi Circus as the subject of *Circus Sideshow* is certain, paradoxically that certainty raises ambiguities. We cannot be sure of how much Seurat knew about this circus: that, for instance, it was an efficient organization, which seems both to have traveled and been well capitalized, with its owner adept at publicity and serving in professional organizations.[74] Vallès's series of articles in 1882 had made much of the divisions between richer and poorer *saltimbanques*, and one of the reactions against Pelez's *Grimaces and Misery* in 1888 had been because it seemed too demonstrably to play up the alienated existence of the traveling shows. In representing the Corvi Circus, Seurat by contrast selected a successful and entrepreneurial enterprise. How justified, then, is one in reading his painting as melancholy or marginal?

Perhaps Seurat's views of the circus were colored by firsthand knowledge of circus life from two acquaintances. One may have been the mysterious artist of circus subjects called Wagner, who was described by the novelist Joris-Karl Huysmans in an August 1888 article in *La Cravache parisienne*.[75] The following month Seurat's friend Paul Signac wrote a letter to the editor explaining that this was Théo Wagner, who performed a trapeze act with the duc de La Rochefoucauld at the Cirque Molier

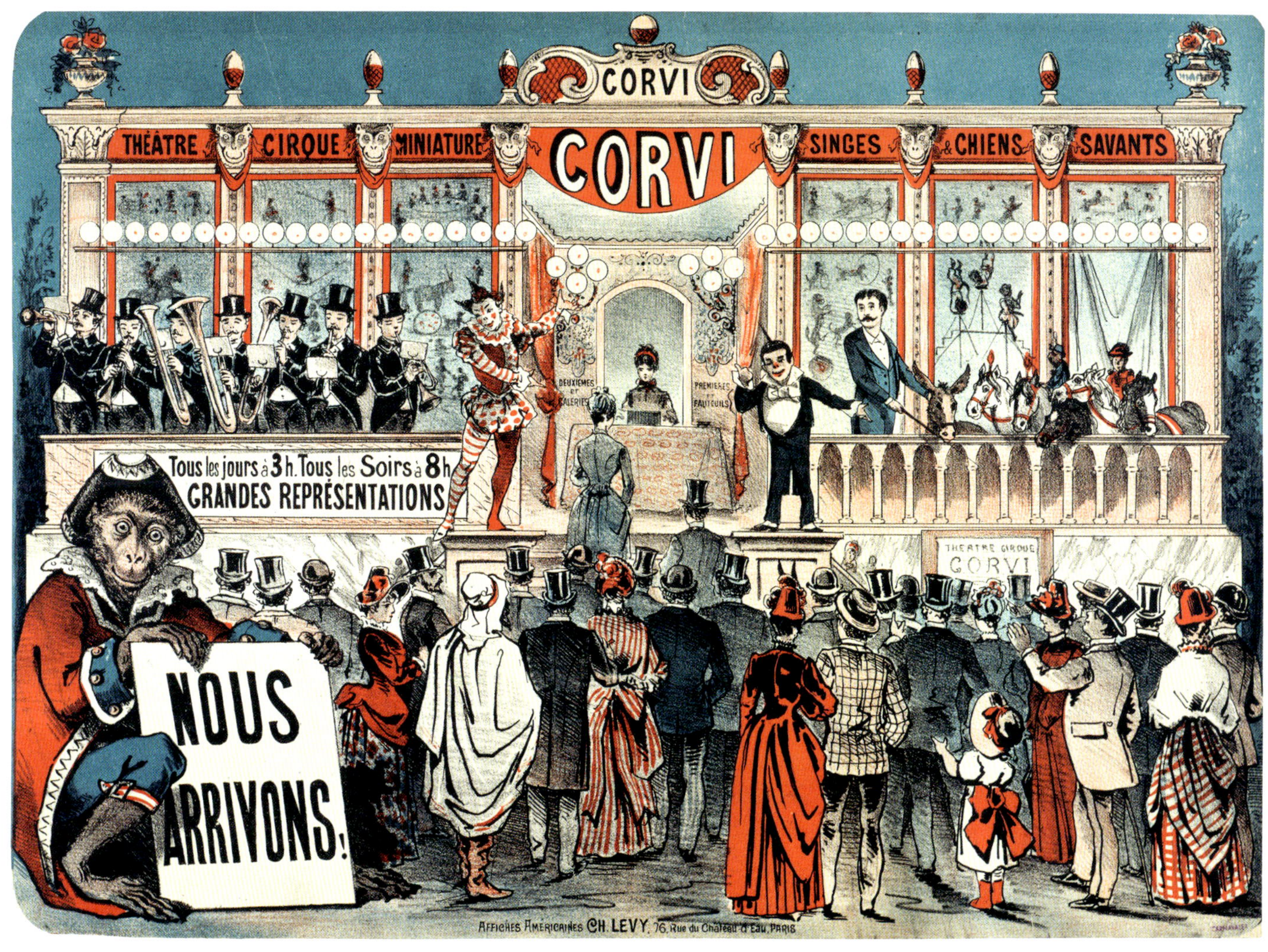

FIG. 45. Affiches Américaines, Charles Lévy, Paris (printer), *Corvi: We're Here!*, ca. 1882–88. Color lithograph, 15 ½ x 21 ¾ in. (39.4 x 55.2 cm). Musée Carnavalet — Histoire de Paris

in Paris and whom Seurat had known when they were students at the Ecole des Beaux-Arts.[76] The other was Léon Pourtau, a musician who in 1885–86 took a year out of the Conservatoire de Paris to play clarinet at a *café-concert* and in the band of a traveling circus. In 1887 Pourtau won first prize for his instrument at the Conservatoire, but he also attended art classes and was a practicing Neo-Impressionist painter, friendly with Lucien Pissarro and Louis Hayet, who introduced him to Seurat.[77] Thus this rather unclubbable artist may well have had inside knowledge of the world of the *saltimbanque*.

Probably stimulated by seeing the Corvi Circus at the Gingerbread Fair in the spring of 1887, Seurat had *Circus Sideshow* ready for exhibition at the Salon des Indépendants in March 1888. Born in December 1859, he was still a young artist when he painted it, twenty-eight when it went on view.[78] Having studied for at least three years at the Ecole des Beaux-Arts in Paris, the nation's leading art school, under the strict Neoclassical eye of Henri Lehmann, in 1879–80 he undertook a year's compulsory conscription in the French army and by 1881 was working independently in the capital.[79] Sharing a studio with Edmond Aman-Jean and Ernest Laurent, he developed his highly individual drawing style based on robust, simple forms defined not by line but modeled in strongly shaded masses with conté crayon on textured Michallet paper. His early paintings, typically small panels of landscapes, sometimes with figures, were also characterized by economical use of form and handled with distinct strokes that made no attempt to describe specific textures but gave a unified surface. By this period Seurat had begun to read and explore theoretical texts about art and color theory, such as Charles Blanc's *Grammaire des arts du dessin* (Grammar of the Arts of Design), first published in 1867, and Ogden Rood's *Modern Chromatics, with Applications to Art and Industry*, published in New York in 1879 and reissued in France in 1881 as *Théorie scientifique des couleurs* (Scientific Theory of Colors).[80]

By 1883 Seurat had begun work on his first major canvas, *Bathers at Asnières* (*Une Baignade, Asnières*) (fig. 46). Rejected by the jury of the Salon in spring 1884, it was then exhibited at the first Salon des Indépendants, a jury-free organization set up by the Paris city council.[81] *Bathers* attracted negligible critical attention. Seurat immediately began work on another canvas of the same size (ten feet wide) and of a similar subject, people at leisure on the banks of the Seine in the western suburbs of Paris. *A Sunday on La Grande Jatte (1884)* (*Un Dimanche à la Grande Jatte [1884]*) was exhibited at the eighth, and final, Impressionist exhibition in the spring of 1886, where its large scale, innovative treatment of touch and surface, and economically, even stiffly, articulated figures drew intense critical attention and instantly established Seurat as the leading figure in Parisian avant-garde painting (fig. 47).[82] Throughout this period Seurat's technique and composition had been in a process of progressive development. *Bathers* was painted in broad strokes, the artist intent on maximizing the effect of summer sunlight by the use of high-key color. With *La Grande Jatte* Seurat began with a similar touch but in the later stages reworked some areas with a dotted mark, the aim being to increase luminosity by having contrasting colors vibrate against each other, so interspersing the natural green of the

FIG. 46. Georges Seurat, *Bathers at Asnières* (*Une Baignade, Asnières*), 1884. Oil on canvas, 79 x 118 in. (201 x 300 cm). National Gallery, London, Courtauld Fund, 1924

FIG. 47. Georges Seurat, *A Sunday on La Grande Jatte (1884)* (*Un Dimanche à la Grande Jatte [1884]*), 1884–86. Oil on canvas, 81¾ x 121¼ in. (207.5 x 308.1 cm). The Art Institute of Chicago, Helen Birch Bartlett Memorial Collection

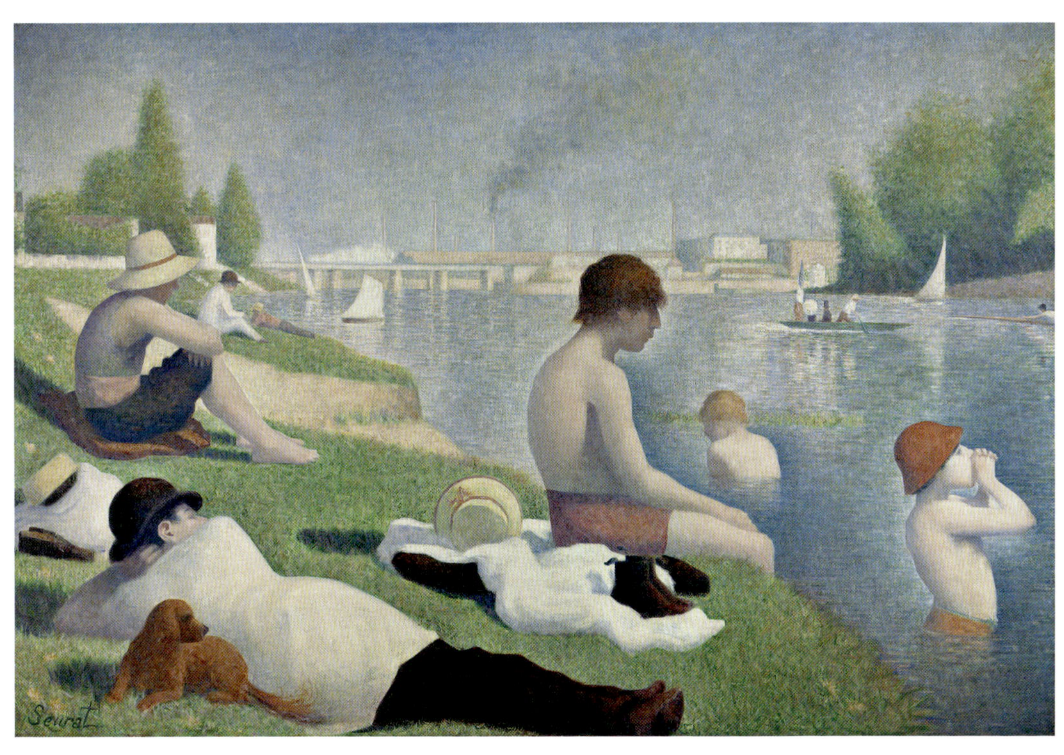

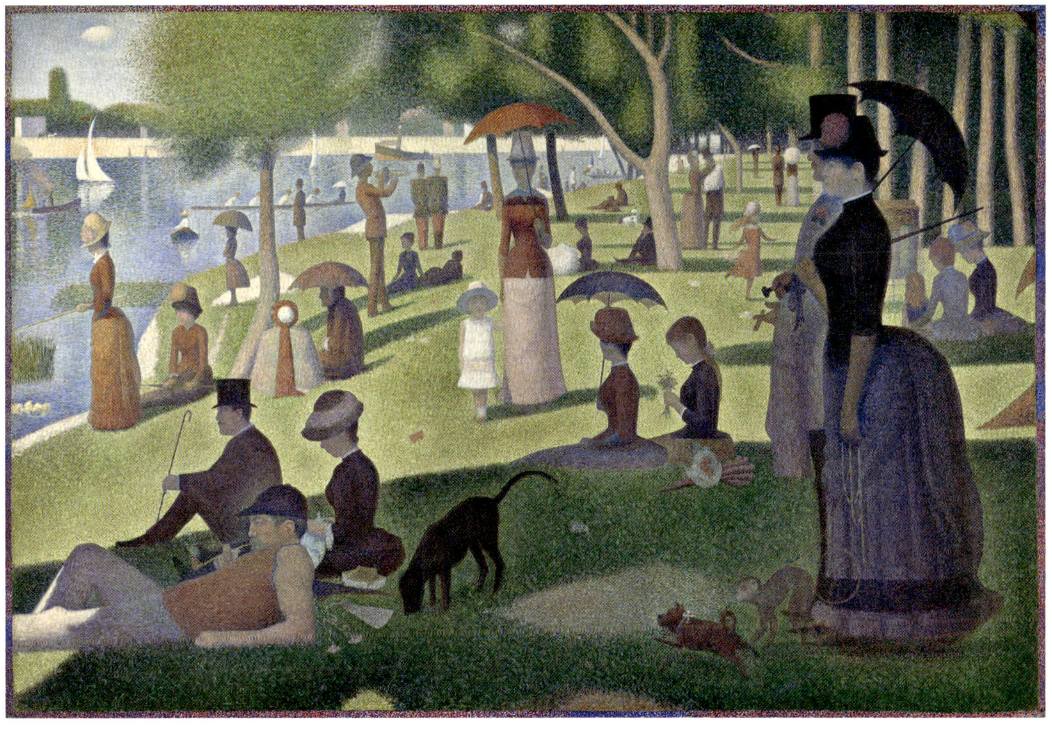

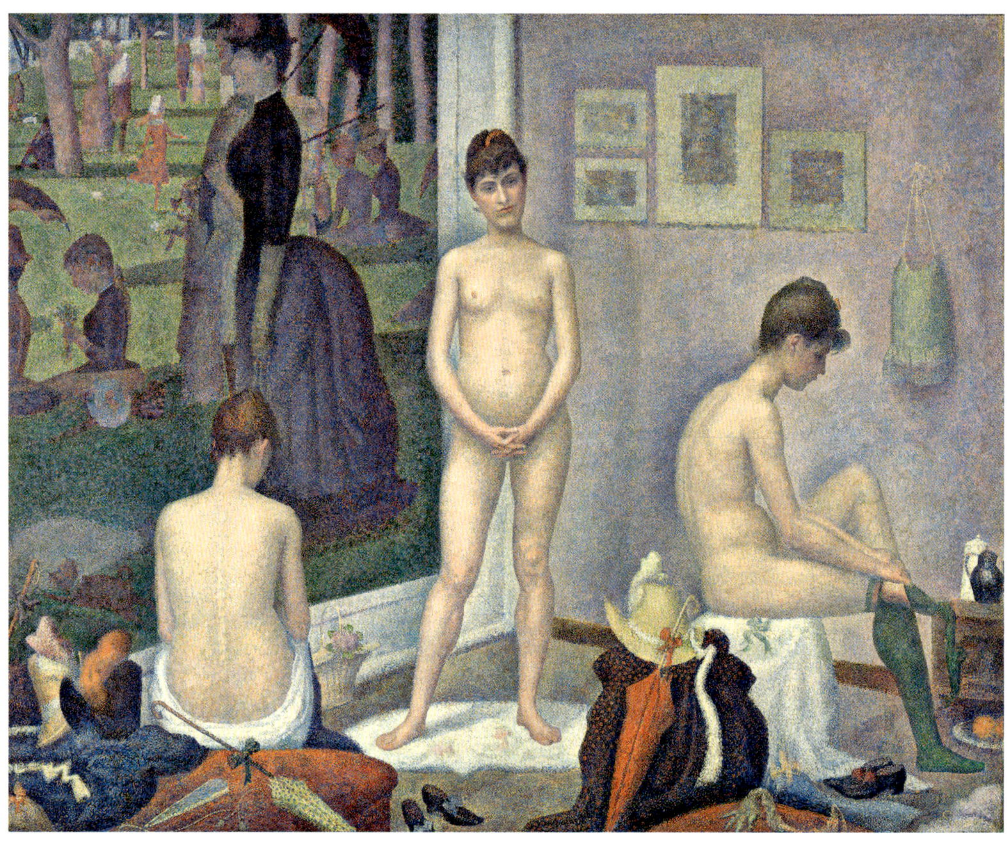

FIG. 48. Georges Seurat, *Models* (*Poseuses*), 1886–88. Oil on canvas, 78¾ x 98⅜ in. (200 x 249.9 cm). The Barnes Foundation, Philadelphia

grass with dots of complementary red. In terms of composition both *Bathers* and *La Grande Jatte* have a degree of fragmentation. The former, with its men and youths alongside each other on the river bank but not engaged by either gesture or gaze, perhaps took on its air of paradoxically isolated sociability due to its preparatory procedure, as Seurat crafted drawings of the figures separately, so that each was transferred to the canvas as an integral individual. *La Grande Jatte* is a more complex composition, with a larger number of figures, requiring more complicated development. In this case Seurat made some drawings of interrelated figures, but nevertheless the final design, rendered strictly planar by the fall of horizontal shadows, is divided into individual figures and groups that are diverse — many in profile, some frontal, a few apparently haphazard — and yet do not give the impression of casual social interactions. There is something oddly mute about both of these two large paintings filled with people in stately social silence. Indeed, when *La Grande Jatte* was exhibited for the second time, in August 1886 at the Salon des Indépendants, one critic wrote that he shared "the hilarity of the public in front of the wooden figures who seem to have come straight from the Gingerbread Fair into this canvas. They're

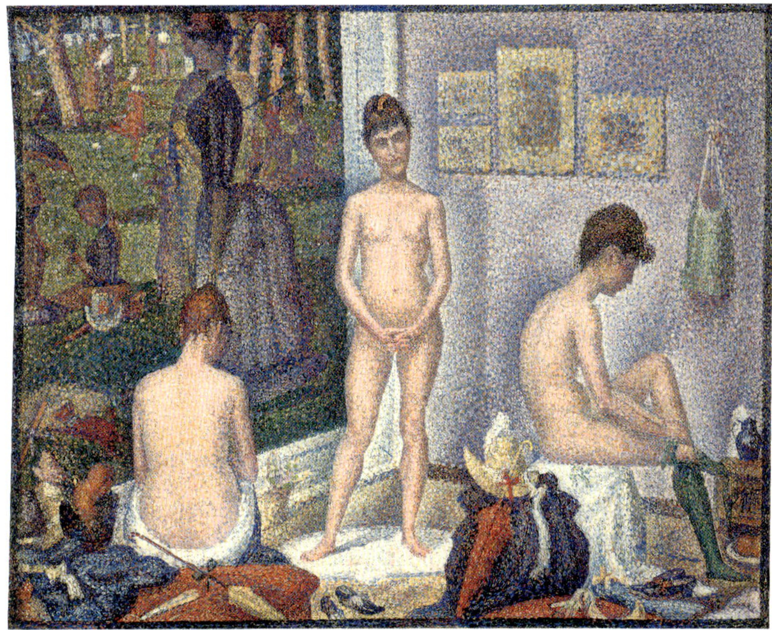 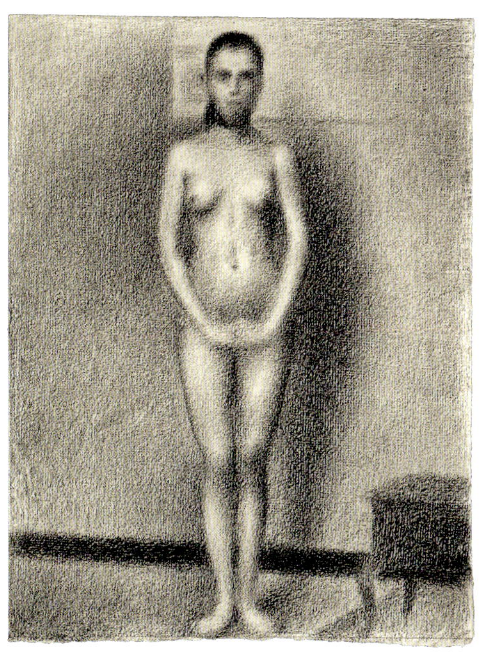

a band of petrified, immobile creatures, mannequins whose role is to grab the public's attention and make them laugh."[83] One wonders if Seurat, who subscribed to a press-cuttings agency, had read this and stored the idea of a fairground scene in his imagination.

Seurat's next large composition, *Models* (*Poseuses*), seems to have been a conscious effort to explore new problems (fig. 48). This studio scene of models showing themselves to the artist takes up an indoor not outdoor subject, in interior light not direct sunlight, and presents naked rather than clothed bodies. With *La Grande Jatte* framed on the wall behind, these contrasts are especially clear. Seurat probably saw *Models* as a progressive next step, taking on the conventional subject of the nude and applying to it, consistently for the first time, his new dotted touch. If *Bathers* and *La Grande Jatte* had been compiled from the disparate elements of multiple drawings and oil sketches, *Models* was in part an attempt to resolve the resultant disequilibrium. Its simpler design of three figures was worked up via oil studies of each separately, as well as a substantial oil study (fig. 49) to work out the details of the ensemble, which were transferred exactly into the final painting.[84] Seurat did make changes as he crafted *Models*, for example, abandoning the very strict symmetry he had essayed in an early drawing of the central model for a more relaxed pose (fig. 50). *Models* is a harmoniously balanced composition, setting the simply rendered pale bodies against the complexity of *La Grande Jatte* on the rear wall and the clutter of discarded clothes in the foreground. That said, it remains marked

FIG. 51. Georges Seurat, *Sidewalk Show* (*Une Parade*), ca. 1883–84. Conté crayon on paper, 12⅝ x 9⅝ in. (32.1 x 24.5 cm). The Phillips Collection, Washington, D.C.

FIG. 52. Georges Seurat, *The Saltimbanques*, ca. 1886. Conté crayon on paper, 9½ x 12¼ in. (24.1 x 31.1 cm). Private collection, New York

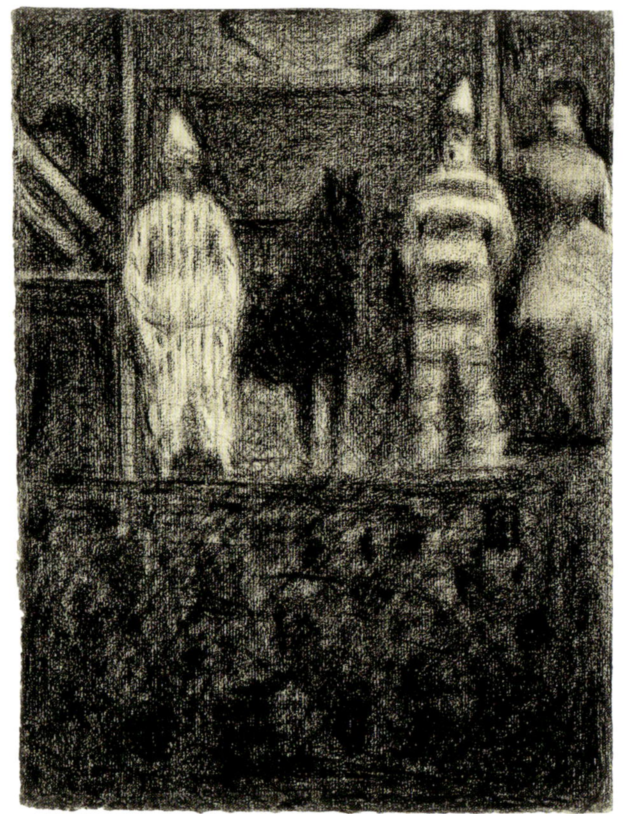

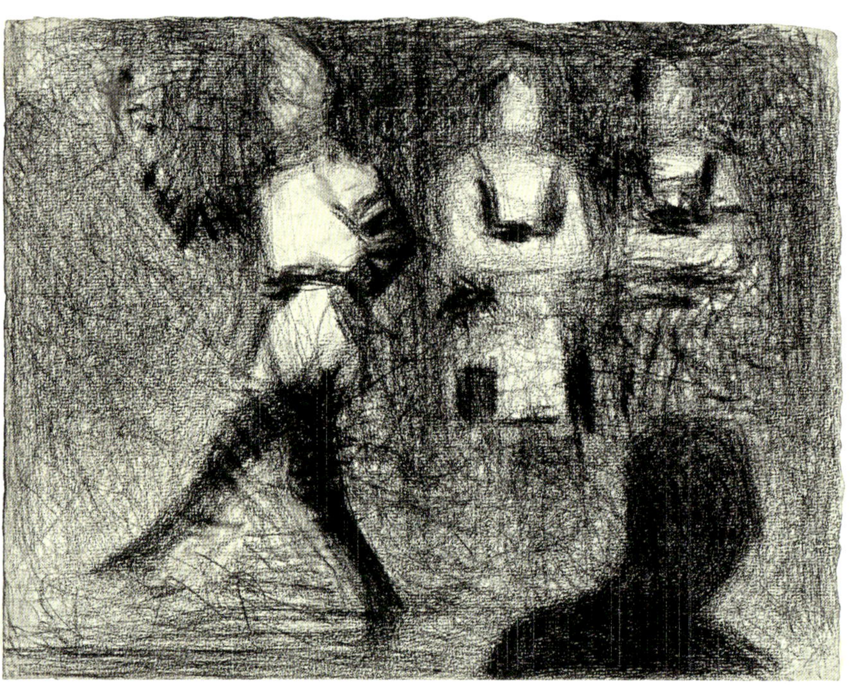

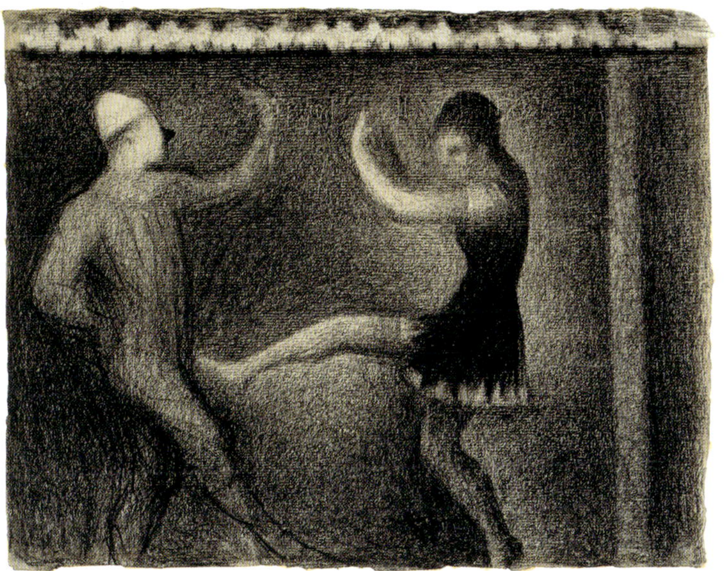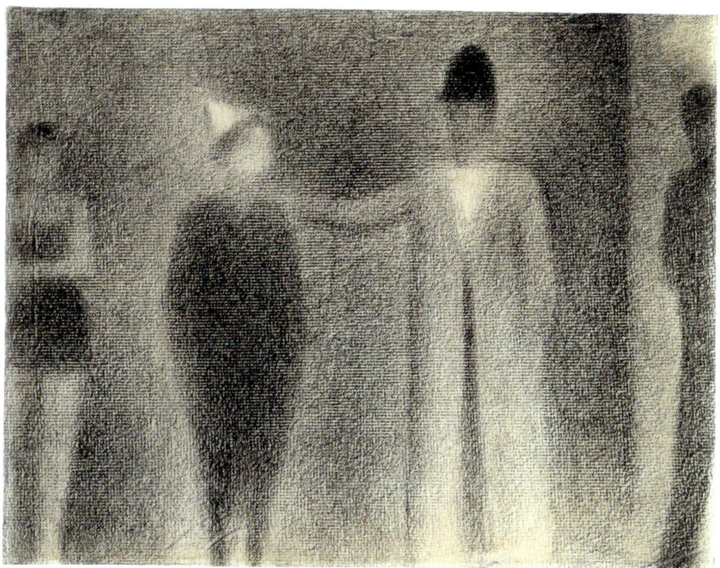

by Seurat's instinct for the profile and the frontal. Initial work on *Models* probably began in late 1886, thus slightly predating *Circus Sideshow*. Visiting Seurat's studio in June 1887, Camille Pissarro mentioned seeing only *Models*, which suggests that *Circus Sideshow* was painted during the second half of that year and completed over the winter; it is likely that to a certain extent Seurat worked on the two canvases in parallel.[85] Vincent van Gogh, who visited Seurat's studio hours before departing for Arles on February 19, 1888, probably saw both paintings in the company of his brother, Theo, just before they were shown at the Indépendants in March.[86] The fact that *Circus Sideshow* is only half the size of Seurat's three preceding substantial pictures might suggest that it was intended to be painted more rapidly to get the subject promptly on show, that he saw it as a more experimental statement, that he chose a smaller canvas to obviate the difficulties created by his cramped studio — or a combination of all three.[87]

Seurat's long-standing interest in the subject of *saltimbanques* is reflected in several drawings in his favored medium of conté crayon made before *Circus Sideshow*. One of a standing drummer was inscribed on the back by his friend Fénéon with the note "Montfermeil 1881, parades saltimbanques, Place des Marronniers," thus demonstrating Seurat's fascination with traveling fairs at the outset of his career.[88] At the 1886 Impressionist exhibition he showed two further drawings on the theme: *Acrobat at a Ticket Booth*, lent by Mme Robert Caze, widow of a writer killed in a duel earlier in the year, and *Sidewalk Show* (*Une Parade*) (fig. 51), lent by the novelist Huysmans.[89] Both sheets may have been drawn about 1883–84, testimony to Seurat's continuing interest in circus life, and the fact that both belonged

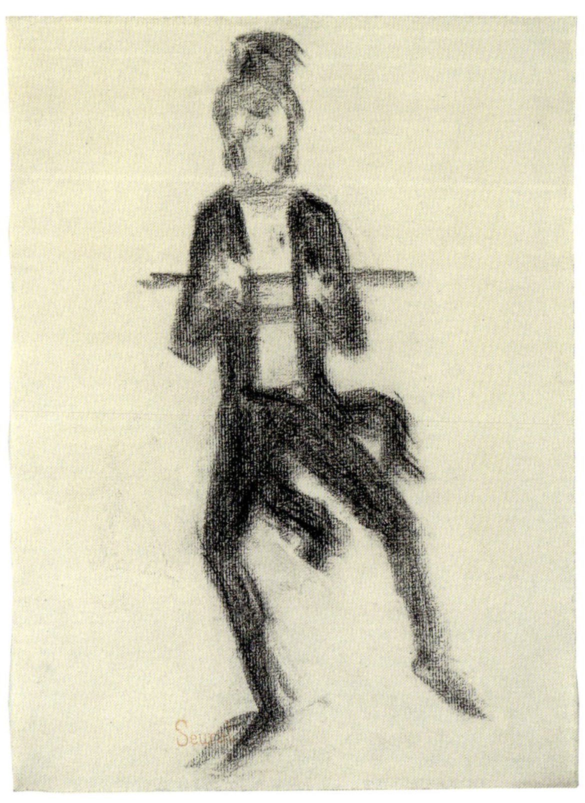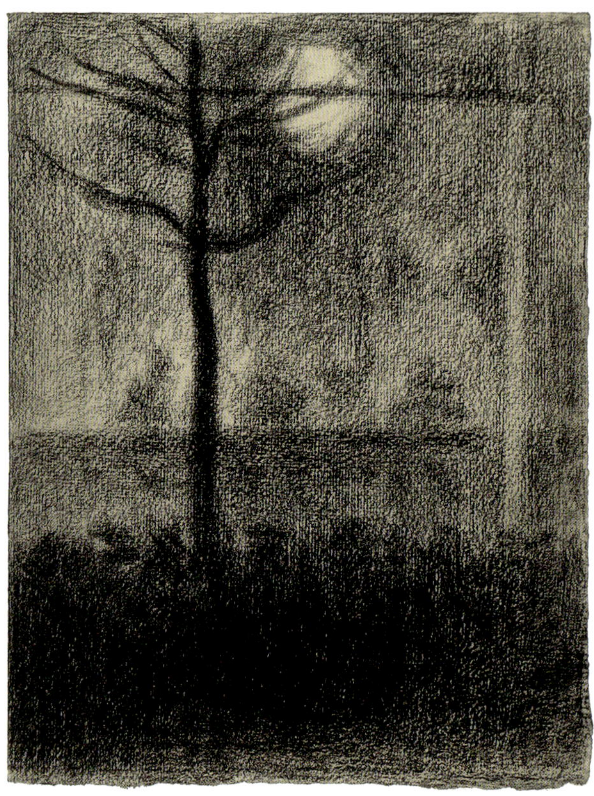

FIG. 55. Georges Seurat, *Dancer with a Cane*, ca. 1888–90. Conté crayon on paper, 12 ⅛ x 9 ⅛ in. (30.7 x 23.2 cm). Private collection

FIG. 56. Georges Seurat, *The Tree*, 1887–88. Conté crayon on paper, 11 ⅞ x 9 ½ in. (30 x 24 cm). Private collection

to naturalist *littérateurs* suggests their shared enthusiasm for such scenes. *Sidewalk Show* depicts four performers on the platform outside a circus tent, a tuba player to the left and a female performer to the right, while between them are two clowns who flank a black pony, one in a costume with horizontal stripes, the other with vertical stripes, the latter with his mouth open to shout. This group fills the upper half of the sheet; the darkly marked lower section offers hints of a crowd in the foreground. Representing what one critic in 1886 described as "two splendid clowns marketing their quack's show to the public," and echoing the conventional schema of crowd, platform, and performers found in caricatures, illustrations, and naturalist canvases, this drawing was a prelude to *Circus Sideshow*.[90]

Several other drawings of *saltimbanque* subjects by Seurat date from the mid- to late 1880s. *The Saltimbanques*, from about 1886, is similar in handling to *Sidewalk Show*, with its quite broad strokes, and introduces the head and shoulders of a figure to anchor the foreground (fig. 52). *Pierrot and Colombine* and *Two Clowns (Une Parade)* were created about 1886–88, so contemporaneously with *Circus Sideshow* (figs. 53, 54). Both employ a softer, more uniform shading, which in its uninsistently subtle monochrome corresponds quite closely to the ambient illumination Seurat

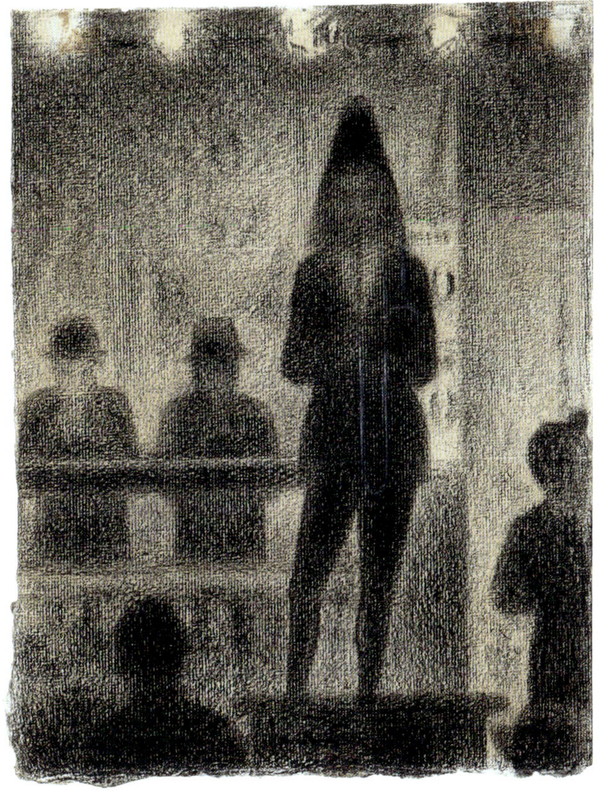 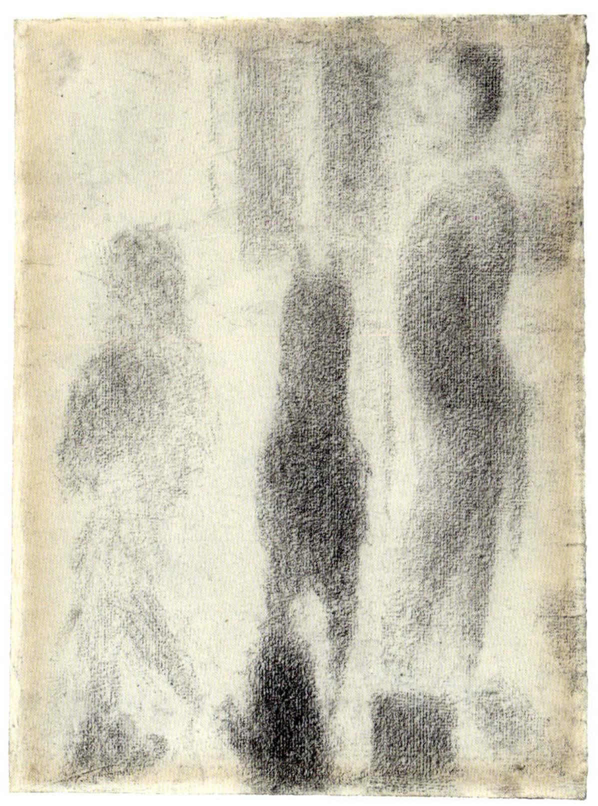

conjured up in color on his canvas. *Pierrot and Colombine*, like the large painting to come, used the ephemeral architecture of the sideshow to create a shallow right-angled armature against which performers are set; here it contains the curving movements of two dancers as they execute their stylized steps. In *Two Clowns* an authoritative figure places his hand on the shoulder of a smaller figure in whiteface, while two marginal characters look on at this silently eloquent gesture of accreditation. A very different drawing, from about 1888–90, of a dancing hoofer in top hat and tails, his cane held horizontally over his chest as his coattails flap haphazardly behind him (fig. 55), shows how Seurat could isolate choreographed actions in movement, an option he set aside in *Circus Sideshow*, where the similarly frontal trombonist is petrified in his pose. Indeed, in terms of their body language the figures in all four of these sheets differ from the physically mute performers in *Circus Sideshow*, who neither dance nor even discreetly touch one another.

Three preliminary drawings in conté crayon survive that relate specifically to *Circus Sideshow*'s compositional genesis (figs. 56–58). They roughly correspond to the tripartite design of the final painting, but it would be wrong to think of them as planned simultaneously and coherently to do that.

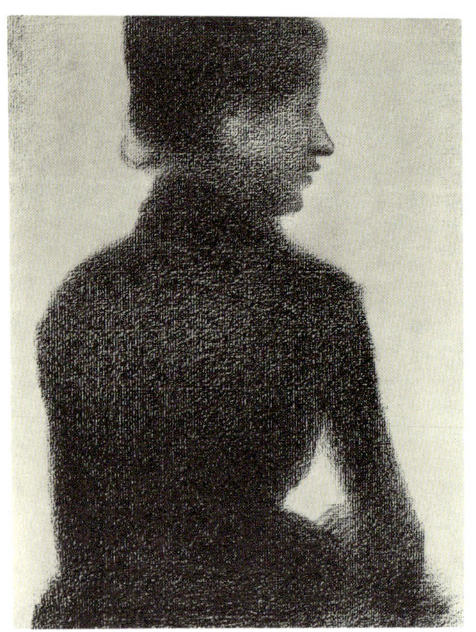

FIG. 59. Georges Seurat, *Woman from Behind*, ca. 1886–87. Conté crayon on paper, 12½ x 9½ in. (31.7 x 24 cm). Destroyed (H662; see César M. de Hauke, *Seurat et son oeuvre*, vol. 2 [Paris. Gründ, 1961], pp. 238–39, no. 661)

We cannot be sure of any particular sequence. The sheet with the skeletal tree, which relates to the left-hand side of the composition, was probably the first to have been made and could have been an independent work in its own right, as it is treated as a balanced whole (fig. 56). The other two sheets seem more probably to have been made with a larger composition in mind. The one featuring the standing trombonist (fig. 57), who wears the conical hat and leggings that were apparently traditional among some *saltimbanque* musicians (see fig. 37), may have been made with the painting in train, to establish the interrelationships of the central grouping. Alternatively, it could have been made independently in response to seeing the Corvi Circus's *parade*, but then caused Seurat to realize that it could act as the focal point for a composition. In this drawing Seurat was especially concerned to register the fall of artificial light in the darkness, as it blurs the contours of the trombonist or picks out the shape of his instrument. The third sheet looks as if it were made — quite rapidly, with its spectral masses — to fix specific formal relationships in the right-hand third of the painting: the buffoon and Corvi facing each other in profile, their placement vis-à-vis the public beneath, and Corvi's with the ticket office windows behind (fig. 58).[91] The sheet included a pony seen frontally, as in popular promotional prints (see fig. 42), but Seurat abandoned that element in the painting. Of the three, this is the only drawing not to include a source of artificial light. Together these evocative drawings magnificently demonstrate the subtle diversity of Seurat's creative practice, as his eye and imagination crafted his emphatic yet enigmatic composition.

As work on the main canvas progressed Seurat may have turned to earlier drawings that he had in folios. The hatless head of the young woman third from the left in the crowd appears to have been taken from a drawing connected to *Models*, as it may represent one of the sitters for that painting (fig. 59).[92] In contrast, the top-hatted man third from the right seems to have been borrowed from an entirely independent drawing of a full-length figure that Seurat had made about 1884 (fig. 60). What this suggests is that the composition of *Circus Sideshow* emerged rather untypically from inconsistent practices, at least compared with Seurat's more systematic use of preliminary drawings for *Bathers* and *La Grande Jatte*, prepared with a specific painting and purpose in mind. Perhaps the painting had a rapid genesis in the second half of 1887. Like the quite steadily developed *Models*, it was necessarily a studio project, a somewhat formal exercise based on the conceptual creation of pictorial architecture. There was no initial response to nature, as with the oil sketches made outdoors for *Bathers* and *La Grande Jatte*; this would have been unlikely anyway, as *Circus Sideshow* is a night scene. Presumably the related drawings of the tree, trombonist, and Corvi were from memory.

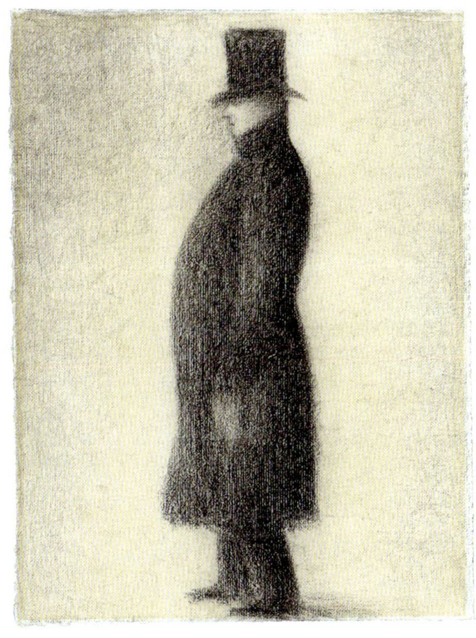

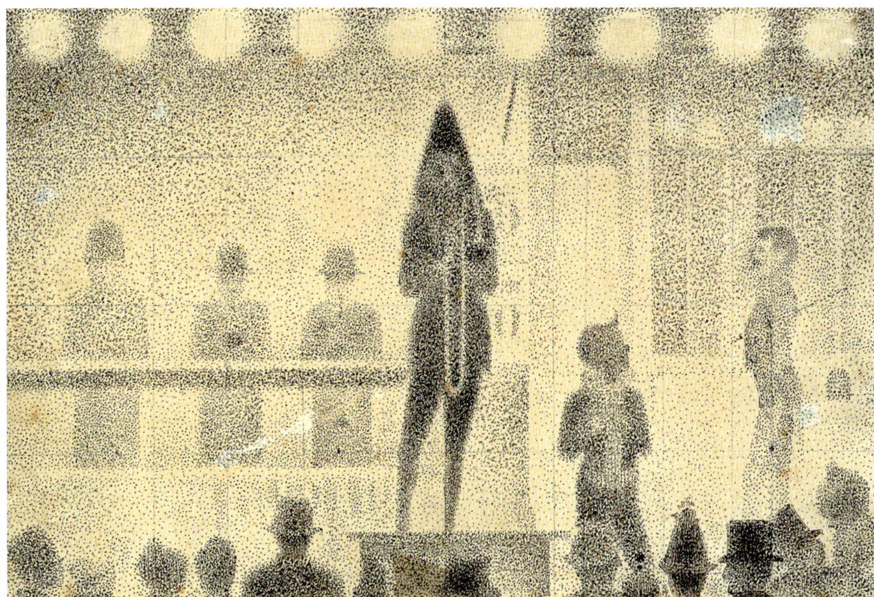

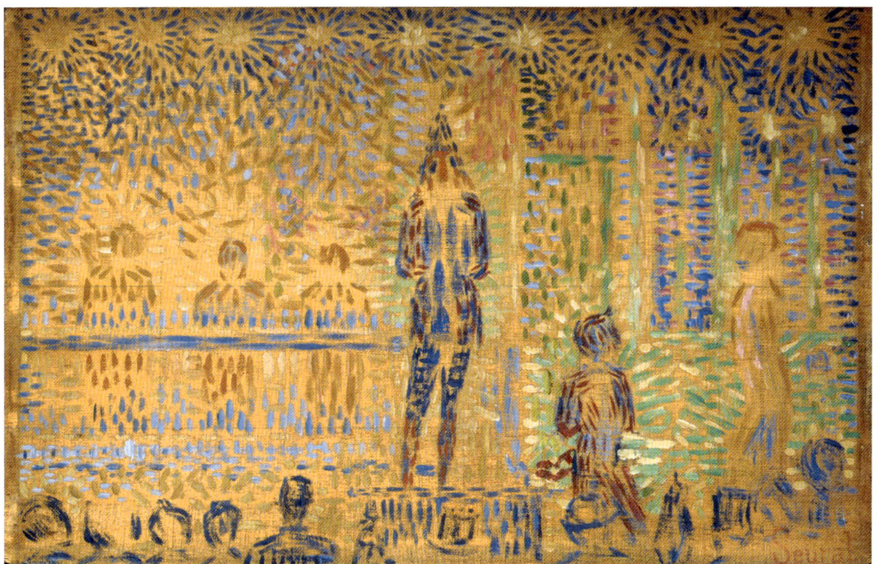

FIG. 60. Georges Seurat, *Man in a Top Hat* (*Le Haut de forme*), ca. 1884. Conté crayon on paper, 12 ⅛ x 9 ⅜ in. (31.2 x 23.8 cm). Private collection

FIG. 61. Georges Seurat, *Study for "Circus Sideshow,"* 1887–88. Ink squared in graphite on paper, 4 ⅞ x 7 ½ in. (12.5 x 19 cm). Menard Art Museum, Aichi, Japan

FIG. 62. Georges Seurat, *Study for "Circus Sideshow,"* 1887–88. Oil on wood, 6 ½ x 10 ¼ in. (16.5 x 26 cm). Foundation E. G. Bührle Collection, Zurich

Additional and intriguing questions about Seurat's preparatory procedures are raised by another drawing quite distinct in method (fig. 61). Executed in pen and ink over a pencil grid, it presents the fundamentals of *Circus Sideshow*'s composition. Further, it is composed of dots in a manner similar to Seurat's divisionist painting technique. The grid divides the surface into four horizontal and six vertical sections, corresponding to the 4:6 ratio of the final painting (see fig. 115).[93] These proportions are also matched by the preliminary oil sketch Seurat made to establish the key color contrasts, which is similarly gridded (fig. 62). On this panel Seurat rehearsed key chromatic elements such as the blues and oranges around the musicians to the left, and the orange-violet of Corvi against the green and deeper violet windows. The oil sketch also fixes the values — the relative lightness and darkness — of figures and background. Thus the trombonist and the buffoon form dark silhouettes against the paler zones behind them, whereas the musicians are closer in value to their back cloth. Even the hole under the cashier's window for exchanging money for tickets is indicated as a dark patch. The figures of the public, though neither as defined nor as dark as the central figures, function chromatically in the same fashion. The dotted drawing corresponds to this in many ways. While it adds little to the system of values, which one might expect to be a drawing's purpose, it does, however, contribute detail. The hats and bonnets of the crowd, the trombonist's instrument and the admission price on the panel behind him, Corvi's baton, and the horizontal pipe at the top for the gas lights, along with the diagonal strut that supports it, all take form in the drawing. A rare exception is a detail from the oil panel that is not in the dotted drawing, namely the buffoon's flowing coattails.

Seurat added elements to the final painting that appear in neither the dotted drawing nor the oil sketch. Corvi himself has a larger presence and new figures appear at the far sides of the canvas: the mother and child paying their entrance fee at the right, the ticket seller at her window, and the ophicleide or saxhorn player cut by the canvas's left edge. Some minor architectural components come in — the balustrade in front of the band and the angled banister behind the trombonist — but the crucial structural addition is the tree, taken from the conté drawing (fig. 56). In the end, the precise creative progression of *Circus Sideshow* remains unknowable, our evidence fragmentary; the inventory drawn up after Seurat's death lists three oil panels and four conté crayon drawings for the painting, but we know only one panel and three such drawings.[94]

Much as Seurat enjoyed the spectacle of *saltimbanques*, his painting is more than a response to what he saw at the Gingerbread Fair. For he was an artist, visually acute, schooled in the analysis of form and composition, with an active memory — a kind of internal museum of images, or *musée imagi-naire*. His creative imagination would have drawn upon works of art that he had seen, admired, and memorized, in a process as much unconscious as deliberate. What may have fueled it as he conceived *Circus Sideshow*? On what did Seurat draw from his *musée imaginaire*? Thanks to the research of Herbert, we know about the portfolio of prints and photographs after art, popular imagery, and cheap broadsides that the artist had collected.[95] These included reproductions of etchings by Rembrandt, and while Seurat did not have a copy of *Christ Presented to the People*, it might reasonably

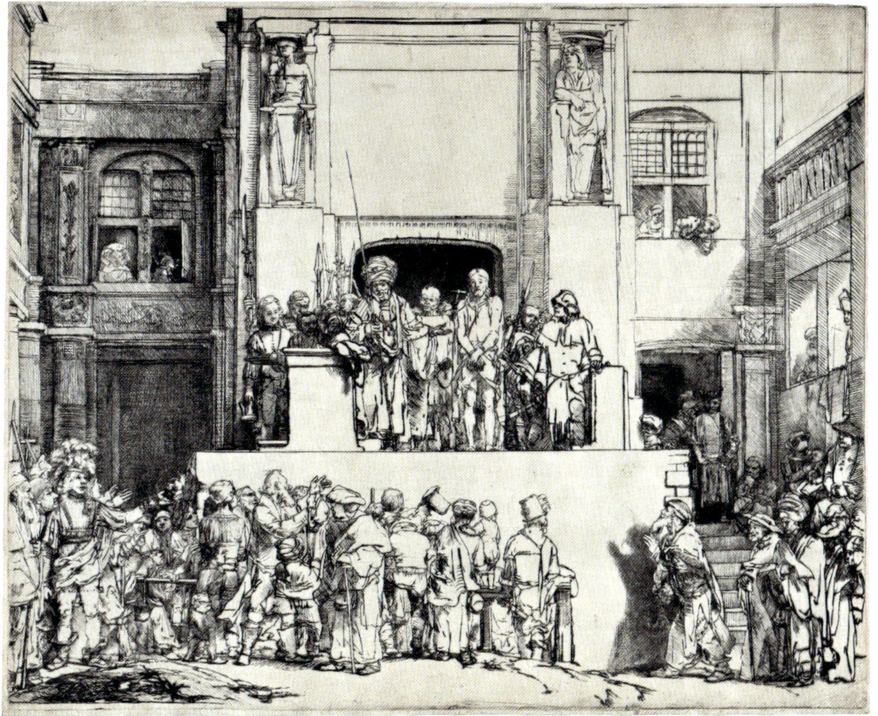

be assumed that he knew this famous drypoint of 1655 (fig. 63), especially as it had been specifically praised in Blanc's *Grammaire*.[96] Rembrandt's balanced, frontal design, with the crowd added in later states of etching below the platform on which Christ stands, established a generic composition to which *Circus Sideshow* is an heir, as well as foreshadowing the painting's implicit theme of the judgment of those onstage by the crowd. The portfolio's inclusion of colored prints from the Napoleonic era after Carle Vernet demonstrates Seurat's taste for naïf popular imagery, and the simple directness and cocked leg of a drum major perhaps finds some echo in the trombonist (fig. 64).[97] Another print from the portfolio is, it can be argued for the first time, of particular relevance: Charles Simon Pradier's engraving of 1832 after Jean Auguste Dominique Ingres's *Tu Marcellus Eris* (*You Will Be Marcellus*) (1811; Musée des Augustins, Toulouse) (fig. 65). This Neoclassical treatment of a subject from Roman antiquity may at first seem very far from *Circus Sideshow*, but it is replete with pictorial parallels: the night scene artificially lit, the frontal figure (here a statue) standing on a central plinth, the dominant character on the right seen in profile, the emphatically lucid structuring of the composition by horizontals and verticals. Ingres's composition in Pradier's engraved version was praised twice by Blanc in his *Grammaire*, who held it up as exemplary in its coordination of composition and format.[98]

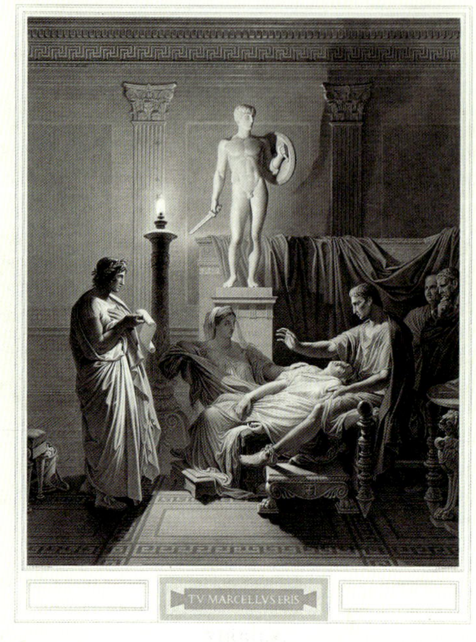

Although none were in Seurat's portfolio, Japanese woodblock prints were widely circulating in Paris in the 1880s and much admired by his contemporaries, including Signac and Van Gogh. Japanese artists were attracted to the subtleties of nocturnal motifs and the simplification of silhouettes, as found in Kobayashi Kiyochika's 1881 *Fireworks at Ikenohata* (fig. 66).[99] Here the line of lanterns and row of heads positioned against the night sky, as well as the off-center tree, have resonances with Seurat's work. Finally, an art form dependent on silhouette, the shadow play, had recently received a new lease on life at Le Chat Noir, a cabaret in the rue Victor-Massé, only a few blocks away from Seurat's Montmartre studio at 128 bis, boulevard de Clichy. He was listed as a customer there in 1888.[100] At Le Chat Noir Seurat may have seen the shadow play *La Tentation de Saint-Antoine* (The Temptation of Saint Anthony) by Signac's friend Henri Rivière, first performed in December 1887 and published the following year as an illustrated book in color. One of the tableaux represents the sin of Pride: on a city street at night, with shop windows illuminated and festive lanterns glowing, silhouetted pedestrians pass the looming black form of an equestrian statue on a plinth (fig. 67). Contemporaries would have recognized the rider as the self-promoting demagogue and nationalist General Boulanger, based on Edouard Debat-Ponsan's portrait (location unknown), which had been exhibited at the Salon that year.[101] Rivière's composition is on a diagonal, so quite different from *Circus Sideshow*, but his shadow plays

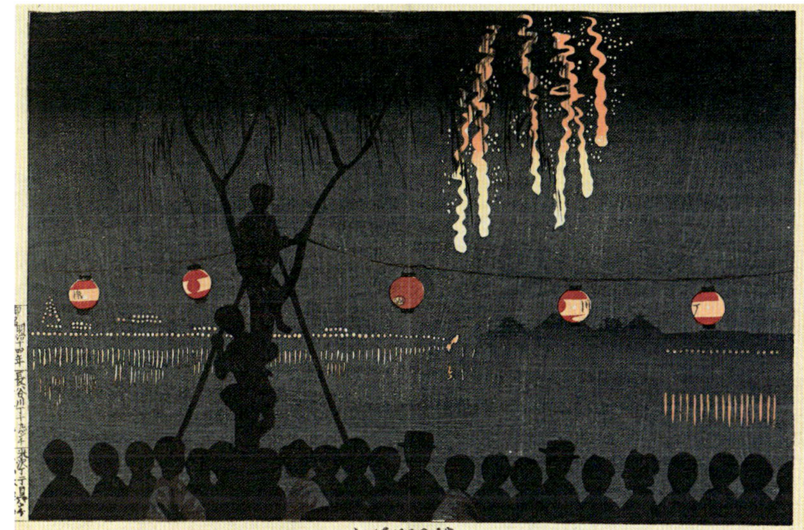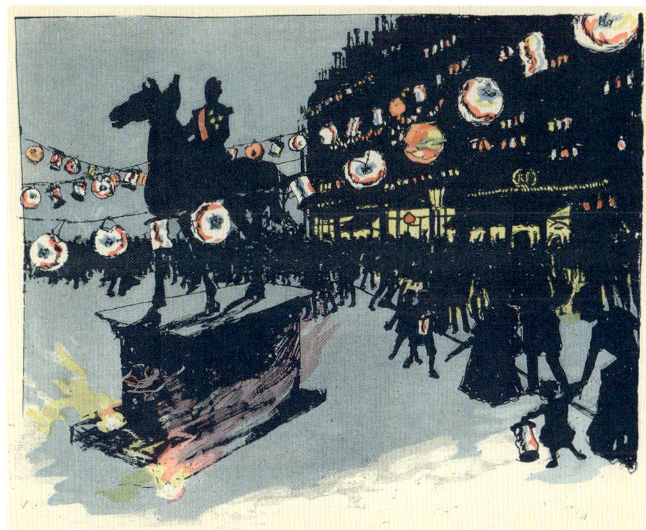

would have reminded Seurat of the dramatic power of the silhouette, an important aspect of the latter's drawing practice and a technique revisited in the foreground public of his painting. Reviewing the potential stimuli of Seurat's *musée imaginaire* is intended here as a suggestive exercise, seeking out the diverse types of visual prompts — some specific, others associative, some cultured, others *populaire* — that might have shaped Seurat's pictorial conceptualization of *Circus Sideshow.*

Turning next to Seurat's distinctive painting technique, we can confirm on the basis of recent examination that *Circus Sideshow* is executed on a very fine canvas, and that the painting has never been varnished, thus preserving a matte effect.[102] Although it was made with a dotted touch, by late 1887 Seurat's characteristic method, the surface was not handled consistently; the oval to the left of center is in large dots, for instance, whereas much smaller dots were used for the dominantly violet square to the right of the trombonist. The touches of separate color employed by Seurat do not merge; rather they interplay, giving vibrancy to the experience of looking at the painting.[103] The canvas is structured in terms of color. The strongest zones of contrasting colors — deep orange-pink and sonorous green — are the vertical rectangles behind and just to the right of the trombonist. This central area also presents the most emphatic value contrasts, notably the dark silhouette of the trombonist against the pale rectangle of the numbered placards announcing admission price. Countering this focal area, the musicians to the left and proprietor and the paying public to the right are quite close in value to their backgrounds. The overall effect of *Circus Sideshow* is to exude the warm tonality of an early summer night, its soft harmony of secondary colors — violets, greens, oranges — unifying, involving, holistic. Even the lefthand tree and central trombonist, at first sight among the darkest elements in the painting, are in deep blue but also very dark violet, almost aubergine, touches, their hint of red adding an underlying warmth. This is picked up in dots of somber pink on the tree and pinks and reds of low value on the trombonist that indicate the light cast by the gas jets.

The silhouettes and profiles of the figures in *Circus Sideshow* are animated by the light falling on them, and the color subtly responds to the different levels of lighting. Those figures deeper in the picture space, and therefore closer to the line of gas jets over the platform, are more illuminated. Thus the mother and child at the ticket window to the right are strongly lit in orange, with red dots on their bonnets, because they are near the jets and another source of light, the globes above the entrance booth. Ferdinand Corvi is farther back in space than the trombonist, so his face is well lit from above, as are the faces of the other musicians. But because the trombonist stands far forward on his dais, he is illuminated from behind and appears to be lifted out from the background, his dark calves outlined by the glow.[104] There is obviously less light on the crowd, standing farthest from the circus's illumination in the gloom of the public thoroughfare, but nevertheless the two hats beneath the trombonist are delineated, again from the right, where the greater light of the entrance falls.

Seurat used light in combination with spatial layering—one figure or form in front of another—to give a sense of compacted depth to his painting. As Pelez also did, he made the most of the flat surfaces of the temporary structure of the circus to set up transitions in the backdrop that are abrupt and visually disconcerting. Thus to the right of the trombonist what appears to be a green door only has the width of half a door. Equally, the pale half-hidden placards, adjacent to the left, seem to have only enough space to give a partial glimpse of the ticketing information. Another strangeness occurs below the musicians, where Seurat painted both the balustrade behind which they stand and the shadows cast toward it by their legs, which are backlit. For light also comes from inside the unseen big top and glows through its tarpaulin walls, increasing the stark silhouettes of the trombonist and crowd.[105]

Primarily, then, *Circus Sideshow* presents an economically simplified ensemble rendered with a relatively systematic touch in order to optimize the overall sense of unity—yet Seurat retained an eye for detail. The woman's head second from the left, for example, has a directional placement of red-pink dots to suggest the waves and shape of her hair, while the upper number cut off by the trombonist's shoulder has an angled point identifying it as a *3*, the price of thirty centimes thus tallying with the entry charges registered by other artists such as Heidbrinck, Dehesghues, and

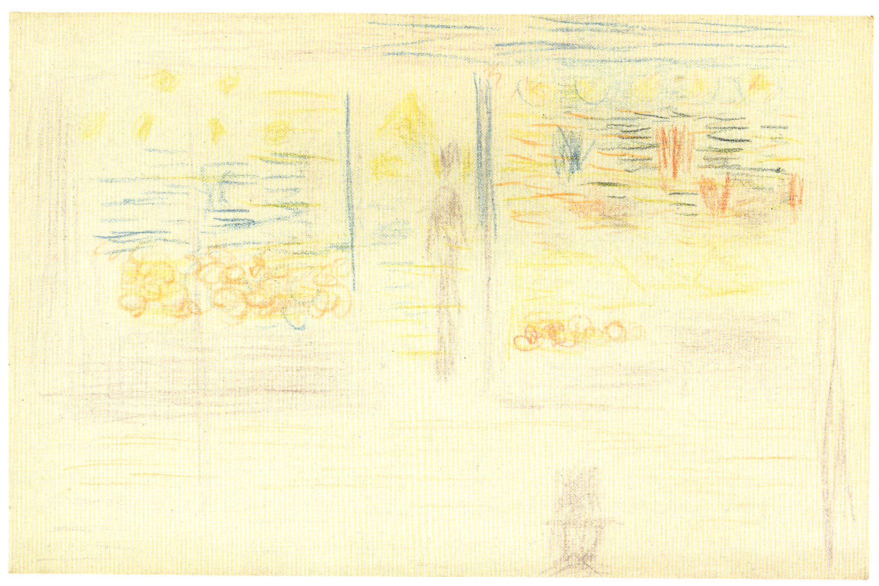

Pelez (figs. 4, 25, 31). At a very late stage in the execution of the painting minute additions were made, such as the pale, almost white, dots to emphasize the profile of the stiff-haired buffoon and his open mouth — as if Seurat wanted to register a shout. Enumerating these details makes one realize how Seurat was negotiating between style and description, operating in the interstices between controlled chromatics, distilled drawing, and the still-insistent requirements of observation and recognition.

As one of the six major figure paintings Seurat made at regular intervals during his short career, *Circus Sideshow* was clearly motivated by his typical imperatives, at once an engagement with a certain kind of social experience — in this case with *fêtes foraines* — and his creative instinct to experiment with stylistic possibilities, for with Seurat subject and style should not be separated. Each of these paintings was a progressive initiative, essaying different types of brushwork, chromatic organization, compositional structure, interplay between drawing and final image, and of course the relevant subject. Lighting was one problem Seurat set himself. After he had reached different solutions to painting strong sunlight in *Bathers* and *La Grande Jatte*, he turned to studio light with *Models* (see figs. 46–48). An intriguing next challenge for his developing technique was to create a nocturne with artificial illumination. Equally, structural issues applied. *Circus Sideshow* shared with the contemporaneous *Models* a strong tripartite character, and Seurat's instinct for such a design can be traced back to a drawing he made in colored crayon about 1882 (fig. 68). Two shop windows flank the central vertical of the customer entering the door, while a top hat marks the foreground plane: the composition is simple but stylized.[106] Both *La Grande Jatte* and *Models* balanced frontality and profile; *Circus Sideshow* was to do the same but with more emphasis on the frontal axis, reinforced by backs as well as fronts. If Seurat's musicians are seen directly from the front, the silhouetted figures in the crowd, notably the bowler-hatted man to the left of the dais and the conically bonneted woman to the right, are seen directly from behind. This is a reverse frontality, but with the same abrupt structural effect. Of course, the compositional device of presenting the backs of the audience was part of naturalist painting's evocation of the actual, of the likelihood of having obstacles between oneself and what one wants to see; in other words, of naturalism's conscious evocation of the physical actuality of daily experience. Seurat took that compositional trope and adapted it with the stylistic vocabulary he had to hand in later 1887 and early 1888.

Naturalism is residual not only in the composition — looking over heads — but also in the viewpoint, for our eye level is that of the public.[107] We look up at the performers on stage, and from our close vantage cannot see the trombonist's feet, hidden by the rim of his plinth. In addition there is a descriptive attention to detail in the figures. The buffoon with the combed-up hair and exaggerated bow tie holds his lapels in a swaggering pose; the girl at left opens her mouth to talk to a neighbor; the man with a baby also seems to be speaking; the woman mounting the stair on the right turns to her male escort. One might argue that *Circus Sideshow* is the most sociable of Seurat's six major figure paintings; there is conversation, the individuals depicted are collectively preoccupied with the same pursuit, and thus there is suggested a fragile, rather formal, sense of community, of shared experience. All this emerges, paradoxically, despite the painting's exuding a powerful sense of ritual, but then that is what the fairs offered: the opportunity for crowds of disparate citizens to mingle and share the same experience at set times of year and in response to established rites and celebrants — *Let's go and see Marseille!* So two kinds of sound are, perhaps too discreetly, suggested: the conversational babble of the public and the pumping music of the circus band. Against that is the very evident stillness of the figures, the absence of gestures (as in previous paintings), and, even more than in *Bathers* and *La Grande Jatte*, the lack of facial character. The members of the crowd have profiles, but these give little away and their identities are essentially established by their hats or lack of them; the musicians' faces are all schemas — the shadow under a nose, two eye sockets, the mouth hidden by an instrument — and only the handsome, moustached Ferdinand Corvi has much by way of characterization: strong chin, Roman nose, carefully coiffed hair.

Seurat's artistic instinct was to seek harmony. In a letter he drafted for the journalist Maurice Beaubourg on August 28, 1890, Seurat summarized his aesthetic ideas with the simple statement "Art is Harmony. / Harmony is the analogy of opposites."[108] Harmonious balance of color and composition was clearly a foremost aim in *Circus Sideshow*, achieved through Seurat's dotted touch and his simplification and repetition of forms. Seurat placed recurring motifs throughout the picture, whether the string of nine gas jets, the pair of facing girls, the row of almost identical musicians whose bowlers rhyme with the painted ovals on the canvas behind them, or the zeroes of the entry prices.[109] He avoided figures that were too individualized, preferring schematic types; he scarcely dipped into the vocabulary of caricature, and made no studies of individual heads whose identity might clash with the whole. Thus he resisted the piecemeal character of contemporary paintings that depicted particularized heads in crowded scenes of urban entertainment, such as Henri de Toulouse-Lautrec's *Moulin de la Galette* (fig. 69). Much has been made by writers of *Circus Sideshow*'s apparent flatness.[110] Indeed, there are no diagonals driving into pictorial

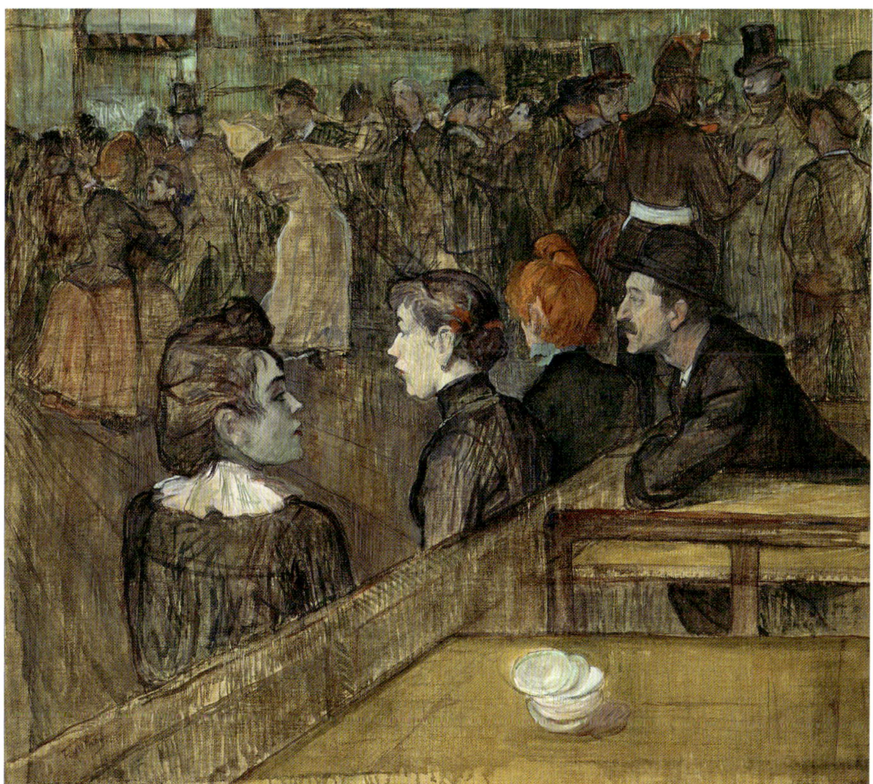

FIG. 69. Henri de Toulouse-Lautrec, *Moulin de la Galette*, 1889. Oil on canvas, 35 7/8 x 39 5/8 in. (88.5 x 101.3 cm). The Art Institute of Chicago, Mr. and Mrs. Lewis Larned Coburn Memorial Collection

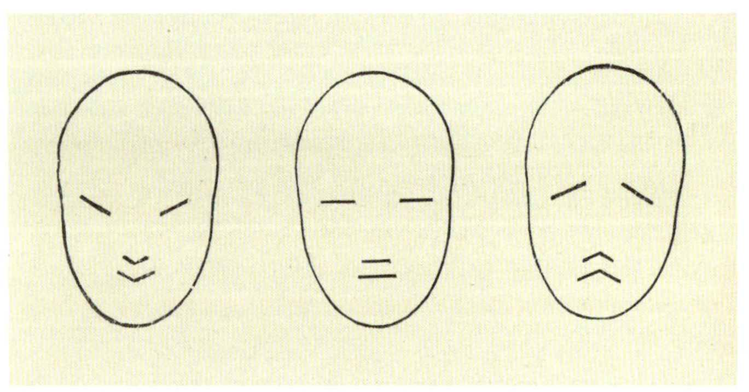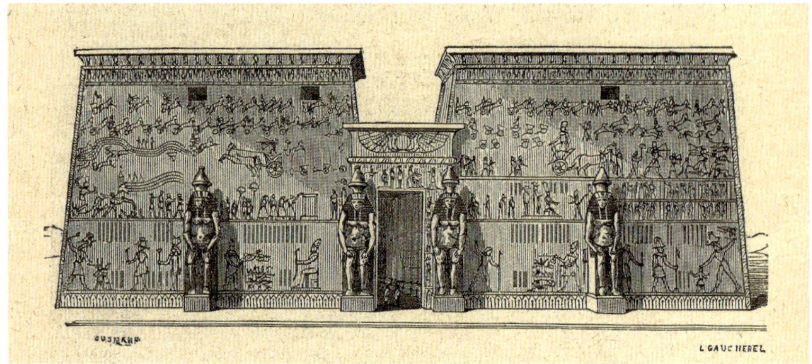

FIG. 70. David Pierre Giottino Humbert de Superville, diagram of three schematic faces, from Charles Blanc, *Grammaire des arts du dessin* (Paris, 1870 [first ed. 1867]), p. 36. Wood engraving. The Metropolitan Museum of Art, New York, Thomas J. Watson Library, Gift of Edward C. Moore

FIG. 71. Léon Gaucherel, Egyptian temple, from Charles Blanc, *Grammaire des arts du dessin* (Paris, 1876 [first ed. 1867]), p. 88. Wood engraving. The Metropolitan Museum of Art, New York, Thomas J. Watson Library, Jacob S. Rogers Fund

depth, such as the riverbank in *La Grande Jatte*, or expansive gestures that imply surrounding space, as in Daumier's *parade* subjects. Here there are only overlaps of figures and forms to suggest that one thing is in front of another. Seurat's evocation of a compressed space is a function of his effort to evoke the inclusiveness of the illuminated twilight and the jumbled, huddled crowd within a harmonious pictorial arrangement.

Seurat acknowledged his interest in aesthetic theory, and it needs to be asked to what extent it had an effect on *Circus Sideshow*. We know that he had studied Charles Blanc's 1867 treatise *Grammaire des arts du dessin*. In an important letter to Félix Fénéon of June 20, 1890, outlining his career, Seurat noted that he had read Blanc as a student, and later Gustave Kahn recalled how well Seurat knew the art historian and aesthetician's texts: there is no doubt that his thinking marked the artist deeply.[111] Early in the *Grammaire* Blanc wrote of the human figure, the fundamental form in art, as being perfectly symmetrical and yet containing disproportions, as arms are longer than torso, and legs longer than arms; so he viewed the body as offering "opposition within symmetry and diversity within equilibrium, [which] gives form to the principle established in antiquity: Harmony derives from the analogy of opposites."[112] Here is the source of Seurat's 1890 summary of his own aesthetic, and in *Circus Sideshow*'s central figure one can see Blanc's concept visualized; the trombonist's head and torso are frontal and symmetrical, their equilibrium mitigated by the arms and one leg being out of alignment, thereby presenting harmony animated, but not disrupted, by contrast.

Blanc's *Grammaire* introduced Seurat to other writings and concepts. An admirer of David Pierre Giottino Humbert de Superville's *Essai sur les signes inconditionnels de l'art* (Essay on the Unmistakable Signs of Art) (1827), Blanc reproduced the Dutch aesthetician's three schematic faces: the first with its simple lines for eyes and mouth angled upwards, conveying expansive emotions of gaiety; the second with horizontal lines, calm; the third with the lines angled downward, sadness (fig. 70).[113] He concurred with Humbert de Superville's belief that certain formal characteristics inherently transmit emotional and moral values, for instance, emphasizing that horizontals "express the soul's repose, the equilibrium of the moral faculties."[114] Blanc also argued that symmetry gave a composition "something sober, calm, majestic, which perfectly suits religious subjects and imposing historical scenes," citing as an example Ingres's *Apotheosis of Homer* (1826–27; Musée du Louvre, Paris).[115] Ingres's painting was a major statement of French Neoclassicism, and in many respects Blanc was a committed classicist, preferring Greco-Roman drapery to modern costume. He also admired Egyptian art, noting that the ancient Egyptians anticipated the Greeks in their scrupulous eye for proportion, as evident in figures in the Louvre's collection marked with grids to ensure the ideal ratio of human limbs.[116] For Blanc the most emphatic characteristic of Egyptian art was its regulated repetition. "It belongs to the register of sublime things, this persistent repetition which makes a procession out of every step, a religious motif from every movement, a sacred cadence out of every gesture," he wrote (see fig. 71).[117] The formal qualities, then, that Blanc lauded as fundamental to art of profound value were symmetry, horizontality, and repetition, all of which are intrinsic to *Circus Sideshow*. One might add that in Blanc's theory the calming effect of horizontality — "the equilibrium of the moral faculties, the sleep of the passions" — is disrupted by the merest indication of a diagonal — "one is struck by the eloquence of such an indeterminate sign."[118] Seurat, of course, introduced a few disruptive diagonals into his design — the banister behind the trombonist's dais, the bracket supporting the gas pipe, Corvi's cane — and these correspond to Blanc's dictum about diversity in equilibrium.

Since his student days Seurat had nurtured an interest in color theory. Blanc's *Grammaire* introduced him to the mid-nineteenth-century ideas of Michel Eugène Chevreul, which centered on a relatively traditional view of how primary colors — red, yellow, and blue — function with their respective secondaries, green, violet, and orange. These pairs, or complementaries, formed color opposites and thus the strongest chromatic reaction to each other; as Blanc put it, the colors exalt their opposites.[119] Seurat's 1890 letter to Fénéon mentioned knowledge of the American Ogden Rood, author of *Modern Chromatics*, whom he had come across in a book review by Philippe Gille in *Le Figaro* of January 26, 1881. Rood's text made important observations, for example, about how color absorbs light, and recommended painting in small dots closely juxtaposing colors.[120] Seurat's letter also noted that he had read studies as well as the writings of earlier artists — in particular Eugène Delacroix, Camille Corot, and Thomas Couture — and that he had been "struck by the intuition of Monet and Pissarro." Clearly

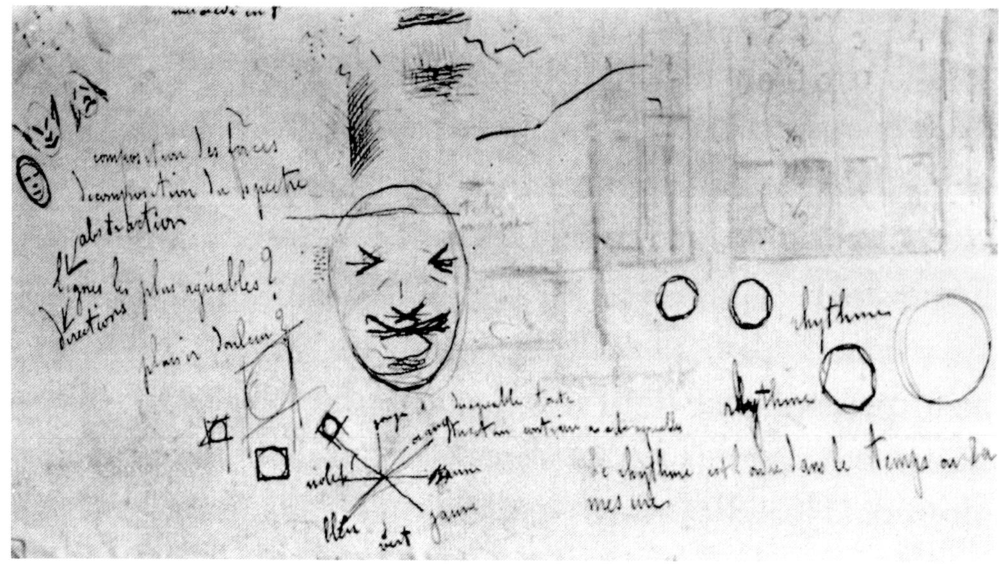

his understanding of how color works was based on the insights of other painters, combined with the theoretical texts he had consulted.[121]

In his letter to Fénéon, Seurat recalled meeting Charles Henry—a theorist influential in his circle—after the 1886 Impressionist exhibition, so in the second half of that year. The meeting may have been through mutual friends such as the poets Kahn and Jules Laforgue; in August 1886 the latter was trying to patch up a row Henry had had with Kahn.[122] Henry was an eccentric figure, interested in both mathematics and aesthetics. Seurat's exact contemporary, he took up a modest position as a librarian at the Sorbonne in 1881; a year after Seurat's death in 1891, he moved on to a research position at the Ecole Pratique des Hautes Etudes.[123] As the title of his first book, the 1885 *Introduction à une esthétique scientifique* (Introduction to a Scientific Aesthetics), suggests, Henry explored the linkages between ideas of beauty, artistic expression, and the laws of science. At this period France was at the forefront of modern science, as seen with the work on bacteria by Louis Pasteur. Another leading field was the *psychologie nouvelle* developed by Jean-Martin Charcot and Hippolyte Bernheim, who investigated the subconscious workings of the human mind. What engaged Henry was how our responses to what we see, and in particular to art, are predisposed by psychological instincts. He was fascinated by the notion that the direction of lines affects the emotional reaction of the viewer, especially when linked to color, and he involved his artist friends in his experiments, Signac helping him measure the angles on Greek vases.[124]

The urge to interlink art and science was widespread in the Parisian avant-garde of the later 1880s. The poet René Ghil's *Traité du verbe*

(Treatise on the Word), published in 1886, exemplifies the trend with its attempt to equate colors and the sounds of words.[125] Such initiatives were undertaken in reaction against naturalism's accumulation of observed and documented fact, as artists sought provable principles that underpin, even predicate, the emotional effects stimulated by works of art. Going further in this direction, the new aesthetic of Symbolism, launched by the poet Jean Moréas's manifesto in 1886, sought to dislodge descriptive naturalism and replace it with a methodology geared to suggestion and to the evocation of the *Idée*, the quintessential emotion or meaning.[126] Both Henry and Seurat, in their different ways, were part of this avant-gardism.

The extent to which Henry's ideas lie behind *Circus Sideshow* is ambiguous. The painting is dominated by horizontality, giving the calm effect described by Blanc, and so does not seem a likely test bed for Henry's theories on angles.[127] That said, a sheet of studies made by Seurat during the genesis of *Circus Sideshow* includes, along with a sketch of the Corvi Circus box office at upper right, citations from Henry's book on scientific aesthetics (fig. 72).[128] It also has a sketch of a schematic face along the lines of Humbert de Superville's trio (fig. 70), and indeed, to judge by their features, the faces in the painting are formed on the model of "calm" horizontality. In addition there is a color wheel (with names of colors written in) and a number of diagrammatic shapes, which suggest that Seurat was grappling with the visualization of Henry's ideas, for his book had no illustrations. If Henry's theories supported what Seurat had already absorbed from Blanc and Humbert de Superville, still Seurat needed to work out if there was anything new to be learned from the work of a contemporary who was much discussed in Symbolist circles.[129]

Henry linked color science with psychology. In his *Cercle chromatique* (Chromatic Circle), published in 1888, for example, he suggested that passing from a dark zone into light can be "douloureuse," or saddening (though common sense says the opposite).[130] He was innovative in his attempt to link the direction of lines to colors, believing that lines moving upward and to the right (clockwise) are agreeable, while those moving downward and to the left (counterclockwise) are disagreeable (which experience affirms). Positive warm colors such as red and yellow should therefore be to the top and right. Seurat was evidently interested in this notion, though the color circle he sketched failed to make sense of Henry's text, placing, as Herbert put it, "yellow at two places and nothing at all . . . where violet should have been," once more suggesting that he was essaying Henry's ideas rather than entirely convinced.[131] Our evidence, then, shows that Seurat was engaged with, but in no way slavish to, Henry's ideas when he painted *Circus Sideshow*. Henry's theories elided with the avant-garde's attraction to the ideal of a scientific aesthetic and thus deserved Seurat's attention, though their overelaboration could certainly irritate — as clear in Fénéon's facetious remark, in a generally laudatory article on Henry in May 1889, about a fictitious "Polish mathematician" who had calculated Henry's angles up to eight trillion.[132]

How, then, does one read the color in *Circus Sideshow*? The painting appears as a harmony of secondaries, in that the combination of violets, greens, and oranges sets the overall chromatic effect. This is particularly apparent just right of and above center, where the numbered placards abut an essentially orange rectangle, and the green door abuts an essentially violet square. However, the painting also reads in terms of primary contrasts, albeit very subtly.[133] Red, yellow, and blue are all present across the canvas's surface: red, especially a rich crimson, is used to define shapes such as the trombonist's upper hand; yellow to indicate light defining or outlining instruments or the oval decoration behind the musicians; blue most notably as the brilliant cobalt blue that gives a slight sense of relief to the foreground figures.[134] According to Henry, dark blue, violet, and green are inhibitory, so disagreeable or sad.[135] All those appear at first glance. But the musicians and their backdrop make a warm zone, which covers about half the surface of the canvas, and there is deeper warmth inside the box office, behind the green woodwork of the entrance. The figures set in the more strongly lit zones of the platform and entryway appear warmer in tone, and thus the painting does not seem so melancholy or unwelcoming, despite the crowd appearing at first sight to be almost fossilized.

How, moreover, does one read the direction of lines in Seurat's painting? Are the diagonals — the cane under Corvi's arm, the banister behind the trombonist, and the bracket holding up the gas pipe — angled in an "inhibitory" way? Or could one argue that — aside from the obvious dominance of horizontals — there is a fairly consistent upward tendency in *Circus Sideshow*, evident in the trombonist's conical hat, the flames of the gas jets, the customers climbing the steps? The little girl whose mother purchases their tickets holds an umbrella with an orange curved handle and crimson fabric that is angled upward in a way that is "dynamogenic" or happy, as a child about to see the circus would be.[136] But the instrument (ophicleide or saxhorn) near the left-hand margin is angled in the opposite direction to the girl's umbrella and is set in relief by dark blue dots; should it be read as happy or sad? Do the diagonals contradict the general upward momentum — offering another paradox in the painting, alongside the frozen jollity — or correspond with it? If we take into account the mix of theories Seurat drew on, perhaps we cannot be doctrinaire about how to read either his colors or his angles.

Interpreting *Circus Sideshow* in its aesthetic context is complex and compels us to confront the painting's paradoxes. To an extent Seurat's method was based on observation of the physical world: Charles Angrand remembered how on night walks back to Montmartre from meetings about the Salon des Indépendants Seurat would note the halo of complementaries around the gas lamps.[137] We have seen how his painting's composition used a trope derived from naturalism, and we will find Neo-Impressionist colleagues such as Angrand and Signac doing the same. Yet there was simultaneously an urge within this group to react against naturalism, articulated for instance in a letter from Hayet to Lucien Pissarro in March 1887 in which he condemned popular naturalist painters such as Emile Bayard and Pierre-Georges Jeanniot.[138] It was an initiative shared by writers such as Moréas, author of the Symbolist manifesto, who damned naturalism as unartistic, middle-of-the-road, "this average art."[139] In *Circus Sideshow* both subject and style — the reduction of figures to ciphers, the silencing of a noisy public event, the compressed space and dotted surface, the fascination with night as a time of disjunction, alienation, and mystery — point to a new but as yet undefined aesthetic.

Friends such as Kahn and the Belgian poet Emile Verhaeren noted that Seurat was interested in the aesthetic ideas of Richard Wagner, the German composer, as were many of his contemporaries in France, including Edouard Dujardin, editor of the *Revue wagnérienne*, which ran from 1885 to 1888.[140] We cannot be sure if Seurat was in tune with Wagner's grand concept of music as a "vehicle of a highly significant moral experience."[141] But Verhaeren recalled Seurat trying to imagine the effect of darkening the concert hall at Bayreuth to demand concentration on the music and the stage. Seurat's own innovation of adding a painted border to his canvases for similar effect was evolving as *Circus Sideshow* was under way; the one along all four edges of the canvas was probably added straight after painting was finished, but the precise timing is not possible to ascertain.[142] The likelihood again is that Seurat developed an aesthetic concept that intrigued him only to the extent that it could contribute to the development of his painting, rendering it more modern by the absorption of progressive ideas.

Modern aesthetic notions might also find common cause with the past art appreciated by Seurat's intellectual mentors. Increasingly a key term used by and of progressive artists in the mid-1880s, and one with significance for Seurat, was *synthèse* (synthesis). At the Impressionist exhibition in May 1886 Octave Mirbeau had used it in relation to Edgar Degas's pastels of women washing, and Jean Ajalbert had referred to *La Grande Jatte* as "truly a work of synthesis."[143] Later that year Camille Pissarro explained newly emerging Neo-Impressionism to the art dealer Paul Durand-Ruel in terms of the search for a "modern synthesis by means based on science."[144] Taken from scientific terminology, *synthèse* meant for artists

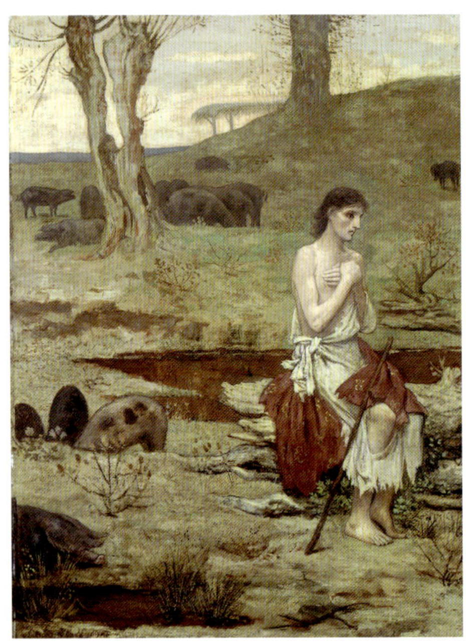

FIG. 73. Pierre Puvis de Chavannes, *The Prodigal Son*, 1879. Oil on wood, 51¼ x 37¾ (130 x 96 cm). Foundation E. G. Bührle Collection, Zurich

the simplification of pictorial elements such as form, color, and detail to enhance the overall unity. It had been used by Blanc as early as 1864 in his obituary of Delacroix, which Seurat told Fénéon in 1890 that he had read. Blanc appreciated the synthetic in art. He found it in ancient Egyptian painting and sculpture, in which "each figure is an emblem, each slave represents thousands of slaves, each priest a whole class of priests."[145] In 1883 Pissarro had encouraged his son Lucien to study Egyptian art for the same reason: "that'll give you the best possible ideas about simplification."[146]

The relevance of Egyptian art for Seurat and the comparable hieraticism of *Circus Sideshow* have, quite rightly, often been noticed.[147] Yet Seurat's use of Egyptianizing motifs needs to be linked to a wider understanding among progressive painters in the mid- to late 1880s that style could gain resonance by simplification (as caricaturists had long understood) and viewed as part of the larger reaction against naturalism and its observation of detail. Further, the synthetic figure had value in itself, emblematic of a type, summarizing the social order. This is where Seurat's representation of figures differs from the deliberately haphazard groupings and actions depicted in the crowds of naturalist painters. In *Circus Sideshow* the lower classes, identifiable by the caps or bowler hats of the men and the girls' bare heads, queue for the cheap seats reached up the steps behind the trombonist's dais, while the bourgeois, with their top hats and conical bonnets, enter the dearer seats by the central stairs. This was the actuality of class and consumption in 1880s Paris, reduced to a regulated synthetic schema along the canvas's lower edge: the social order registered pictorially, without disharmony.

In the *Grammaire* Blanc argued that the painter should avoid "excessive, convulsive movements"; we don't paint portraits of people laughing, he wrote, because such moments are accidental, not summative.[148] These ideas were influential through the mid-1880s. Writing about Pierre Puvis de Chavannes in 1884 Armand Dayot praised the artist's ability in paintings such as *The Prodigal Son* (fig. 73) to convey sadness in the figures, "so moving in their expressive impassivity," merely by "the harmony of lines"; such restraint obviated the need to heighten emotional effect by exaggerated gesture.[149] In *Circus Sideshow* Seurat also achieved intensity of emotion by economy of line and coordination of color, the reduction of means of expression to heighten expressive effect. This was in accord with Blanc's definition of style: "it is truth enhanced, simplified, released from all insignificant details, to present its original essence, its typical aspect."[150] Seurat's professor Lehmann had the same instinct for expressive compression, demanding of his students at the Ecole, "and the idea? the idea?"[151]

Seurat took a scene he had observed on the streets of Paris, a subject and a composition rooted in naturalism, and submitted it to his own stylistic imperatives and some of the progressive theories circulating in the avant-garde circles within which he moved. His creative momentum tallied with what Kahn had recently written in an attempt to further define the nascent aesthetic of Symbolism: "The goal of our art is to objectify the subjective (the exteriorization of the Idea) instead of subjectifying the objective (nature seen through a temperament)."[152] Reading, training, and his early practice as an artist, together with the current aesthetic confrontation between established naturalism and emergent Symbolism, all coalesced with Seurat's mastery of his creative means and eye for unified style to produce a painting harmonious and hypnotic in its mute authority.

Circus Sideshow on Exhibition

Circus Sideshow was first exhibited at the fourth Salon des Indépendants, which opened on March 22, 1888, in the Pavillon de la Ville de Paris on the Champs-Elysées. The Indépendants had been established in reaction to the apparent severity of the jury at the official Paris Salon in 1884, which had rejected a large number of works, including Seurat's *Bathers*.[153] The Paris municipal Council, which held more radical republican views than most French governments, responded with a gesture of *égalité* by setting up an annual exhibition that had no jury, allowing both experimental artists and amateur painters to show their work independently of establishment control. This liberal attitude was echoed in Ernest Hoschedé's preface to the catalogue of the 1888 Indépendants, in which he attacked the so-called République des Arts dominated by a clique of senior artists and state functionaries such as the *directeur des beaux-arts*, and demanded "absolute liberty" for artistic aspirations.[154] Such egalitarianism necessarily meant the inclusion of some very bad painting, as the critic Arsène Alexandre bemoaned in his column for the daily *Paris*, unfavorably comparing some works on view — coincidentally enough — to the painted decorations of fairground stalls.[155]

Seurat exhibited ten works. Two were substantial paintings: *Models* at over eight and *Circus Sideshow* at over four feet wide. The remaining eight were all conté crayon drawings, four on the subject of the *café-concert*, or music hall (see figs. 75–78), and four of single figure types: two of women reading, one of a man eating, and another of a street sweeper.[156] Seurat had shown no major figure painting in Paris since submitting *La Grande Jatte* to the second Salon des Indépendants in August–September 1886, so the presentation of two significant canvases with contrasting subjects was a tactic to demonstrate his innovative stylistic development and assert his position in the Parisian avant-garde. The eight drawings formed what would be the most concentrated public display of his draftsmanship in

FIG. 74. Georges Seurat, *Eden Concert*, ca. 1886–87. Conté crayon, gouache, chalk, and ink on paper, 11 5/8 x 8 7/8 in. (29.5 x 22.5 cm). Van Gogh Museum, Amsterdam (Vincent van Gogh Foundation)

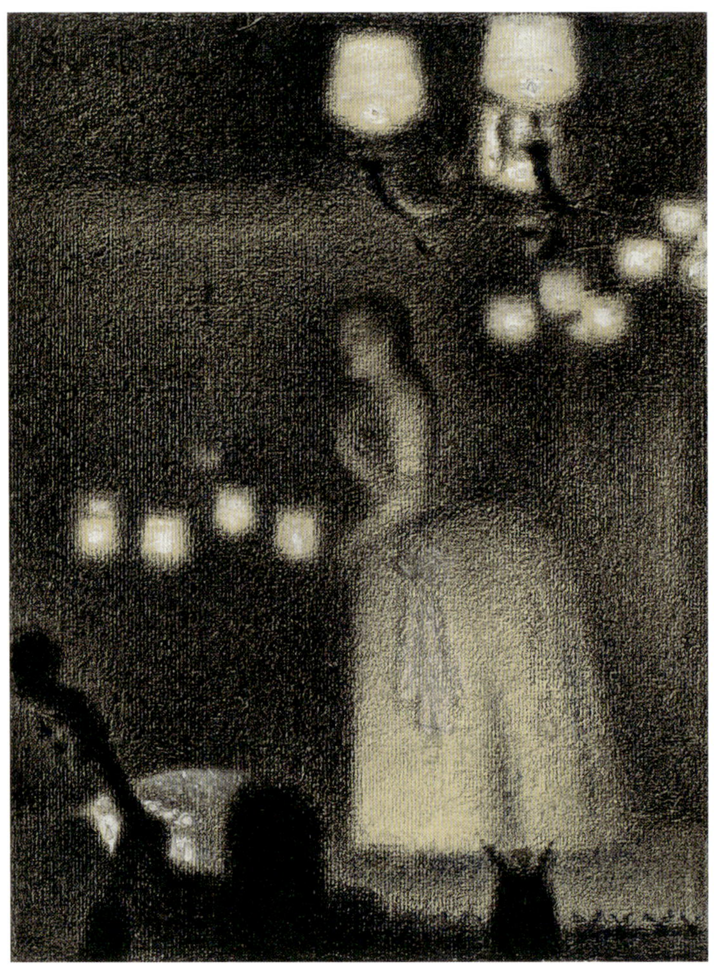

his lifetime, and the group of four *café-concert* subjects was an important element within it.[157] Together with *Circus Sideshow*, the *café-concert* drawings formed a core to his otherwise diverse submission, concentrating his interest in popular entertainment.

As with the circus, Seurat had been drawn to the theme of the *café-concert* for some time; colored-crayon drawings of singers date from the early 1880s, and at the third Indépendants in the spring of 1887 he had presented the conté crayon *Eden Concert*, soon purchased by Theo van Gogh, always the astute art dealer (fig. 74).[158] The exhibited drawings — clearly considered important finished works by Seurat — represent nighttime scenes at local venues in Montmartre, which he visited easily from his neighboring studio and named in his titles. In them Seurat experimented with compositional formulas for depicting performers (always women) on stage, seen above or through foreground figures. Two of the

Seurat's Circus Sideshow

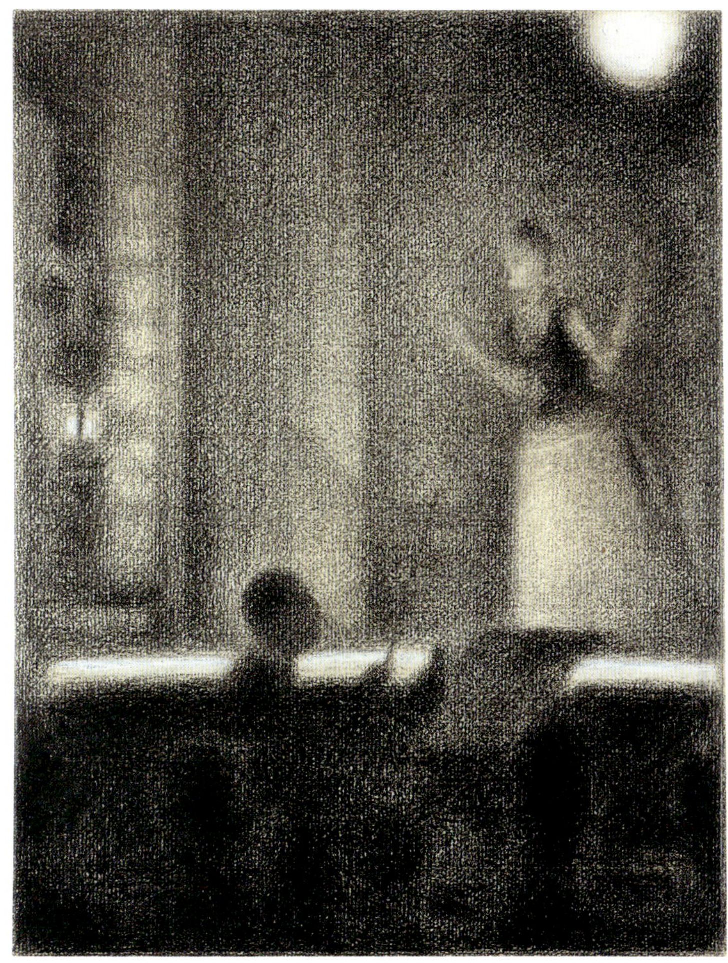
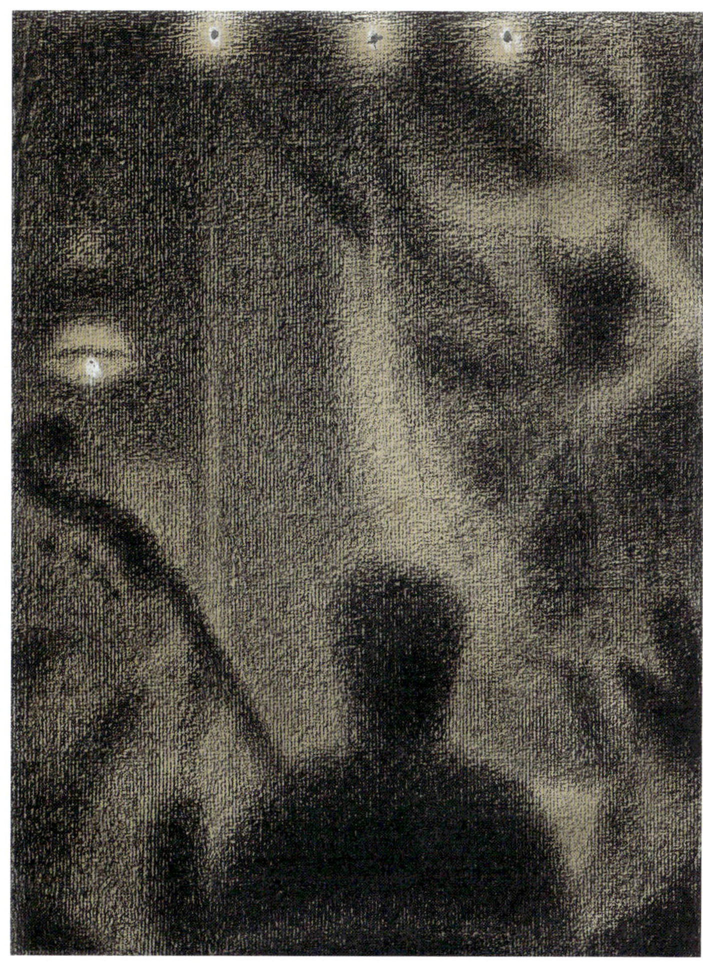

FIG. 75. Georges Seurat, *At the Gaîté Rochechouart*, ca. 1887–88. Conté crayon with gouache on paper, 12 x 9¼ in. (30.5 x 23.5 cm). Museum of Art, Rhode Island School of Design, Gift of Mrs. Murray S. Danforth

FIG. 76. Georges Seurat, *At the Divan Japonais*, ca. 1887–88. Conté crayon on paper, 12⅜ x 9¼ in. (31.5 x 23.5 cm). Private collection

drawings shown in 1888—*At the Gaîté Rochechouart* and *At the Divan Japonais*, the former with a singer and the latter with a dancer—share *Eden Concert*'s composition with the performer positioned in profile and musicians beneath her seen either from the side or abruptly from behind (figs. 75, 76).[159] By contrast, the other two, *High C (Forte Chanteuse)* and *At the Concert Européen*, as well as the contemporaneous *At the Concert Parisien*, depict a female singer frontally, viewed through or around the heads of the audience (figs. 77–79). All were modeled on conventional images in the illustrated periodicals of the 1880s, using the nuanced dark matter of black conté and Seurat's subtle strokes and shading, sometimes touched with gouache to lift out the lights, to transform cliché into graphic magic, distilling from a topos quintessential forms.[160]

The three drawings with frontal singer make the public subservient to the performer. In *High C* (fig. 77) the emphatic, almost sacerdotal, gesture

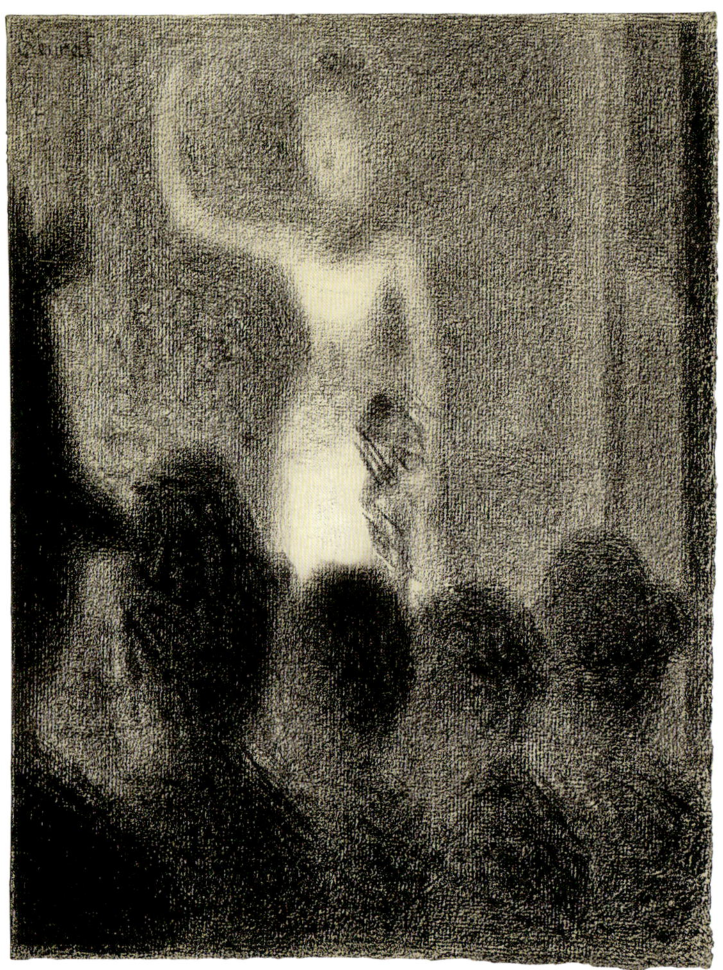

of the singer's raised arm reduces her audience to hypnotized heads. *At the Concert Européen* (fig. 78) sets the listeners askew from the singer, perhaps responding to the effect of mirrors on the walls of the venue, but nonetheless they are mesmerized by the ritualized W-shaped gesture of lyrical appeal made from center stage. The diva in *At the Concert Parisien* (fig. 79) is almost lost in the gloom, but she still commands the felt- or bowler-hatted males, their simply stamped shapes like gingerbread figures from the Gingerbread Fair. The other three drawings, with the performer in profile, focus on the dynamics between performer and musicians, and on the lighting of these dark interiors. The singer in *At the Gaîté Rochechouart* (fig. 75) repeats the gesture of the one in *At the Concert Européen*, though here she responds to the conductor and his orchestra in the darkness of the pit, yet dominates from her position on the light-flooded stage. *Eden Concert* (fig. 74) is even more hierarchical, the singer in her exaggerated

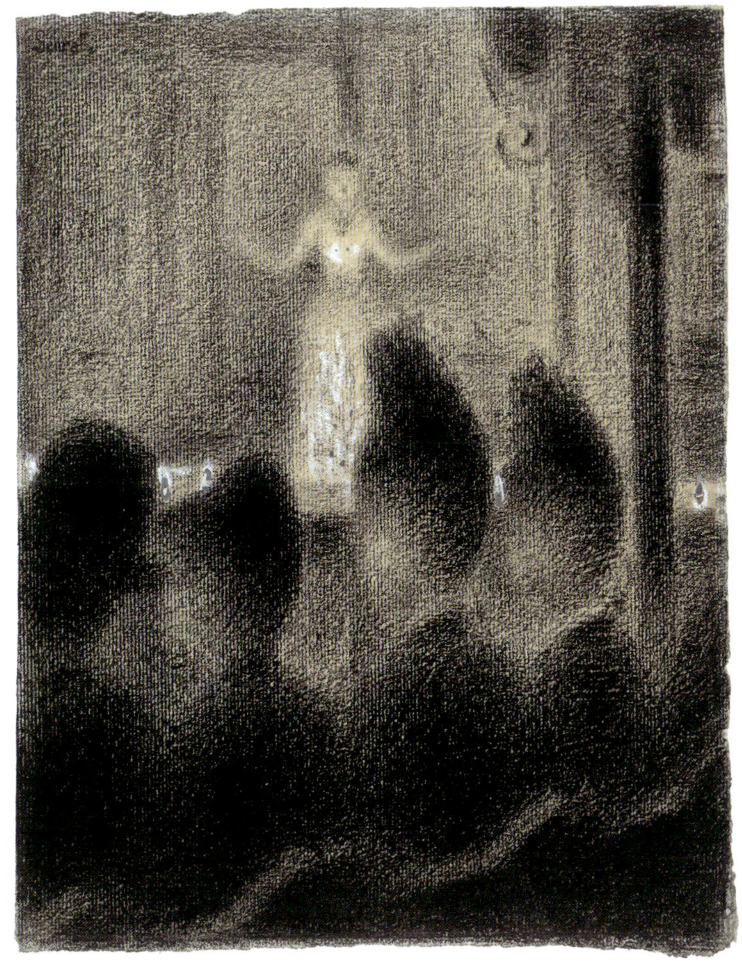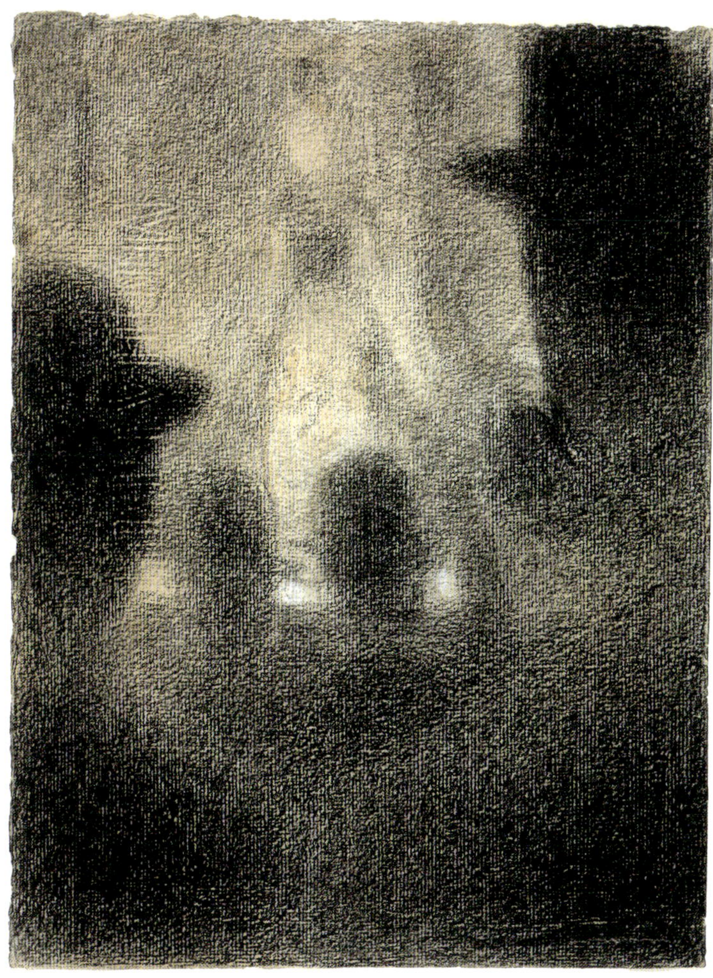

bustle a domelike form lit by the floating lights that irregularly frame her, like lamps held up by acolytes around some strange priestess. *At the Divan Japonais* (fig. 76) continues the fascination with the profile, the dancer's flamboyantly flourished arm illuminating the arc of her petticoats in a gesture of sexual attention repetitively and ritualistically demanded. That this drawing, with its wry interplay of the bass's neck and dancer's kicked-up leg, would be developed into Seurat's next major painting, *Chahut* (fig. 6), suggests once again how fluid and cross-referential were his creative processes.

One might read the *café-concert* drawings as images of anonymity and alienation in the modern city, and thus as a parody of vivid naturalist compositions and their lively transmission via journalistic imagery. The *café-concert* scenes of Degas, with their expressive singers and engaged audiences (see fig. 80), show by contrast how still and cold Seurat's depictions are. The

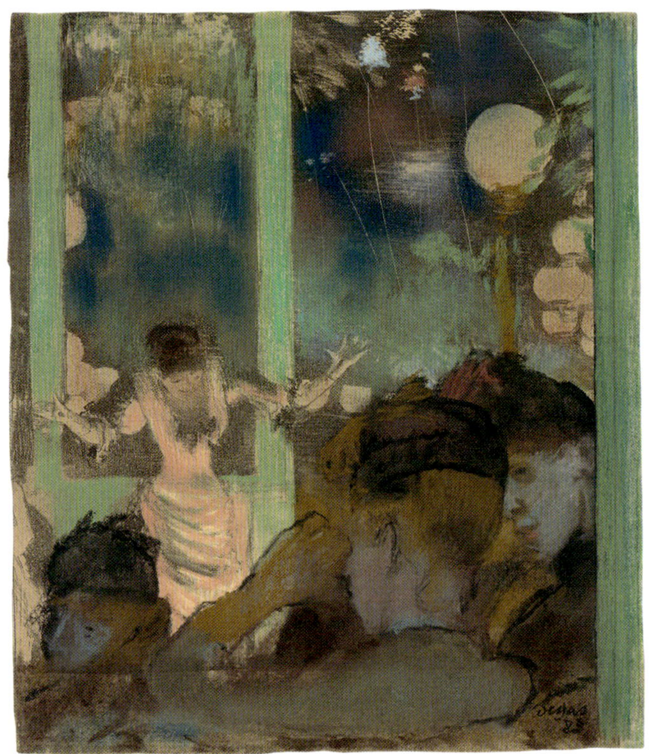

drawings can also be viewed in terms of Symbolist aesthetics as a refinement of the idea (*Idée*) of performance and public, or as part of a search for formal synthesis of this essential relationship. Certainly the *café-concert* drawings have more than composition in common with *Circus Sideshow*. The singers' gestures are just as stylized, in the appeal of their open arms or the solipsism of the hand raised to the breast, as Corvi's proprietorial posture or the nonchalant stance of the trombonist. The hieraticism of profile and frontality in both painting and drawings echo the interest in Egyptian hieroglyphics fostered by Blanc. They share too a subject drawn from popular entertainment, from mass not elite culture, yet counter that apparent relish for the *populaire* by rendering the figures as little more than ciphers, their absorption in the spectacle petrified, their stasis paradoxically at odds with the exuberance of the event.

The critical response to Seurat's submissions to the 1888 Indépendants was uneven, and is difficult to explain. *Models* was positively received, as were the drawings—but not so *Circus Sideshow*, which was scarcely mentioned. Reviewers' prejudices certainly played a part. The illustrator Henri Somm was simply antagonistic to Neo-Impressionism, dismissing Seurat's painting technique as "multicolored and mathematically contrasted lentils."[161] The conservative Maurice de Faramond made no comment on the picture, and the radical republican Gustave Geffroy gave it one critical sentence: "*Circus Sideshow* has . . . scant allure, poverty of form, a wan and uncomfortably contrasted look."[162] Meanwhile three critics who had written supportively of *La Grande Jatte* in 1886 dealt with *Circus Sideshow* briefly and noncommitally. Paul Adam offered two sentences: "Nearby a *parade* of *saltimbanques* flooded with gaslight attracts one's attention. It's an important study in relief and shading." Jules Christophe provided the curt comment "*Circus Sideshow*, a curious attempt at a nocturnal effect."[163] Seurat's friend Fénéon observed simply, "a *Circus Sideshow*, interesting as the application to a nocturne of a method designed to optimize daylight effects only."[164] "Néo"— apparently Seurat's staunchest ally Signac writing under a pseudonym — was even less generous, telegraphically noting, "A *Circus Sideshow,* nocturne."[165] There were some neutral notices from other friends, such as Rodolphe Darzens's brief "*parade* at a fair: it's a study of artificial light in the open air; the flickering light and the uncertain shadowy outlines are exactly conveyed."[166] It was Kahn who gave the painting most credence, in *La Revue indépendante*, with the following description: "Another canvas, *Circus Sideshow*: three feeble fellows blow their brass instruments, against the garish hoardings of the Corvi Circus; a buffoon played by an amusing adolescent does his *parade*; in front a crowd makes its presence felt with a few emergent heads. In his new research on the effects of gaslight, M. Seurat doesn't quite achieve the harmonious and seductive impression of his *Models*, but the attempt was difficult and the painterly qualities remain."[167]

What caused this silence and negativity, even in quarters usually sympathetic to Seurat's work? To start, it seems that *Circus Sideshow* was upstaged by Seurat's other exhibited works. The drawings were praised, even Faramond admiring their "intense Parisianism,"[168] while the larger *Models* apparently imposed itself as the more important canvas and the successor to *La Grande Jatte*, which is represented as a painting within a painting in its background. For critics following Seurat's progress, this was clearly the sequel, both in the refinement of his technique and in its application to an indoor subject. Moreover, the straightforwardly descriptive character of *Models* could be read in familiar naturalist terms, especially by critics alert to social signs and conditions. The anonymous reviewer for *L'Echo du Nord* wrote about the women's "lamentably rachitic skeletons" and Geffroy diagnosed "the malnourishment of skinny girls who've grown up too fast."[169] Seurat's avant-garde friends, for their part, fixated on the nocturnal effects of *Circus Sideshow*. Fénéon clearly felt that Neo-Impressionism was designed for the painting of daylight, and therefore that *Circus Sideshow* was a non sequitur. Even the more supportive Darzens and Kahn used words — "étude," "recherche"— that suggested the experimental quality of an initiative not fully resolved. It may be simply that *Circus Sideshow* struck critics as odd, daunting even, its space difficult to read, its common fairground subject presented with untypical decorum, its composition adopted from naturalism and caricature for a painting that was neither quite descriptive nor comic. Whatever the reasons for the painting's comparative neglect in 1888, it seems to have had an impact on the artist. In neither of the letters Seurat wrote about his work and career in 1890, to Fénéon on June 20 and Maurice Beaubourg on August 28, did he mention *Circus Sideshow*, nor did he exhibit it again in his lifetime.[170]

Reactions and Rivals

Seurat's preoccupations in creating *Circus Sideshow* — his fascination with nocturnal effects, his search for *synthèse*, his instinct to make something suggestive from low-grade popular entertainment — corresponded with those of his contemporaries in the Parisian avant-garde, several of whom were engaged with similar experiments and subjects during the later 1880s.

Among those contemporaries, the older American painter James McNeill Whistler was held in high regard. Based in London, in 1883 he had resumed exhibiting regularly at the Paris Salon. A display of fifty small oils, watercolors, and pastels at the Exposition Internationale de Peinture et de Sculpture staged by the Georges Petit gallery in May to June 1886 demonstrated the contained resonance of his nocturnes, close-toned marines, and street scenes, and he was much admired by young writers and artists in Paris for his evocative simplicity; indeed the encapsulation of Whistler's work in the *Petit bottin des lettres et des arts* that year — "From symphonies of shadows emerge beings of delicate and serpentine elegance, distant and disconcerting" — succinctly set a suggestive standard to which younger artists might aspire.[171] Whistler's "10 O'clock Lecture" was translated into French by his friend the poet Stéphane Mallarmé for the *Revue indépendante,* and Gustave Kahn recalled discussing with Seurat this exquisite and antinaturalistic text, which so savored the subtleties of Velázquez's nuanced tones, the economy of Japanese prints, and the poetry of night.[172] Seurat painted two marines — *Evening, Honfleur* (1886; The Museum of Modern Art, New York) and *The Channel at Gravelines, Evening* (1890; The Museum of Modern Art, New York) — that make a bow to Whistler in their nocturnal subjects, discreet tonalities, and careful equilibrium. However, not all of the younger generation were so convinced; Signac, reviewing the exhibition of the Brussels-based avant-garde group Les XX in February 1888, found the Whistlers too black.[173] Some of Whistler's nocturnal shopfront paintings show how dark his work could be (see fig. 81); their simple

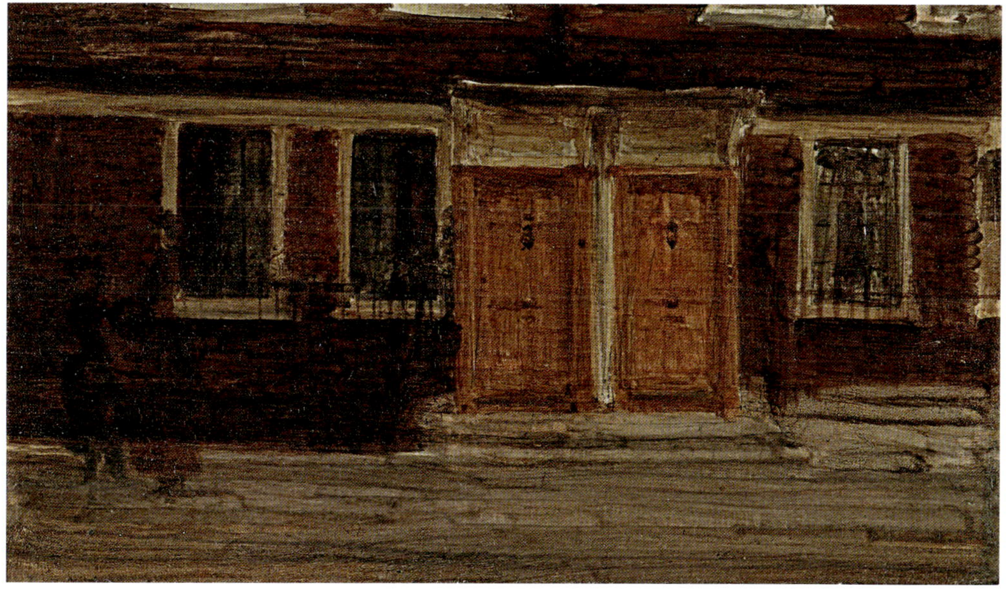

FIG. 81. James McNeill Whistler, *Street in Chelsea*, 1880–87. Oil on wood, 5 ¼ x 9 ¼ in. (13.3 x 23.5 cm). Iris and Gerald Cantor Center for Visual Arts at Stanford University, Committee for Art Acquisition Fund

gridlike designs may have resonated with Seurat. To young painters for whom color was the key, there were other roads to be taken.

But those roads were neither necessarily convergent nor shared. The studios of the boulevard de Clichy and the southern slopes of Montmartre were full of young men in their twenties, not long out of art school, conscious of the tensions in the Third Republic between the claims of *liberté* on the one hand and the entrenched elites on the other. They were alert to new opportunities such as exhibition groupings like the Indépendants, a burgeoning art market on the lookout for fresh talent, and the support available from the plethora of new journals stimulated by the Republic's liberalization of the press in 1881 and their equally young writers, as keen to assert their independence as their painter peers. These artists did not always see eye to eye. In March 1887, to give one example, Camille Pissarro, a convert for the last eighteen months to Seurat's Neo-Impressionism, visited Signac's studio to see his latest painting, probably *The Dining Room* (1886–87; Kröller-Müller Museum, Otterlo), a bourgeois interior with figures stiffly drawn and dotted like *La Grande Jatte*. Louis Anquetin and Emile Bernard, both former colleagues from Fernand Cormon's teaching atelier, were there too and did not disguise their disapprobation; "they're very difficult, those fellows," reported Pissarro to his son Lucien.[174] As it happens, in 1886 and 1887 Bernard had been interested in *fête foraine* subjects as he experimented with stronger contours and simpler drawing. He made many drawings and in 1887 a painting, *Saltimbanques*—dedicated to Vincent van Gogh—which prefigures Seurat's *parade* subject but differs

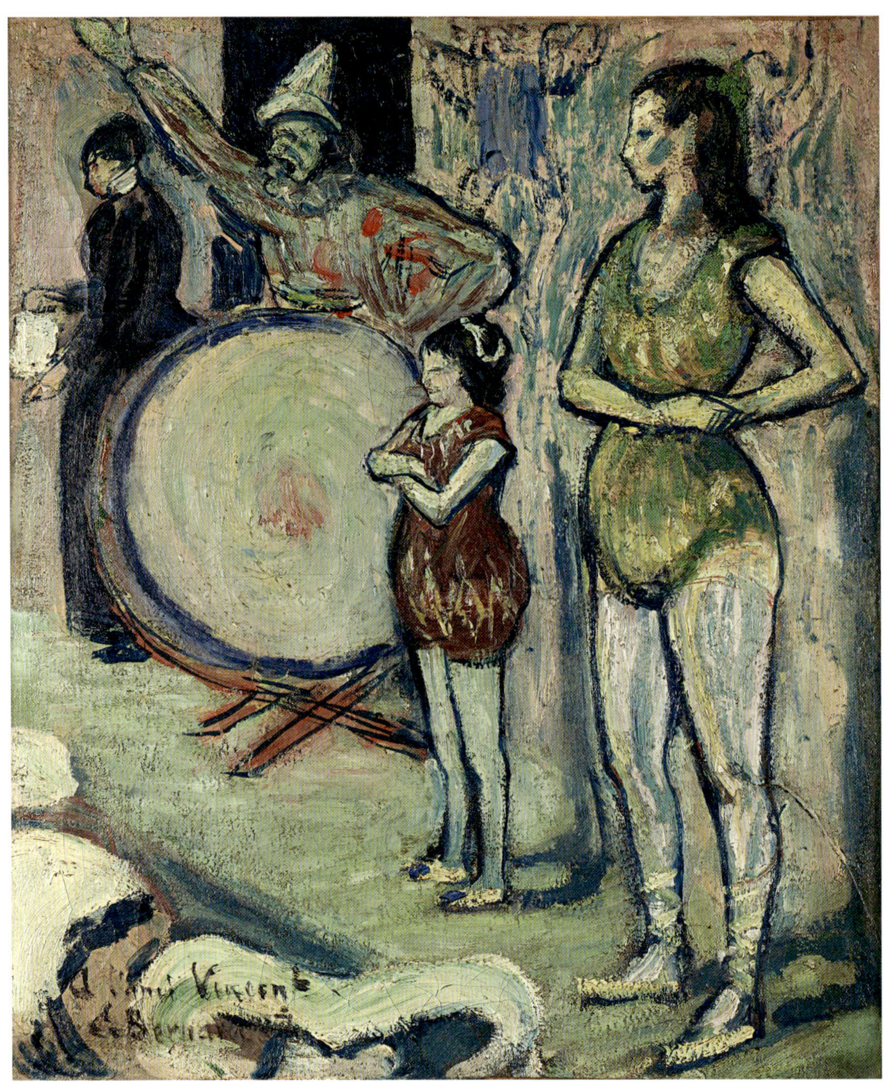

from it particularly in the bold and highly simplified contours of its figures and unsystematic chromatics, to say nothing of the clown's assertive gesture and the diagonal design (fig. 82).[175]

Anquetin's search for a personal style took on a distinct identity in 1887, with paintings marked by his study of stained glass and Japanese prints and characterized by insistent but supple outlining of the forms, enclosing quite flatly painted zones of color responding to an overall harmony. His *Avenue de Clichy* (*Street — Five O'clock in the Evening*) shows a Paris boulevard at dusk, the blue and violet gloaming of the twilit street offset by the orange and yellow light of a butcher's shop at the left (fig. 83). The painting was shown at the Les XX exhibition of February 1888, where

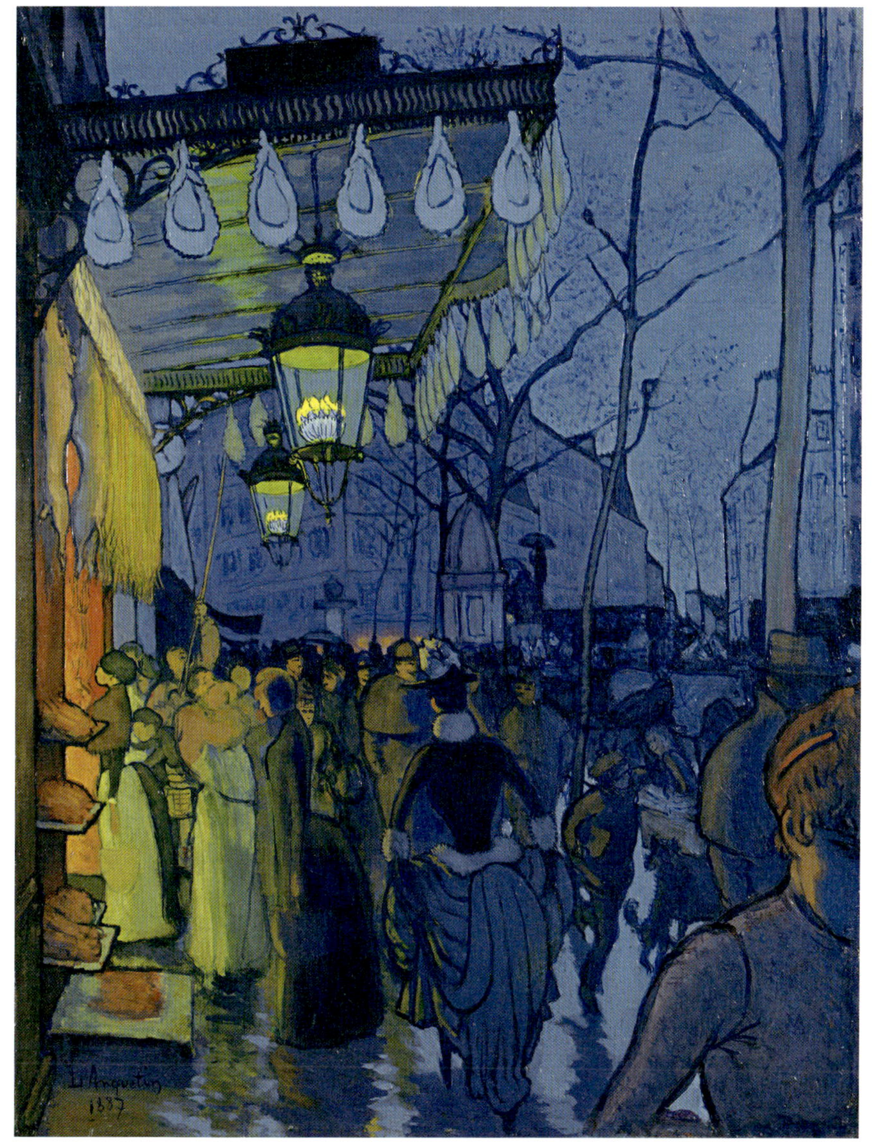

the Belgian critic Verhaeren was unimpressed, finding Anquetin's canvases full of "garish effects" which "seem merely decorative."[176] Signac, writing under his pseudonym "Néo," took the opportunity to get his own back for Anquetin's snub of his work the previous spring, scorning this "self-conscious originality" as "so pitiable."[177] In spring 1888 Anquetin's canvas was exhibited at the Salon des Indépendants in direct competition with *Circus Sideshow*, each offering modern solutions to painting a nocturne of urban bustle and artificial lighting. The critic Gustave Geffroy recognized the rivalry, seeing Anquetin's canvas as "designed to trouble those practicing pointillism."[178] Kahn's review ran in the spring issue of *La Revue indépendante*, and, while citing no specific picture, he acknowledged that Anquetin was "an experimenter," even if he had not yet been able "to provide the results of a resolved aesthetic."[179] In the previous issue Edouard Dujardin, an old school friend of Anquetin, had focused a whole article on his recent paintings. Seeking to characterize Anquetin's style of emphatic contours encompassing modulated color, he came up with "cloisonnism," a term borrowed from ceramics and clearly intended to be distinct from and rival to "Neo-Impressionism," the term generated by Fénéon to identify the dotted touch and divisionist chromatics of Seurat and his colleagues.[180] Dujardin's argument was fundamentally antinaturalist: painting cannot reproduce nature as it has neither movement nor sound; it can only be "symbolique," using its means simply, as does Japanese art, to suggest "the feeling of things" with "the fewest possible outlines and characteristic colors."[181] Seurat would have had some sympathy for the appeal to simplicity, to *synthèse*, but would have rejected the notion that color should be similarly reductive.

Despite antinaturalist rhetoric, it was difficult for some painters to shed naturalism's influence. Kahn's imputation that Anquetin had not yet achieved a coherent style is borne out in *Avenue de Clichy*, where graphic and chromatic simplification announce the new cloisonnism, but the steep diagonal of the street, which gives a sense of the momentum of the passing moment to the running boy and the woman cropped by the lower right corner, underpins what is still fundamentally a naturalist composition. Similarly, Signac's *Place de Clichy,* dated "87" at lower right, wavers between two aesthetics (fig. 84). This quiet scene of a *fête foraine* at midday combines its tentative use of dashes and dots of color — mid-blue and muted orange, greens, and reds — with its figure and carriage naturalistically cut off by the lower edges. The same tendency carries over to another painting of 1887 by an artist in Seurat's circle, Charles Angrand's *An Accident* (fig. 85). It represents the kind of likely actuality — a crowd gathered around an unseen incident outside a pharmacy — typical of naturalism. Yet Angrand was aiming for something different, which he expressed to a friend as "the synthetic expression of things . . . almost hieratic."[182] The ordered horizontals of cab horse and shop facade, the repetition of the pharmacy's colored flasks, and the sharply simplified drawing of the figures make good Angrand's claim. When his canvas was shown at the Indépendants in spring 1887 Fénéon recognized that, in addition, this recent convert to Neo-Impressionism had ambitiously painted the effect of artificial light in a canvas that would be seen in natural light.[183] On show at the time Seurat probably started *Circus Sideshow, An Accident*, by dint of its synthetic handling of a naturalist composition and its daring experiment with painting artificial illumination, set

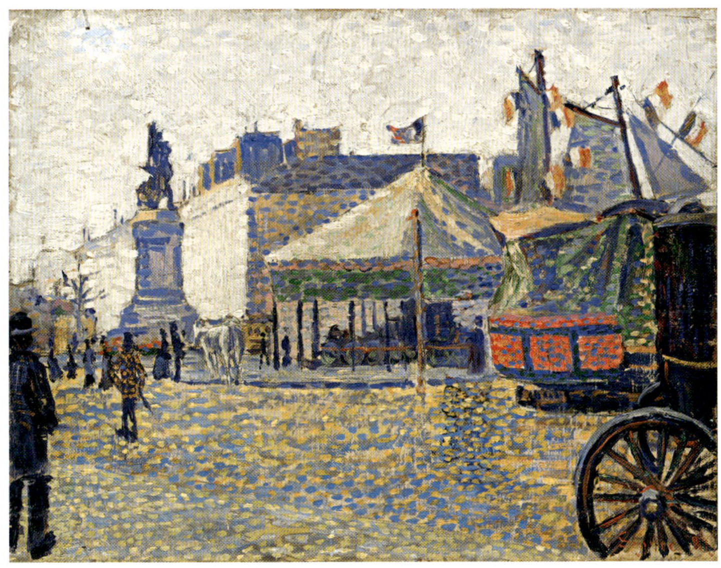

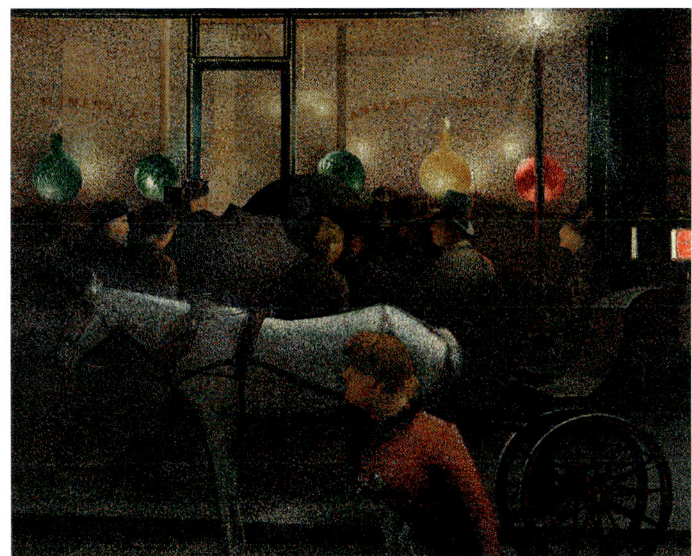

him a specific challenge. Within the ranks of the competitive avant-garde, Seurat did not just stimulate rivalry; he too had to fight for position.

Collaboration was also possible. In January 1888 young Georges Pissarro wrote to his father Camille that he, his older brother Lucien, and his friend Louis Hayet had been going to draw at La Cigale, a *café-concert* on boulevard de Rochechouart.[184] As Neo-Impressionists, both Lucien and Hayet were working with a dotted touch and divided color. But when one compares their two small pictures of the same *café-concert*, presumably La Cigale, it is clear that the results of the technique were far from uniform (figs. 86, 87). Both depicted the singer under a red proscenium arch, seen over the heads of the public, adapting the same generic composition that Seurat did for *Circus Sideshow* and some of his *café-concert* drawings. As occasional illustrators for periodicals such as *La Vie moderne*, they would have been familiar with this often-employed trope. But whereas Lucien's gouache is executed in a relatively uniform touch, represents the foreground figures in some detail, and concentrates the play of light on the stage, Hayet's was made with diverse dots and divergent dashes, the figures softened by the enveloping illumination. Lucien's picture may have been among the group of *café-concert* drawings shown in three frames at the 1888 Indépendants. "Néo," writing in the leftist *Cri du peuple*, read them as social critiques—"The middle classes stupefying themselves in front of sad beers and plaintive divas"—but surprisingly made no such observation about *Circus Sideshow* or Seurat's *café-concert* drawings.[185]

Hayet had developed his own approach to divisionism, writing in later autobiographical notes that as early as 1887 he and Seurat had discussed

FIG. 86. Lucien Pissarro, *At the Café-Concert*, 1888. Watercolor and gouache on silk, 7¼ x 8⅞ in. (18.4 x 22.5 cm). The British Museum, London

FIG. 87. Louis Hayet, *At the Café-Concert*, 1888. Gouache over pencil on paper, 6⅜ x 8 in. (16.2 x 20.3 cm). Private collection

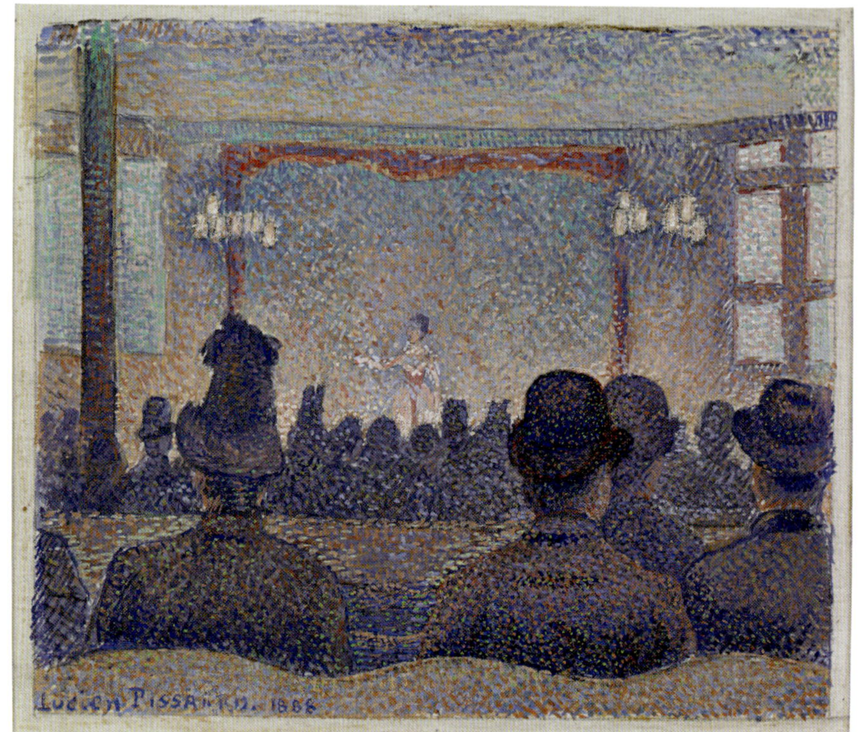

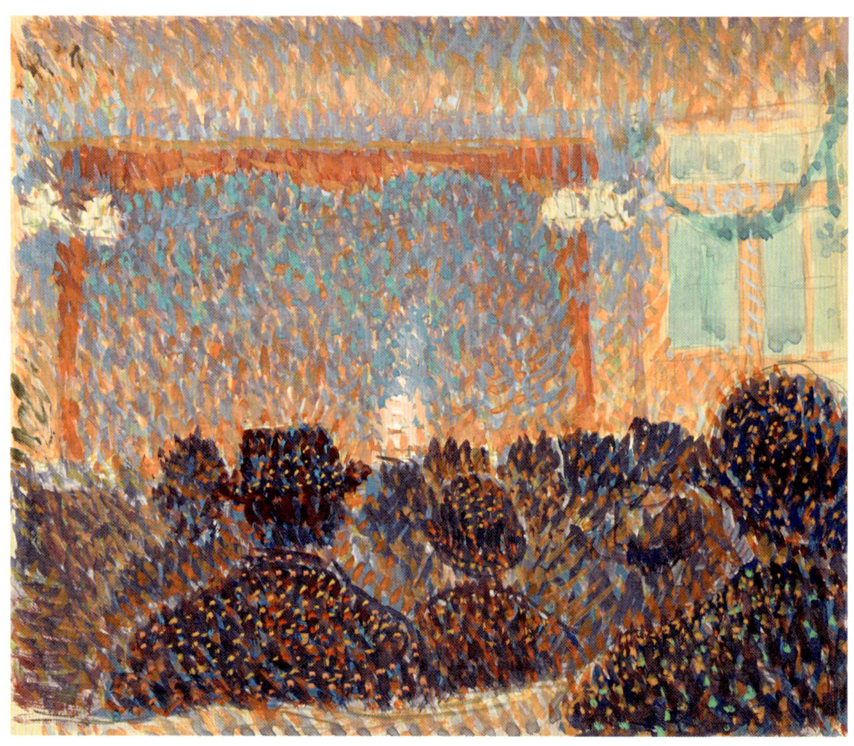

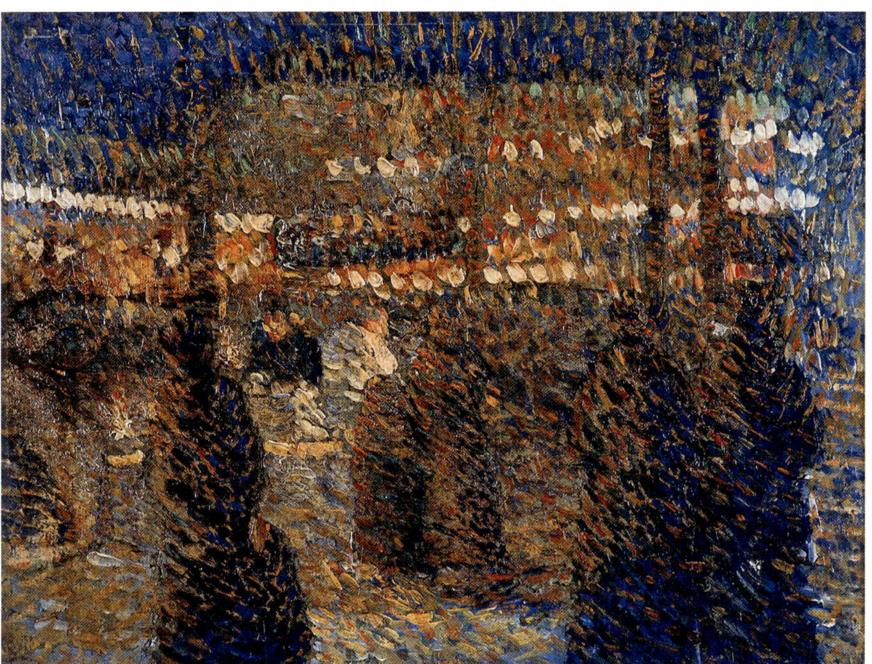

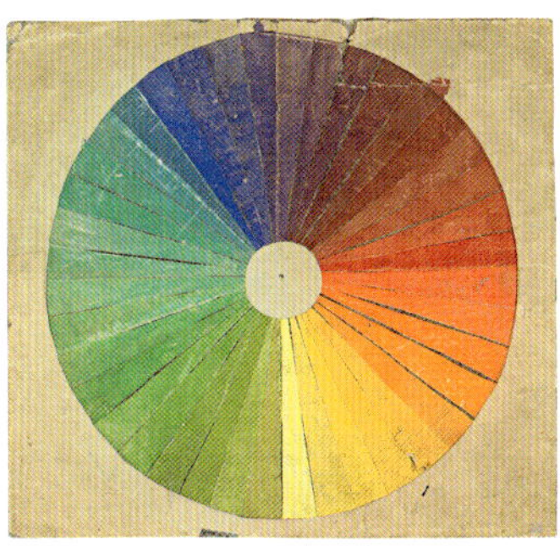

their differences.[186] Nevertheless, during his military service in 1886–87 Hayet painted several exquisitely nuanced color wheels that he gave to fellow "Néos" such as Seurat, Signac, and the Pissarros to aid their chromatic researches (see fig. 88).[187] While Seurat's "unitary" system was based on using complementary colors to enhance chromatic effects, Hayet preferred a "mode pluraliste" that favored the use of similar colors and allowed dashes and flecks as well as dots.[188] This technique can be seen in his small *Fair at Night* (*Fête foraine la nuit*) (fig. 89), where the male figure striding forward on the right, for example, is painted in a solid touch of deep blue, animated by slashed marks of dull and bright orange, while the sky above the fairground is in various rich and dark blues, licked by almost vertical orange strokes. Hayet shows his interest here in how artificial light at night can decompose forms, rather than simplify or silhouette them as in *Circus Sideshow*. A larger nighttime fairground scene, probably made in 1888 and apparently not exhibited (fig. 90), represents a *parade*, with identifiably working-class types of men, women, and children casting their shadows toward the viewer, the red costumes and yellow lights of the circus stage counterpointed against the public's resonant blues. Perhaps it was made quite independently of the more stylized *Circus Sideshow*, or as a competitive corrective manifesting Hayet's *mode pluraliste*. Certainly in 1889 Fénéon criticized another Hayet, *Place de la Concorde* (private collection), for being too close to Seurat's canvas in its cropping of figures,

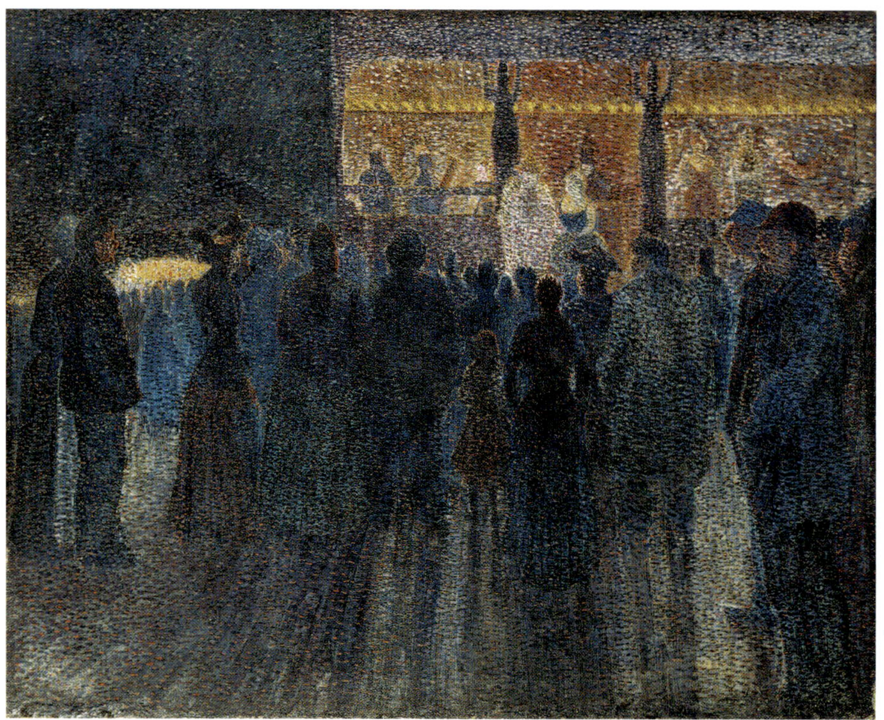

so dialogues and rivalries within the avant-garde did not go unnoticed.[189] By contrast, Maximilien Luce's later *Paris: Boulevard at Night* carried on the Neo-Impressionist fascination with night, albeit less ambitiously, with a much more informal touch and color (fig. 91).

Paradoxically, a painting that seems to have absorbed something of the hieratic quality of Seurat's picture was made by a cloisonnist opponent—Emile Bernard. In 1888–89 he produced *At Le Tabarin* (fig. 92), a work distinguished by strongly frontal and silhouetted forms, repetitive motifs along the upper edge, and an overall composition that looks like an homage to the symmetries of Seurat's painting. Apparently Seurat's *Circus Sideshow* held lessons even for his antagonists.

Crucially, the Parisian avant-garde was not only pictorial but also literary, and Seurat numbered poets like Kahn and Laforgue among his friends. In writing as well as painting, a change of aesthetic from descriptive naturalism to suggestive Symbolism was being registered. Zola's naturalist novel *Nana*, published in 1880, deployed frankly factual, often long sentences: "Two little trees stood out sharply, in a raw green; a Morris column was so white under the strong lighting that one could read the posters from a distance, like in daylight; and beyond the thickening night punctuated by lights, a constantly moving crowd in the gloaming."[190] But writers of Seurat's generation, such as Jean Moréas, Paul Adam, and especially

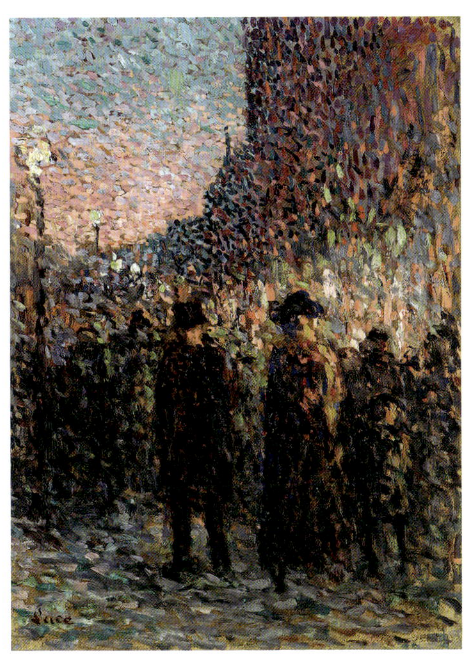

FIG. 91. Maximilien Luce, *Paris: Boulevard at Night*, ca. 1893. Oil on paper, laid down on canvas, 17 ¾ x 13 ⅛ in. (45.1 x 33.2 cm). Museo Soumaya. Fundación Carlos Slim, Mexico City

FIG. 92. Emile Bernard, *At Le Tabarin*, 1888–89. Oil on canvas, 10 ⅝ x 24 ½ in. (27 x 62.2 cm). Mr. and Mrs. Barron U. Kidd

Dujardin, used staccato sentences and many repetitions to suggest mood and the fragmented perception of urban experience. In Dujardin's innovative stream-of-consciousness novella *Les Lauriers sont coupés* (The Bay Trees Have Been Pruned), published in 1887, the second paragraph exemplifies the new style and culminates in the Symbolist key word "Idée": "it's today; it's here; the hour is sounding; and, around me, life; the hour, the place, an April evening, Paris, sunset on a clear evening, the monotonous sounds, the white houses; the shadowy foliage; . . . the streets and the multitudes . . . everywhere Paris is singing, and, in the fog of perceived forms, the idea is softly framed."[191] Dujardin was a close friend of Anquetin's, and in places his prose is overtly pictorial, as in this observation of color under gaslight in a restaurant: "The mirror in front of me reflects the golden frame; the golden frame which is thus behind me; these light effects have a reddish cast, the lights a scarlet tinge; it's the gaslight all pale yellow that illuminates the walls; also yellowed by the gaslight, the white linen, the mirrors, the glassware."[192] The young writers of the 1880s, like the painters, were adapting style — whether sentence structure or synthetic form, repetitive words or dotted surface — and sometimes using the same devices — hypnotic repetition, suggestive imprecision — to forge new means of expression that drew away from the certitudes of naturalism into a more allusive, associative aesthetic. *Circus Sideshow*'s genesis during this phase of cultural transition is given perspective when one acknowledges the parallel literary context.

The *parade* itself was a frequent subject in writing of the later 1880s. Poems such as Arthur Rimbaud's "Parade" and Laforgue's "Soir de carnaval" ("Evening at the Carnival") have been proposed as possible literary stimuli for Seurat.[193] One might add Maurice Vaucaire's poem "Parade," published in 1886, with its stenographic simplicity akin to Seurat's pictorial

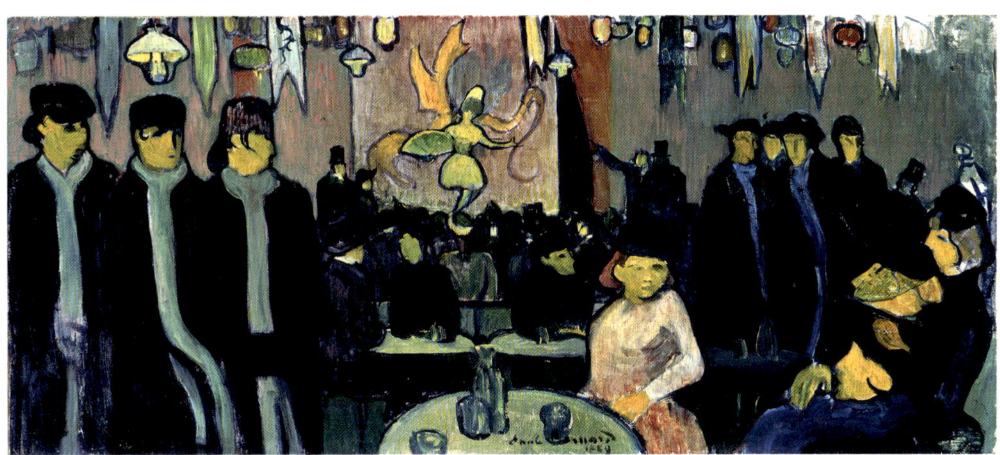

style: "Helmets, bonnets, hats, in front of the sideshow, / Hungrily pressing themselves on the creaking stairs."[194] Or Jean Lorrain's of the same title, using the latest medical terminology to epitomize the *parade* as "unique and divine modern hysteria."[195] In his private diary the poet Albert Samain recorded observations of Paris life made at a particular time and place: "October 1st—Sunday. Outer boulevard, avenue de la République. Five o'clock in the evening. Up toward the square a fair is taking place, strident and tempestuous. . . . A band . . . passes, playing 'En rev'nant de la revue' and the crowd follows, dark, grumbling, drunk. . . . With the harmony of the time of day and the setting, the atmosphere is complete. And it's the blossoming of the Paris working class that I breathe there, amongst these factory girls' skirts, under the delicate late September sky, in air lit up by the animation of this district *en fête,* by the sounds of this facile, soggy music."[196] Quite independently, but contemporaneously with Seurat's work on *Circus Sideshow*, this poet of the same age drew together allusions to the rousing theme song of the populist General Boulanger ("Returning from the Review") and the fragile nature of the Republic as well as to the collective enjoyment of the Paris *peuple*, but from an exterior elitist position, observant but detached. Seurat's painting shares something of the sensibility of such contemporaries—Dujardin's search for a new language to articulate refined modern sensation in the city, Samain's sensitive but aloof response to the solidarity and the fragility of popular culture.

The Show Goes On

After its curiously unremarked appearance at the 1888 Indépendants, *Circus Sideshow* slipped into the shadows of Seurat's growing reputation. Even the biography published by Jules Christophe in 1890 listed only "a circus sideshow" with no further comment.[197] When Seurat died suddenly of fever in March the following year, obituaries by supporters such as Christophe and Fénéon neglected to mention the picture in lists of his major canvases.[198] Téodor de Wyzewa merely listed it. Only Kahn gave the painting a modicum of appreciation, describing it in relation to *Chahut* (fig. 6) as "his first night effect, so deliberately pallid and sad."[199] At the memorial retrospectives of Seurat's work organized in 1892 by the Indépendants in Paris and Les XX in Brussels, *Circus Sideshow* was again overlooked. Paris critics such as Charles Saunier and Remy de Gourmont did not refer to it in their reviews; nor did fellow painter Maurice Denis or old ally Fénéon.[200] The Brussels reviewers, seeing the painting for the first time, were more attentive. If Pierre Olin only listed it and Seurat's friend Emile Verhaeren made no mention, Albert Arnay enthused about "how the

FIG. 93. Henri Gray, *The Saltimbanques, Cirque d'Hiver*, 1892. Color lithograph, 50 x 36 in. (127 x 91.5 cm). Zimmerli Art Museum at Rutgers University, Museum Purchase

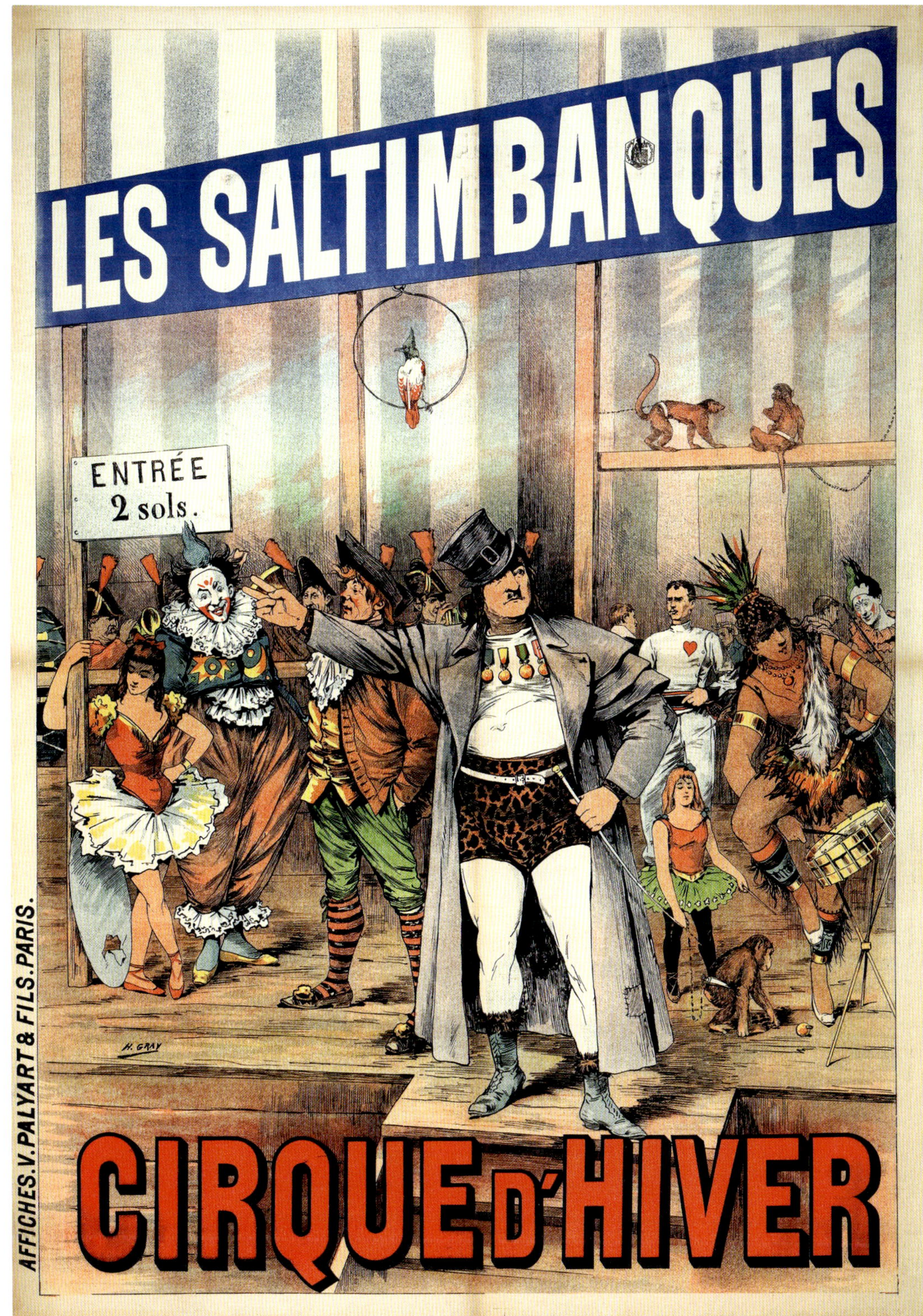

LES SALTIMBANQUES
ENTRÉE
2 sols.
H. GRAY
AFFICHES.V.PALYART & FILS.PARIS.
CIRQUE D'HIVER

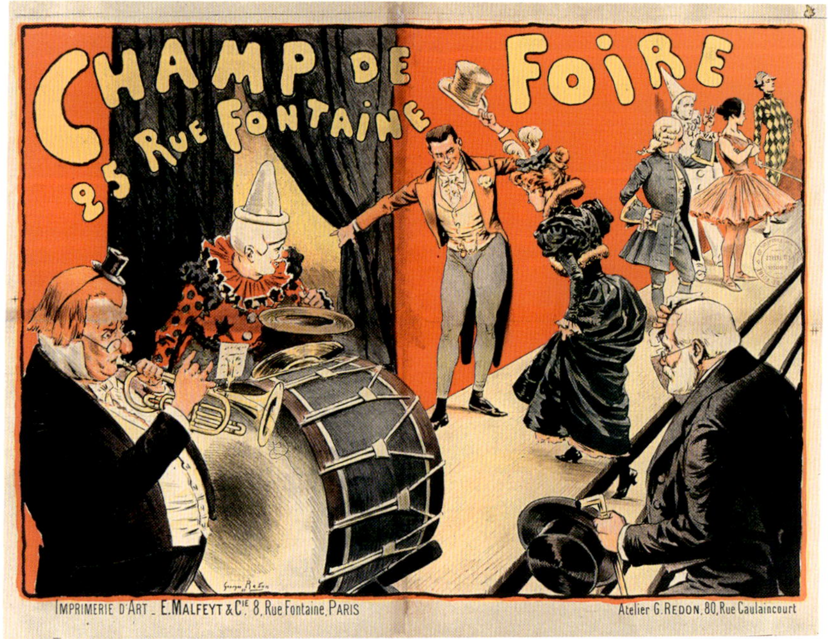

FIG. 94. Georges Redon, *Champ de Foire: 25, rue Fontaine*, 1897. Color lithograph, 25 ⅝ x 33 ⅞ in. (65 x 86 cm). Bibliothèque Nationale de France, Paris

bands of gaslight define the rectilinear modality of this fairground scene!" and Eugène Demolder admired the subtle ambient light, though telling his readers that the painting was not as "décisif" as *Circus* (fig. 7), which he considered the outstanding painting.[201] Gathering together Seurat's small but remarkable oeuvre, the retrospectives reminded viewers of his extraordinary stylistic adventure over the short period from *La Grande Jatte* to *Circus*, and reintroduced *Bathers*, unseen since 1884. Within that trajectory, *Circus Sideshow* seems to have appeared as a parenthetical essay in artificial illumination, a painting of night.

Nevertheless, the subject of the *parade* continued to have a vivid fascination for other artists in the decade or so after Seurat's death, not least because of the growth of popular entertainment as a veritable industry. The 1890s was the great era of the poster, mass-produced but of high quality, attracting creative talents eager to establish their artistic reputations through success in the commercial world. The poster was of course modern printing technology's extension of the time-honored *parade*, the function of both being to pull the public into the show. Henri Gray's advertisement for the Cirque d'Hiver, one of the well-capitalized permanent circuses in Paris, promoted a spectacle of traditional acts—clown, buffoon, female acrobat, and performing animals—joined by a "redskin," a novelty introduced to Parisian audiences by Buffalo Bill's Wild West show, and led by the blustering wrestler in his leopard-skin trunks (fig. 93). In his poster for the venue Champ de Foire, Georges Redon had the dandified buffoon

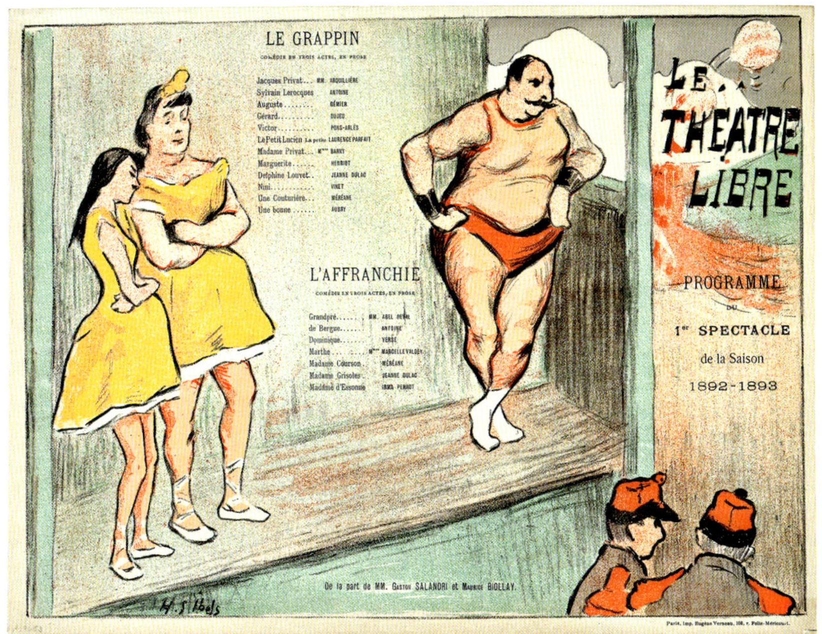
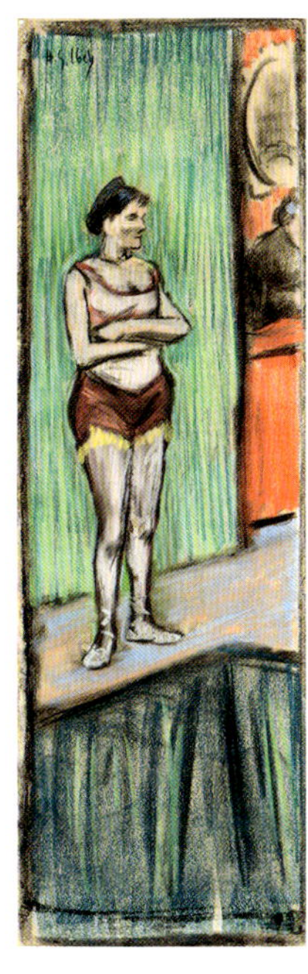
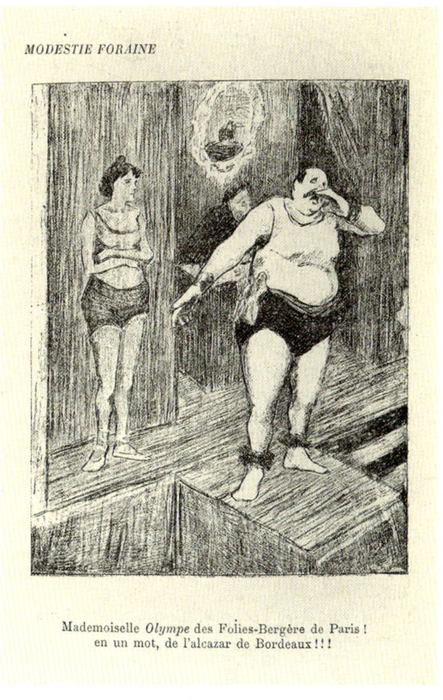

Mademoiselle *Olympe* des Folies-Bergère de Paris!
en un mot, de l'alcazar de Bordeaux!!!

FIG. 95. Henri-Gabriel Ibels, program for *The Grapnel* (*Le Grappin*) and *The Emancipated* (*L'Affranchie*) at the Théâtre Libre, 1892. Color lithograph, 9½ x 12⅝ in. (24 x 32 cm). Zimmerli Art Museum at Rutgers University, Museum Purchase

FIG. 96. Henri-Gabriel Ibels, *Mademoiselle Olympe*, 1893. Pastel over charcoal on paper, 21 x 6¾ in. (53.3 x 17 cm). Zimmerli Art Museum at Rutgers University, Museum Purchase, Lillian Lilien Memorial Art Acquisition Fund

FIG. 97. Henri-Gabriel Ibels, *Mademoiselle Olympe from the Folies-Bergère in Paris! in other words, from the Alcazar in Bordeaux!!!* from *Les Demi-cabots* (Paris, 1896), p. 226. Lithograph. Zimmerli Art Museum at Rutgers University, Museum Purchase, Norma B. Bartman Research Library Fund

guide a bourgeois theatergoer into the tent while clown musicians and other performers promote what the spectacle has to offer (fig. 94). Both posters thus use the imagery of the *parade* to duplicate the job of the *parade*.

In a decade that saw the rise of socialism in France and growing tensions between capital and labor, artists of leftist sympathies were drawn to the imagery of the *fête foraine*, not least because *saltimbanques* immediately conjured up associations of marginality and alienation. Henri-Gabriel Ibels, a member of the group known as the Nabis, used circus motifs repeatedly throughout the 1890s, fusing naturalist compositions with synthetic drawing and sharp color. A lithographic program he designed for two plays produced at the Théâtre Libre in November 1892 features a pair of female performers and a male wrestler on a raised platform with two soldiers strolling by (fig. 95). A variation of it soon appeared in a Paris periodical and later in a book Ibels illustrated, *Les Demi-cabots*, as he often recycled his imagery.[202] *Mademoiselle Olympe*, a pastel he made about 1893, uses a narrow vertical format to isolate the young woman acrobat and a purplish tone for her body to suggest deprivation (fig. 96). The figure clearly satisfied Ibels, as she too reappears, in a plate ironically captioned "Mademoiselle Olympe from the Folies-Bergère in Paris! in other words, from the Alcazar in Bordeaux!!!" in *Demi-cabots* (fig. 97).[203] This collection of texts about performers at *café-concerts*, circuses, and fairs was written by several authors, including Ibels's brother André. In his contribution Georges d'Esparbès described the people of the traveling fairs as continuing a tradition that went back to the Middle

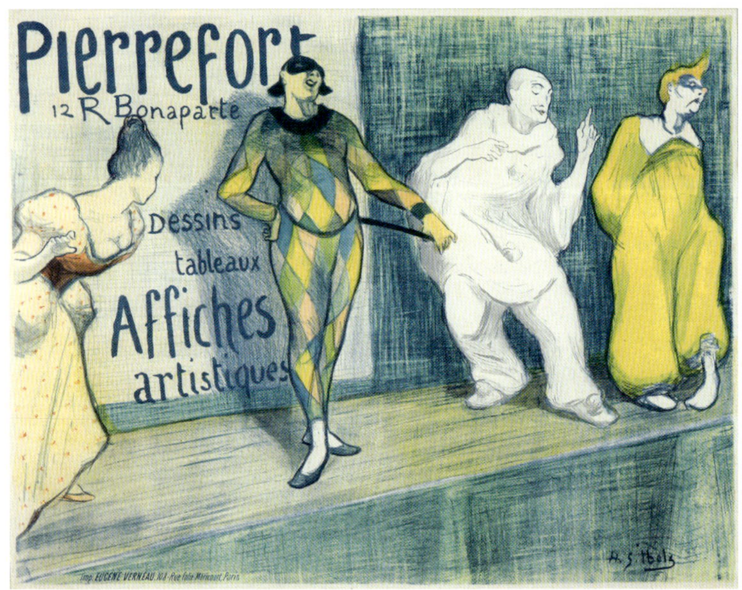

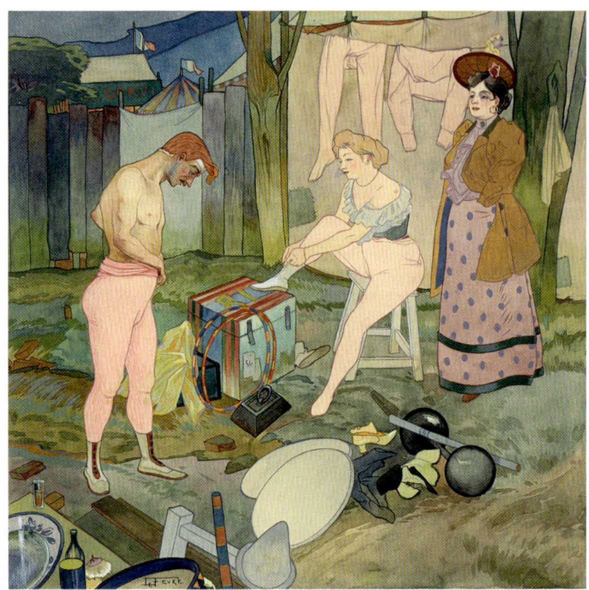

FIG. 98. Henri-Gabriel Ibels, *Pierrefort*, 1897. Color lithograph, 24 1/4 x 31 5/8 in. (61.6 x 80.3 cm). Mr. and Mrs. Jack Rennert, New York

FIG. 99. Georges de Feure, *The Corvi Circus* (*Le Cirque Corvi*), ca. 1893. Gouache, watercolor, and pencil on paper, 15 5/8 x 16 in. (39.5 x 40.5 cm). Sterling and Francine Clark Art Institute, Williamstown, Massachusetts

Ages and reiterated the enduring myth of the sad clown, writing of "the sufferings that are on display in this city of Laughter" and how "under those spangled costumes, a misunderstood heart sobs."[204] The way that Ibels repeatedly used the same cast of melancholy figures in his circus images — the paunchy strong men, the bored dancers on display in their short skirts, the languid acrobat — recalls Daumier's similar deployment of favored types. Ibels's tone was not always the same, however, and in his lithogaph *Pierrefort* of 1897, again reproduced in different formats, he played up the sinister side of the *saltimbanques* (fig. 98). Georges de Feure, in a highly finished gouache of about 1893 that shares Ibels's simplified drawing, relied on color to give an edge to his description of performers preparing backstage at the Corvi Circus (fig. 99). His palette — the ambient blue of the evening offset by strident pinks, sharp violets, and stark yellows — uses ostensibly festive hues to spotlight the vagrant life of the *saltimbanques* and infer the existential paradoxes of the performer.

Other artists played up the vibrant and caricatural aspects of the *parade*, notably Pierre Bonnard, Ibels's fellow Nabi. In his painting *Fairground Sideshow* (*Parade*) Bonnard adopted the conventional formula of performers seen over the public's heads, but brought his particular brand of humor to the painting of the clown's scrawny body and ridiculous trousers (fig. 100). The large lamps directly in front of the clown indicate compression of space and add another comical touch. The quirky drawing made to illustrate *Fairground Stall* (*La Baraque*), a piece of music for children from the playful 1895 piano suite *Petites scènes familières* (Little Scenes of

FIG. 100. Pierre Bonnard, *Fairground Sideshow* (*Parade*), ca. 1892. Oil on cardboard, laid down on parquet board, 14 ⅜ x 11 in. (36.5 x 28 cm). Private collection, courtesy Luc Bellier

FIG. 101. Pierre Bonnard, illustration for *Fairground Stall* (*La Baraque*), from Claude Terrasse, *Petites scènes familières* (musical compositions), 1895, p. 41. Lithograph, image 4 ⅛ x 8 ½ in. (10.6 x 21.7 cm). The Museum of Modern Art, New York, Gift of Abby Aldrich Rockefeller, 1948

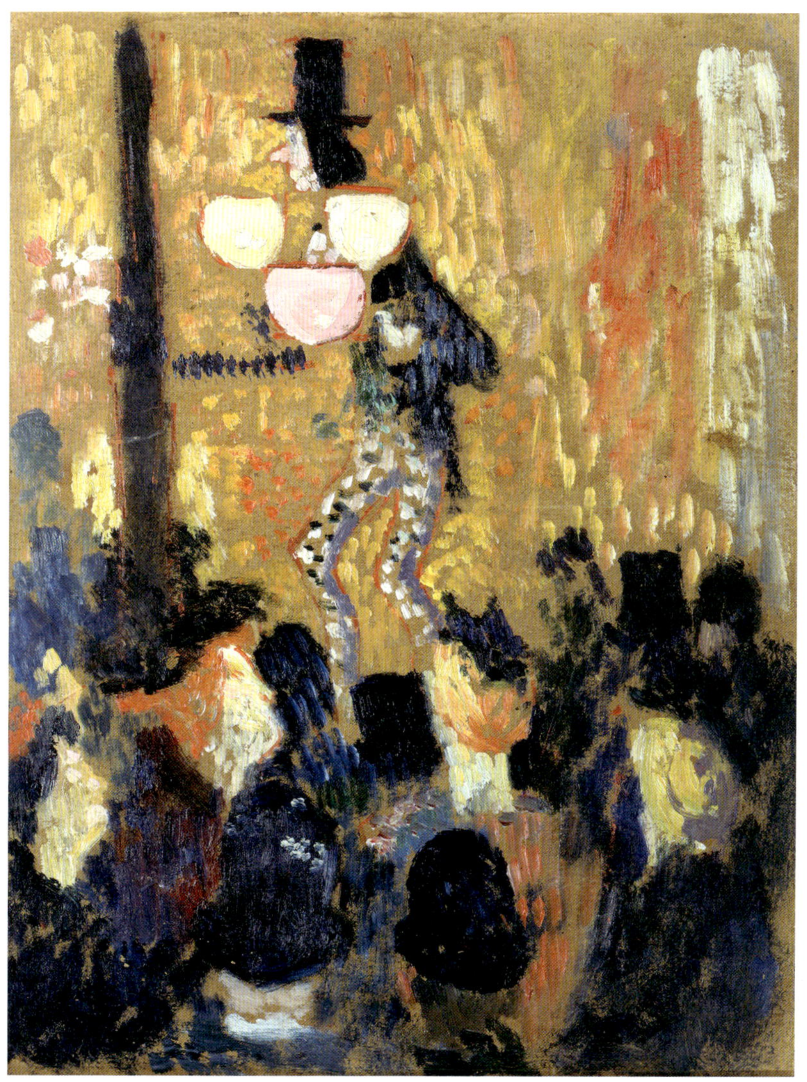

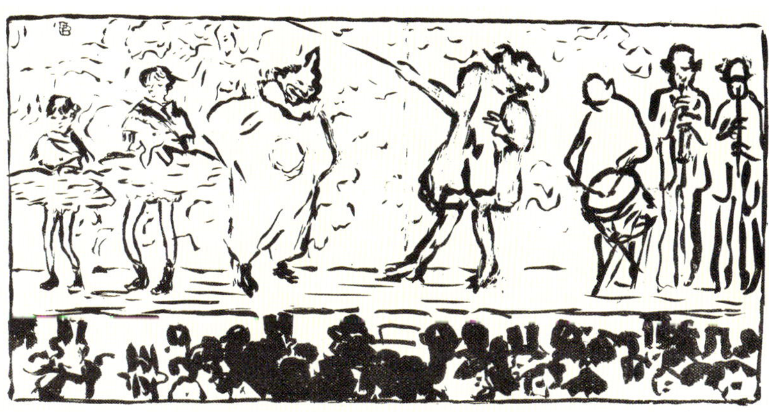

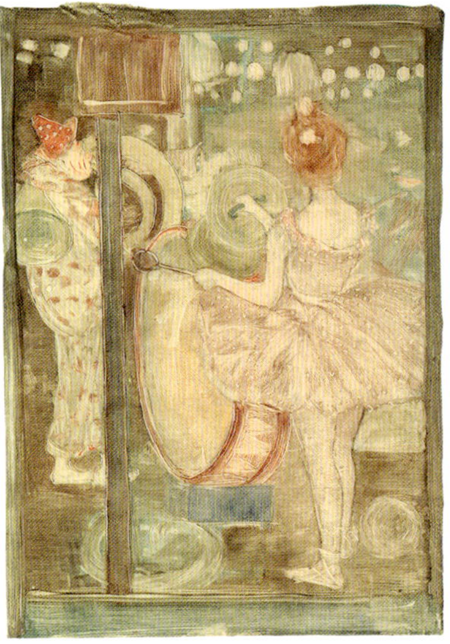 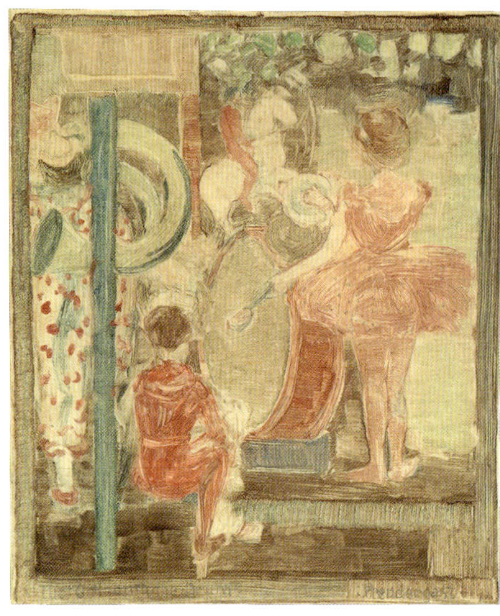

FIG. 102. Maurice Prendergast, *Circus Band*, ca. 1895. Color monotype with pencil additions, 12 ⅜ x 9 ½ in. (31.4 x 23.9 cm). Max N. Berry

FIG. 103. Maurice Prendergast, *Girl with Drum*, ca. 1895. Color monotype with pencil additions, 10 ⅜ x 9 ⅛ in. (26.4 x 23.1 cm). Max N. Berry

Family Life) by his brother-in-law, the composer Claude Terrasse, relishes the fun of the fair by depicting silly legs and gross costumes (fig. 101). Also in the 1890s the American Maurice Prendergast, then resident in Paris, made warm-toned monotypes that seek to capture fairground jollity, with a brass-playing clown in a polka-dot outfit and a tutu-wearing girl banging on the big bass drum (figs. 102, 103).[205] While Prendergast probably had no knowledge of *Circus Sideshow*, the flatness of space and repetition of forms in his work show how such devices were becoming widespread in modern picture making. However, the subject of the *parade* had always been multivalent, and the dark side found in, say, Penguilly-L'Haridon's 1846 painting (fig. 17) resurfaced in an album of etchings on the age-old allegory of the Dance of Death by Lyon artist Marcel Roux, published in 1905. One plate depicts a nighttime fairground with a mixed public of bourgeois and workers, adults and children, watching a performance as the skeletal figure of Death fatally taps a man on the shoulder (fig. 104). The vivid preliminary drawing treats the subject broadly (fig. 105), whereas the detail of the finished print gives sharp focus to the fearsome threat.

The *parade* was such a common attraction in nineteenth-century French popular culture and so insistent a subject in art, both high and low, that it is no surprise that on his first visit to Paris in 1900 the young Pablo Picasso took up the theme (fig. 106). *Circus Sideshow* was on public view that year for the first time since 1892, at a small retrospective staged by *La Revue blanche* in late March and early April, but he did not arrive in the city until October.[206] Nevertheless, he adopted the by-then formulaic design. The liveliest section of Picasso's painting is the stage: its coral

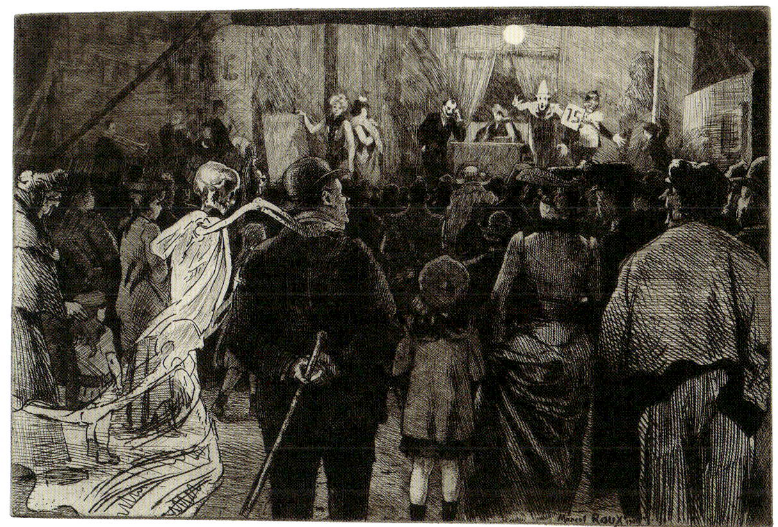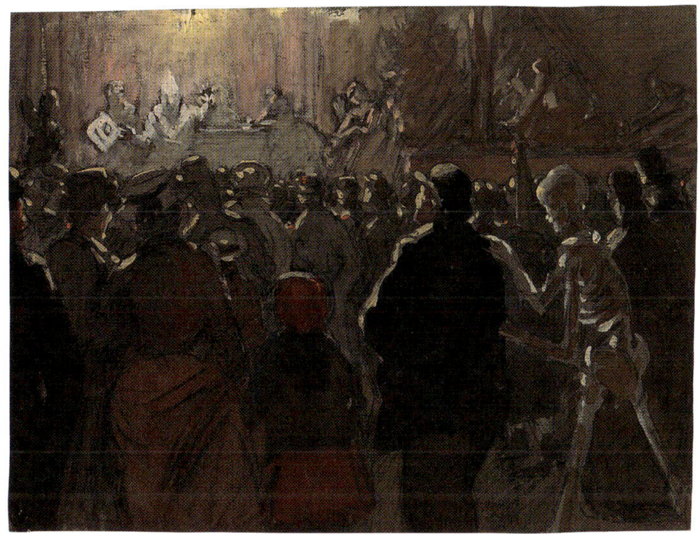

FIG. 104. Marcel Roux, *The Fair: Those Death Takes by Surprise* (*La Fête: Ceux qu'elle surprend*), from *Danse macabre*, 1905. Intaglio and etching, 17 ¾ x 22 ⅞ in. (45 x 58.2 cm). Bibliothèque Municipale de Lyon

FIG. 105. Marcel Roux, *The Fair: Those Death Takes by Surprise* (*La Fête: Ceux qu'elle surprend*), 1905. Charcoal and chalk on paper, 8 ¼ x 11 ⅛ in. (20.8 x 28.1 cm). Bibliothèque Municipale de Lyon

backdrop and peppermint green railings frame an Arab dancer in scarlet pantaloons, a proprietor in evening dress, a stout brass player, a white-faced clown, and a burly strong man. If these characters are picked out, the crowd below is more generalized, a rank of dark costumes and caps from which only a few schematic faces emerge, yet evidence enough for the viewer to contrast a blue-clad worker to the left and a top-hatted bourgeois to the right. The presence of a smiling woman facing us from the lower right-hand corner shows that naturalism's vocabulary of the partial and the momentary was still a viable stylistic option in 1900 for a tyro like Picasso. So too was caricature. The many images of *saltimbanques* and *parades* that Georges Rouault painted during the first decade of the twentieth century (see fig. 107)—grand of gesture and heir to Daumier in their globular grotesquery—are a celebration of the popular culture of the working-class suburbs of Paris in which the artist was raised and an acknowledgment that, as Rouault put it in 1905, "we're all of us clowns more or less."[207] Both he and Picasso continued to explore the *parade* and its timeless evocation of the pathos of comic spectacle well into the twentieth century. With Picasso's costumes and sets for the ballet *Parade*, which premiered in Paris in 1917 with music by Erik Satie and scenario by Jean Cocteau, the show went on.

HOW, THEN, might we leave *Circus Sideshow*? As a painting of many paradoxes, to be sure. It reprises a theme common in caricature, but any comic element—the suavely sinister trombonist, the cipher customers, Corvi as grandiose as in his own publicity—is played deadpan. The strict spacing of the performers isolates them from each other, but in the interests of

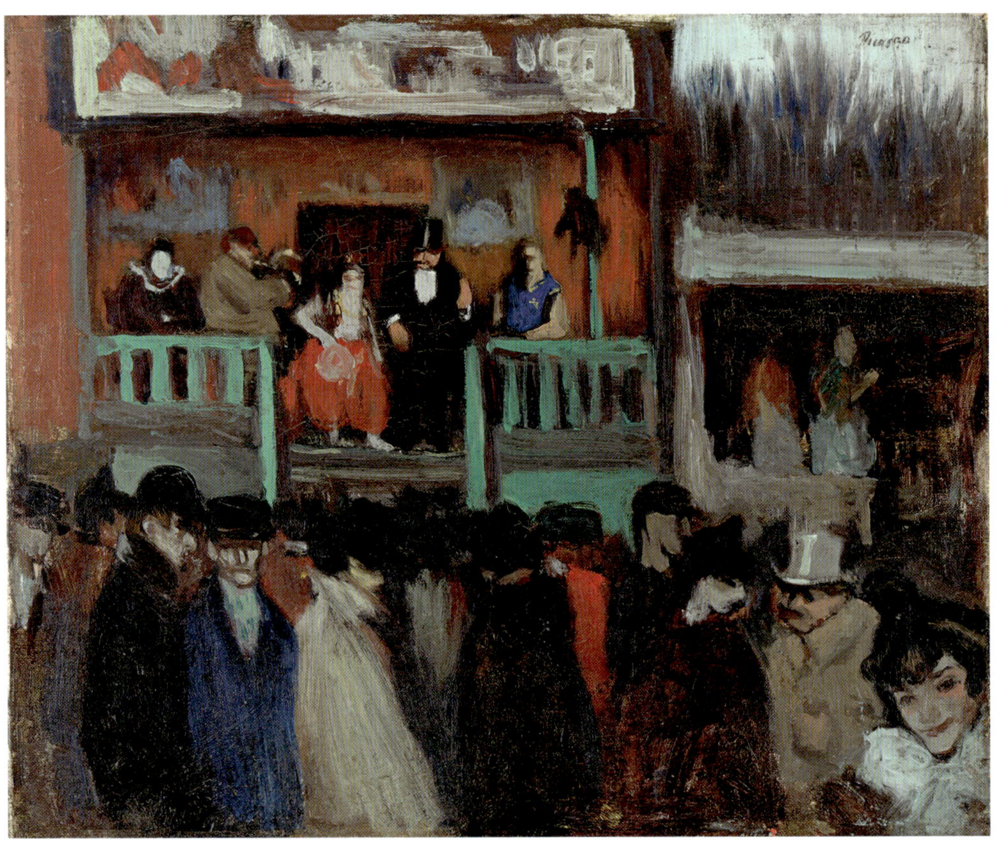

pictorial equilibrium rather than any lachrymose evocation of the sad clown myth. To a certain extent it is fascinating as a transitional painting. There is something still residually naturalist in its composition and its egalitarian subject. After all, truth-to-life was how many evaluated paintings in 1888, as the response to *Models* at the Indépendants demonstrated. At the same time, it was not yet clear what a Symbolist painting was or how it might look. Other paintings made in 1887 and 1888, *Circus Sideshow*'s contemporaries, share that equivocal character of style in the process of being shaped; that can be said of Anquetin's *Avenue de Clichy*, combining the naturalist moment with cloisonnist drawing and synthetic color (fig. 83), or Paul Gauguin's *Vision of the Sermon (Jacob Wrestling with the Angel)*, fitting the actuality of looking over heads to undescriptive color and an imaginary event (fig. 108). If *Circus Sideshow* created a tension between naturalism and a more synthetic approach, then those polarities continued. Over thirty years later, in wake of World War I, Lucien Simon's rendering of a *parade* (about 1919) and Picasso's *Three Musicians* (1921) demonstrate that those stylistic options still marked out the frontiers of painting (figs. 109, 110). In 1887–88 Seurat had been pioneering a path where they branched.

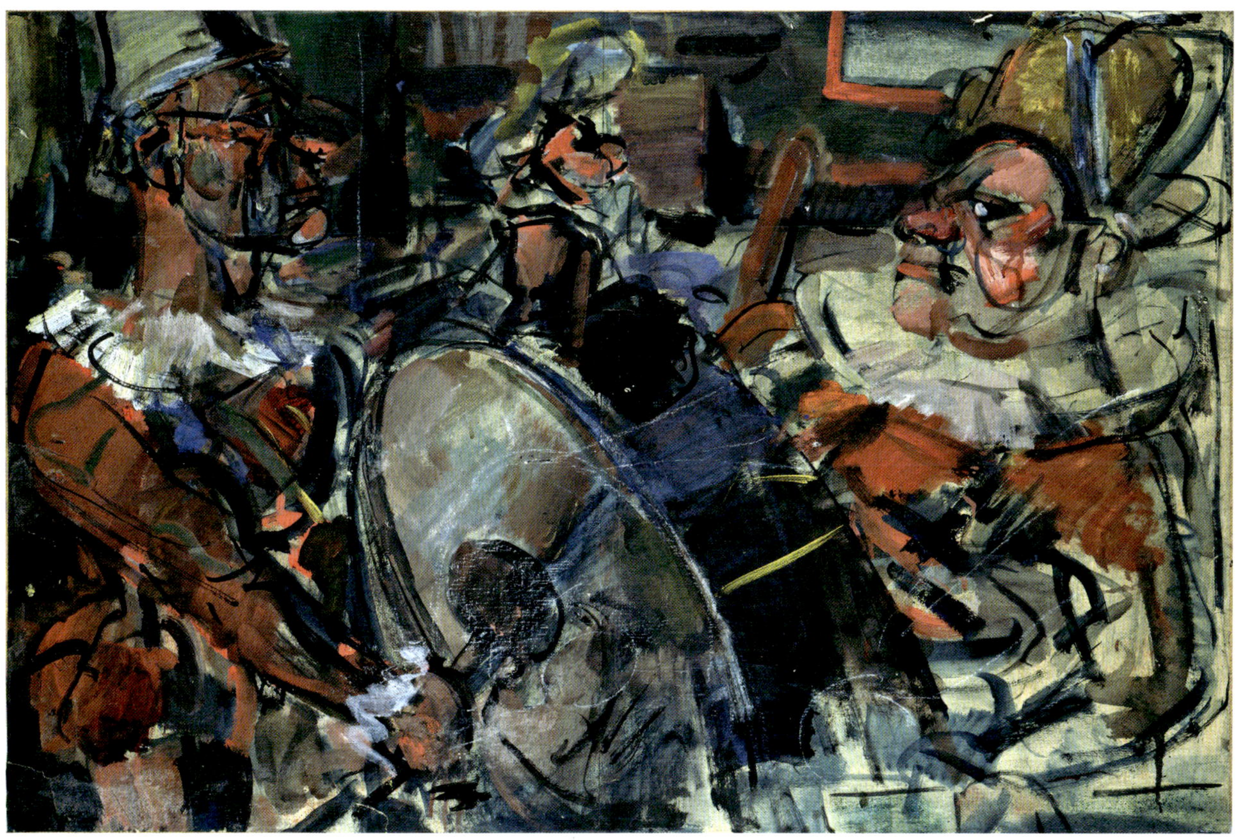

Once again, we can usefully return to Charles Blanc, for whom "Painting raises people's moral standards through its mute eloquence."[208] Perhaps the silence of *Circus Sideshow* is not a deficiency, the result of some perverse decision to suppress animation and noise, but actually a moral decision of some kind, to suggest what Blanc calls a "monde idéale," an ideal world where art and its audience engage in easy if undemonstrative harmony. Seurat's later pictures such as *Chahut* and *Circus* were judged in moral terms by his contemporaries, and have been by subsequent writers. Is such a dimension too strong for *Circus Sideshow*? In his 1890 biographical article Jules Christophe, no doubt briefed by the artist, wrote about Seurat's search for harmony; the same idea is in Seurat's letter to Beaubourg. Perhaps the painting's subtle orchestration of complementaries and uniform dotted surface, together creating a dulcet ambient light that embraces its exchange between performers and public, was intended to evoke a social as well as pictorial harmony. The dominant horizontals convey the mood of calm evoked by Blanc and Humbert de Superville, while repetition enhances what Blanc had called the ceremonial effect. Christophe ended his account of Seurat's method with the remark: "it's logical, too much so, perhaps."[209]

FIG. 108. Paul Gauguin, *Vision of the Sermon (Jacob Wrestling with the Angel)*, 1888. Oil on canvas, 28 ⅜ x 35 ⅞ in. (72.2 x 91 cm). National Galleries of Scotland, Edinburgh, Purchased 1925

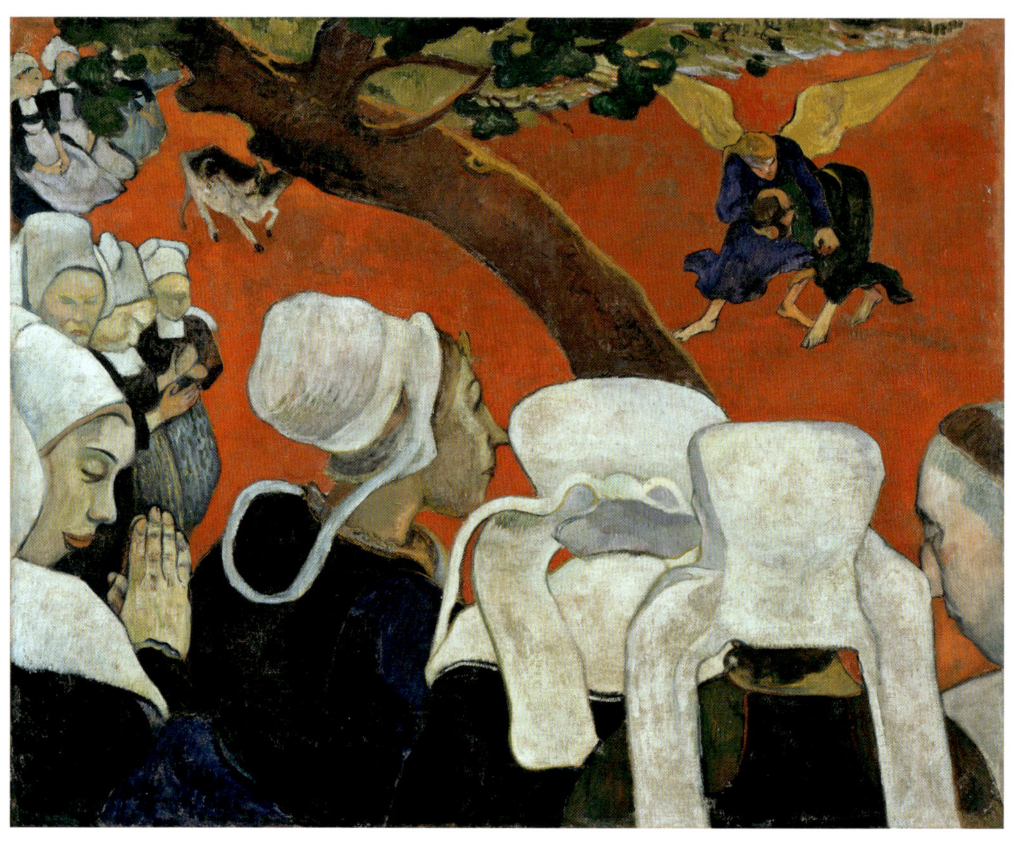

FIG. 109. Lucien Simon, *Fairground Sideshow (Parade de foire) in the Finistère*, ca. 1919. Oil on canvas, 51¼ x 84⅝ in. (130 x 215 cm). Musée des Beaux-Arts, Pau

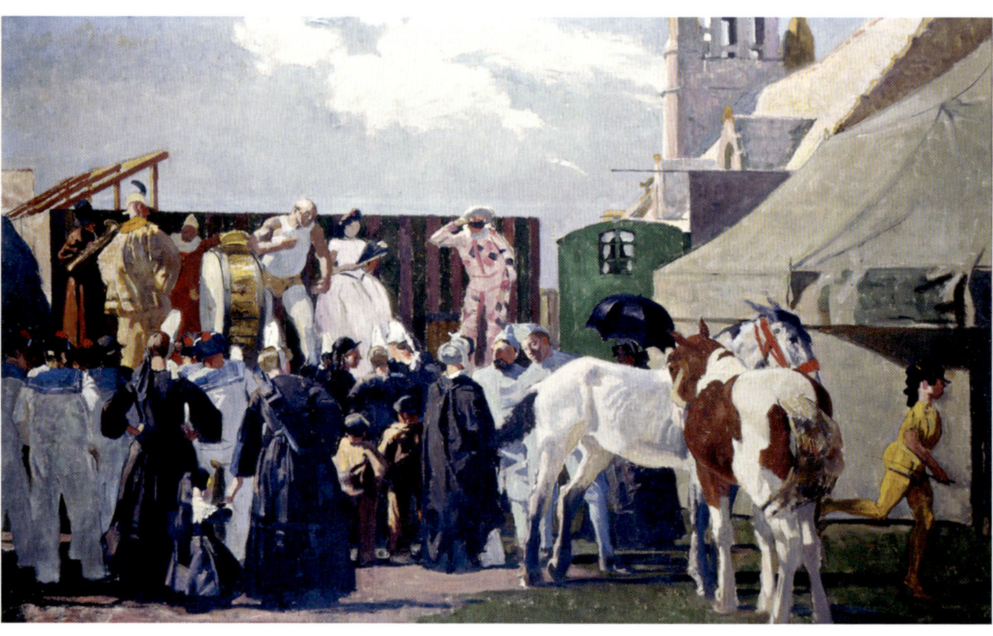

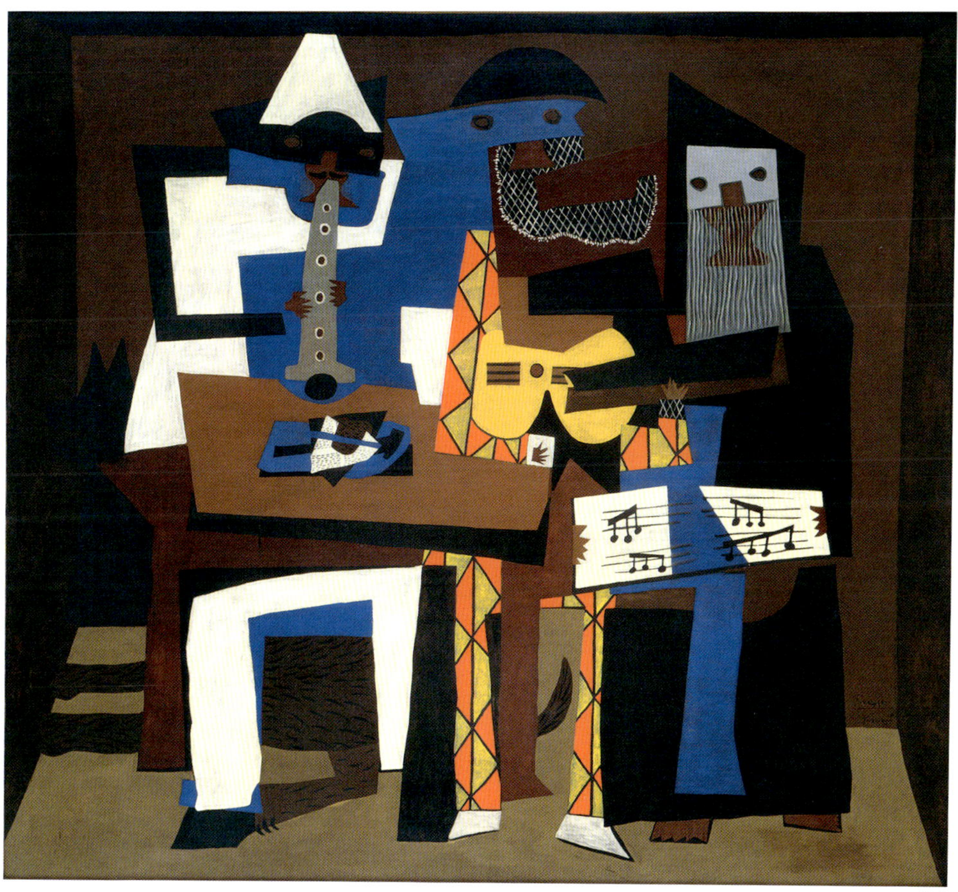

But does that notion of the application of a particular technique, of a "scientific aesthetic," do justice to such an inscrutable and beautiful painting, which presides with calm authority over any room in which it hangs?

We should return to the paradoxes of the painting. It was not a mistake to create a silent, gestureless *parade*. According to Blanc, painting should be muted, gesture downplayed. So *Circus Sideshow* is, if not an ideal, then an exemplary work: exemplary as a representation of artificial illumination at nighttime, as a depiction of a *parade*, as an image of a crowd in modern Paris enjoying popular entertainment and social congress. Exemplary in steering a path between the caricatural and the descriptive, suggesting both but taking on the guise of neither. For *Circus Sideshow* is the lodestar of a new initiative, a work that describes a recognizable world but in a way that gives primacy of place to painting—to the unity of touch, the embrace of color both soft and sharp, the hypnotic reflex of repetition, the steady serenity of the horizontal, the delight of delineation, and the gentle effect of the obscure—and returns us to the mysterious fascination of looking.

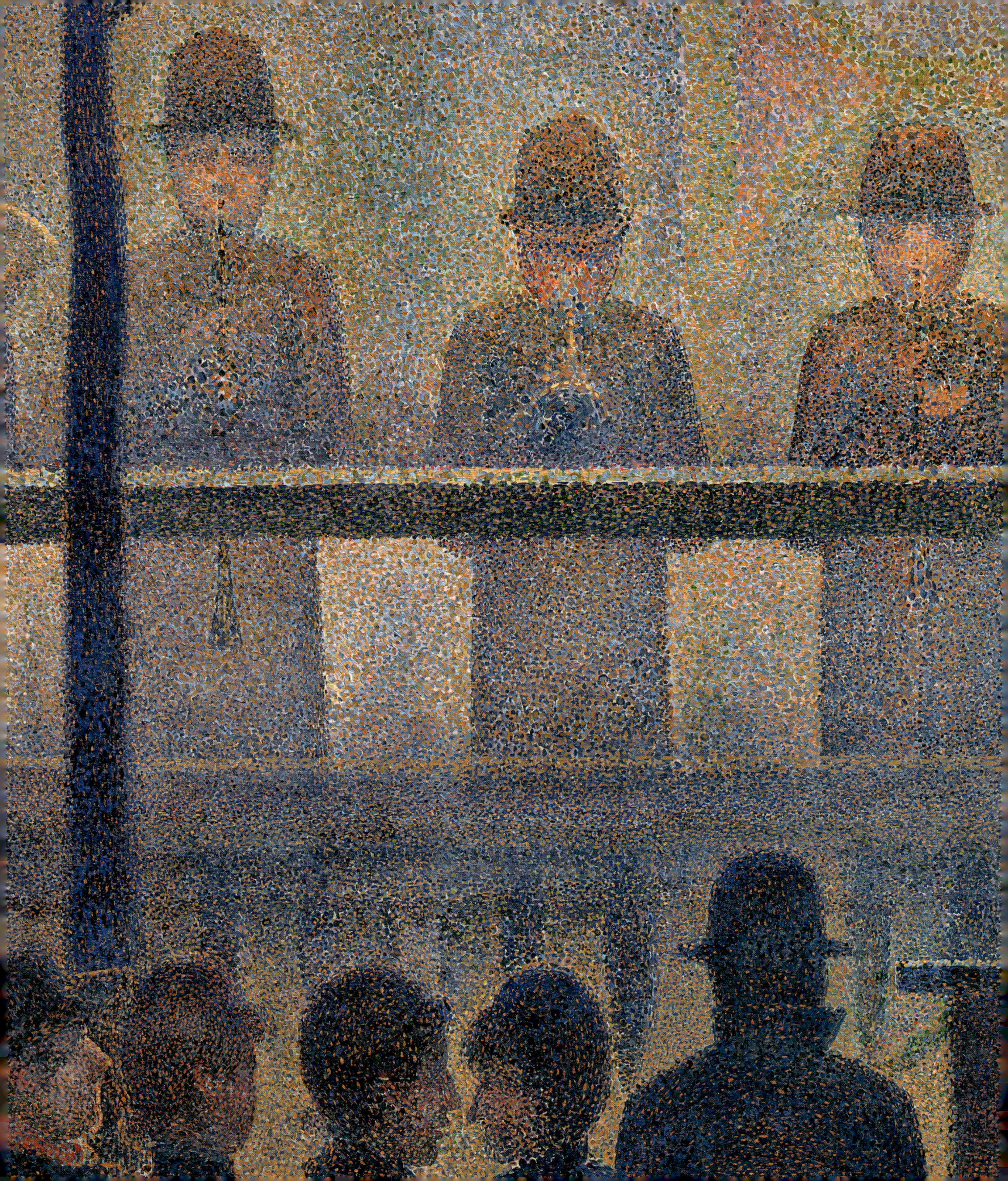

CIRCUS SIDESHOW COMES TO TOWN

SUSAN ALYSON STEIN

GEORGES SEURAT ROSE RAPIDLY in the ranks of the avant-garde to assume celebrity status and a devoted following by the time he was twenty-six, and just as quickly slipped into "oblivion, silence," as Paul Signac lamented in the wake of his friend's sudden death at age thirty-one in 1891. Between the unjust fickleness of the art world and the cumbersome size of Seurat's major works, prospects looked dim for ensuring that posterity would recognize him as "one of the geniuses of the century." In advance of the wholesale dispersal of the "principal works . . . jammed higgledy-piggledy . . . one on top of the other" at the time of the *Revue blanche* retrospective in 1900, "Seurat's poor mother [had] worried about what would happen to his large canvases" when she was gone. "She would like to leave them to some museum. . . . But what museum today would agree to take them," Signac quipped.[1]

As fate would have it, there would indeed be takers for all six of the great figure compositions. Signac lived long enough to see all but one find its way into a public collection during the 1920s. At the tail end of a decade that witnessed the arrival of *Bathers at Asnières* in London's Tate Gallery, *A Sunday on La Grande Jatte (1884)* in the Art Institute of Chicago, *Models* (*Poseuses*) in Philadelphia's Barnes Foundation, *Chahut* in The Hague's Kröller-Müller collection (for the museum then under construction in Otterlo), and *Circus* in the Louvre (see figs. 46–48, 6, and 7), the one outlier of the group — *Circus Sideshow* — came to town, seemingly destined to find a permanent home in New York.

In 1960, sixty years after Seurat's *Circus Sideshow* (*Parade de cirque*) was sold from his estate to the Parisian dealers Josse and Gaston Bernheim-Jeune, it entered the collection of The Metropolitan Museum of Art as part of the illustrious bequest of Stephen C. Clark. It has now held pride of place in the Museum for roughly the same period of time that had formerly been divided between a dealer's private stock in Paris (1900–1929) and a collector's Manhattan town house (1932–60). If the painting

had enjoyed a quiet early history in France, with a smattering of attention by virtue of its inclusion in a dozen venues and even a lingering neglect, the opposite was true beginning in 1929, when the picture changed hands and the dealer M. Knoedler and Company steered its course to more friendly shores.[2]

Circus Sideshow debuted on this side of the Atlantic rather momentously at the inaugural exhibition of the Museum of Modern Art in New York. It commanded a prime spot within the one-hundred-work show — "Cézanne, Gauguin, Seurat, Van Gogh" — which celebrated the founding fathers of modernism, linking Seurat for posterity with the mighty triumvirate of the 1913 Armory Show.[3] Hailed by the museum's young director, Alfred H. Barr Jr., as "one of the most important paintings" by "one of the great artists of modern times," *Circus Sideshow* was installed on the central axis of a suite of six rooms in temporary quarters in the Heckscher Building (730 Fifth Avenue), a few blocks and ten years away from the Modern's eventual site (fig. 111). This "place of honor" ensured that Seurat's genius — as demonstrated in his "composition without parallel" — would not be ignored as it had been upon the painting's first showing in Paris.[4] Indeed, it was so "conspicuously hung," as the *New York Times* reported, that it immediately "catches the eye of the incoming visitor."[5] All told, 47,293 visitors were introduced to its eye-catching virtues during the exhibition's monthlong run (November 7–December 7, 1929).[6]

Veritably overnight, a painting that had failed to elicit the interest bestowed upon the artist's other large-scale compositions received its fair share of attention. Chosen to preside over the newsworthy event and awarded the only detail in the catalogue, "Side Show (La Parade)" found from the start a no-holds-Barred champion in the Modern's founding director. Barr set the buzz in motion, contributing pieces to such popular magazines as *Vanity Fair*, *Vogue*, and *Charm* peppered with names and numbers that made for a seductive equation. "Seurat is a master of spacing, of atmosphere, of composition in

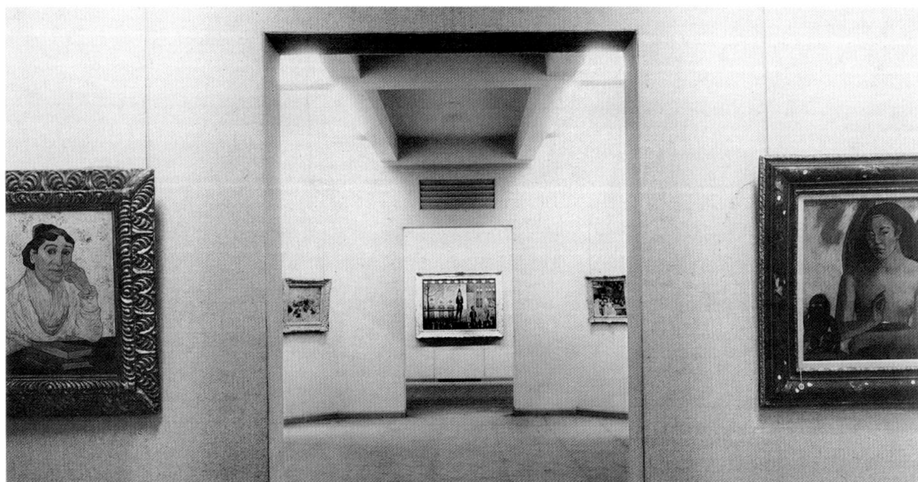

depth and pattern. . . . And in his major works such as *La Parade* we discover that great art can be, as in the painting of Leonardo, Raphael, and Poussin, the result of exquisite calculation."[7] In a town where "money talks vividly," he guaranteed that his sense of the picture's greatness would not fall on deaf ears: "More fabulous still," than the sums fetched for works by Van Gogh, "are the prices asked—and paid—for Seurat's work. *La Parade*, the most important painting in the exhibition might well bring a quarter of a million dollars—considerably more than a fine Rembrandt or Rubens or Titian."[8] Handily reinforced by the marketplace,[9] Barr's estimation of Seurat's genius tallied entirely with that of modernist supporters who rallied to Seurat's cause, not least the influential British critic Roger Fry; he effectively picked up where Barr left off, publishing a full-length article on "La Parade" at the end of the show, which serves as a resonant coda.[10]

Circus Sideshow arrived at the right place and time to become known and admired. Over the previous decade, Seurat's sluggish reputation, buoyed by the vogue for Neoclassicism, had been resurrected and vaulted to new heights, ushering in a keen era of appreciation for the "neglected master."[11] The painting enjoyed its star turn on the heels of the publication of the first American monograph on the artist, written by Walter Pach (1923); Seurat's first one-man show in America at the Joseph Brummer gallery in New York (1924); and the stunning acquisitions, in quick succession, of major works by Philadelphian Albert C. Barnes and New Yorker John Quinn, whose bequest of *Circus* (fig. 7) to the Louvre

in 1924 was as topical as the Birch Bartlett gift of the artist's huge sunlit park scene (fig. 47) to the Art Institute of Chicago two years later.[12] The seventeen Seurats secured by Barr for the Modern's opening exhibition offer a telling indication of the traction Seurat's art had gained by the late 1920s. Most of the loans came from local collectors and were relatively recent acquisitions (some just months old), with six contributed by "the daring ladies" who spearheaded the new museum—Abby Aldrich Rockefeller, Lillie P. Bliss, and Mary Quinn Sullivan—and the rest largely furnished by founding trustees, such as the study for *Bathers at Asnières* lent by Stephen C. Clark (now, Nelson-Atkins Museum of Art, Kansas City).[13] Insofar as the vast majority of these works have since enriched the holdings of American public collections, this foothold was prescient of the future.

Yet, at the time, as Barr bemoaned, aside from *La Grande Jatte* in Chicago and *Models* in the Barnes, Seurat was nowhere to be seen in "our own great museums of New York, Boston, and Washington." In his view, "Seurat as much as any painter since the baroque, belongs in museums where his clarity of thought and austerity of purpose, his evident understanding of his great ancestors, would powerfully influence students and the public." So wrote the Wellesley College professor-turned-museum-director who now had but one painting and one museum in mind.[14]

Some seven weeks after the close of the inaugural exhibition, in late January 1930, *Circus Sideshow* was proposed as a cornerstone acquisition for the new Museum of Modern Art, eliciting pledges of support. But in the end, trustees demurred at the asking price of $100,000, a hefty sum especially in the aftermath of the stock market crash (Black Tuesday fell nine days before MoMA's opening).[15] Barr had no better luck in May 1931, when he asked Stephen C. Clark to consider buying the work himself, doubtless aware of Clark's recent acquisition of the artist's greatest drawing—the conté crayon portrait of schoolmate Aman-Jean (fig. 112)—if not of the collector's ambition to buy only "top notch examples of first class men" and "to get rid of those that are not." Indeed, that summer Clark brought home Cézanne's *The Card Players* (The Metropolitan Museum of Art, 61.101.1) and relinquished his small Seurat oil study to the marketplace.[16] The following spring, he reconsidered the purchase of *Circus Sideshow*, bringing his shrewd businessman's acumen, in a depressed market, to the table. After months of protracted negotiation, in November 1932 he secured the "immortal masterpiece," touted by the dealer M. Knoedler and Company as the "last of [Seurat's] six large canvases that is not yet in a public museum," for less than half its original asking price ($47,000), ensuring that it remained in New York, with the very best chance of finding its way into a museum.[17]

At the time of his purchase, the civic-minded heir to the Singer Sewing Machine Company and elder brother of Sterling Clark (who founded the eponymous Art Institute in Williamstown, Massachusetts) had just turned fifty, was at the height of his enthusiasm for Matisse, and was actively involved in fostering the growth of New York's newest museum, where he would later serve as chairman of the board and president.[18] Beyond setting the pace for fellow trustees when he initiated the Modern's paintings collection with his anonymous gift of Edward Hopper's *House by the Railroad*, Clark had resolved to set the bar (or, as it were, Barr) high for his own collection. "One of the reasons which induces me to make this offer for the Seurat," as he advised the dealer, is that "I am trying gradually to get only the finest examples of artists who seem to me to be in the first rank."[19] Such dictates prevailed as Clark extended holdings rich in works by both established and emerging American greats—from Homer to Hopper—with "superlative" paintings by the Post-Impressionists celebrated in MoMA's opening show, bracketed by choice examples by Renoir and Degas at one end, and Matisse and Picasso at the other. Clark professed "no desire to form a noted collection and none of the collector's spirit which prompts so many people to buy examples of more or less mediocre artists for the purpose

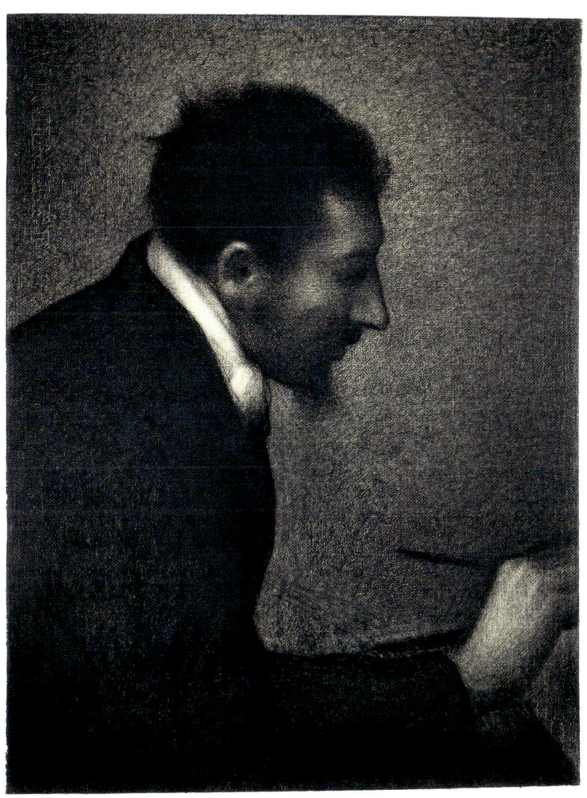

FIG 112. Georges Seurat, *Aman-Jean (Portrait of Edmond François Aman-Jean)*, 1882–83. Conté crayon on paper, 24 ½ x 18 ¾ in. (62.2 x 47.5 cm). The Metropolitan Museum of Art, New York, Bequest of Stephen C. Clark, 1960 (61.101.16)

of rounding out a collection."[20] Nor did he feel any compunction to keep lesser works once he had found an unrivaled gem. As he refined and edited his holdings, fifteen museums would become beneficiaries of well-placed gifts. By 1932 Clark had advanced an impressive track record of donations (to the Yale University Art Gallery, at his alma mater; the Addison Gallery of American Art in Andover, Massachusetts; and the Museum of Modern Art)[21] and had extended his support of New York's cultural institutions to include its most well-established museum; he became a trustee of The Met the very month he began to pursue the Seurat in earnest, which, given the painting's ultimate destination, seems providential.[22]

As part of the collection of one of the most public-spirited and discerning art patrons of his day, *Circus Sideshow* continued to enjoy the limelight and a certain cachet

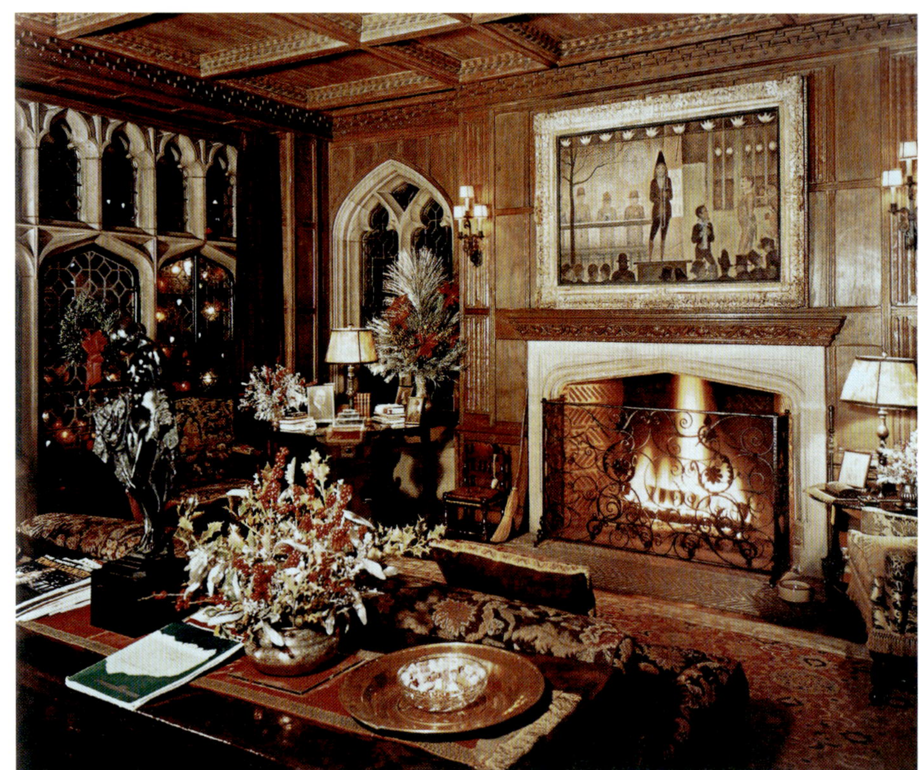

FIG. 113. The library in Stephen C. Clark's Manhattan town house at Christmastime, ca. 1960

FIG. 114. "French Paintings from the Bequest of Stephen C. Clark," The Metropolitan Museum of Art, New York, October 17, 1961–January 7, 1962

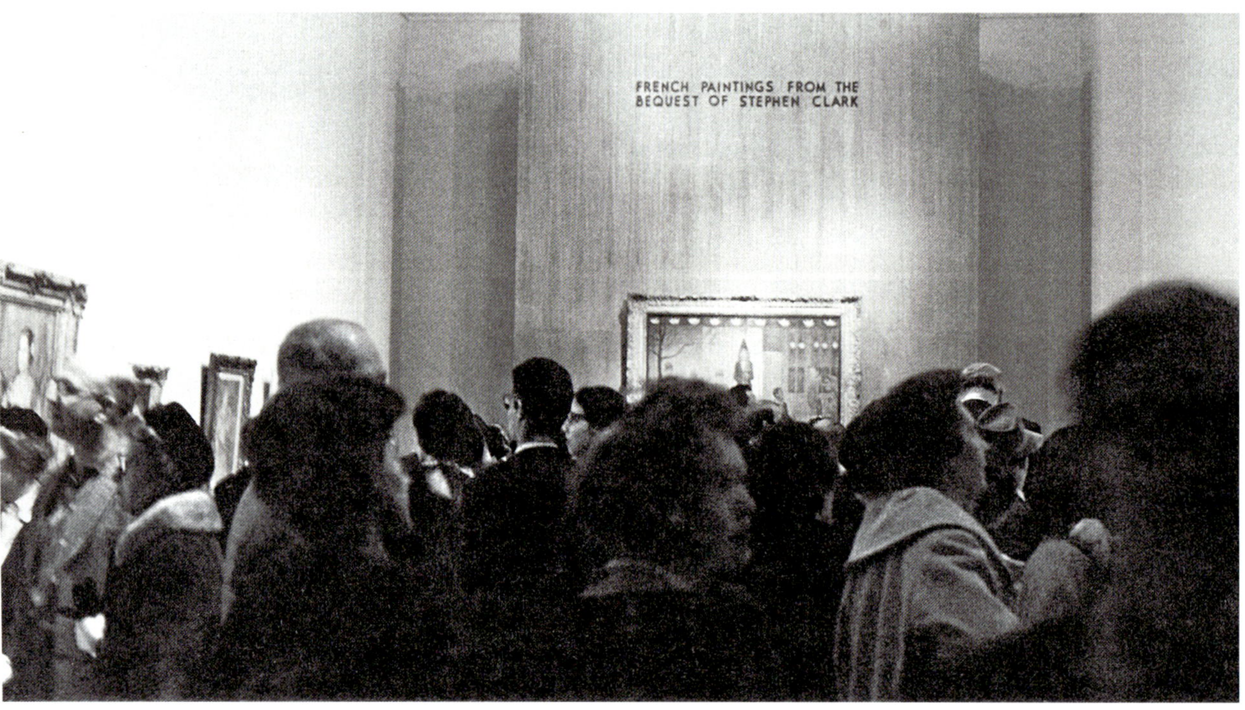

for the next three decades. It was regularly lent to exhibitions held at the Modern (1933, 1934–35, 1939, 1940, and 1955) and to various other New York venues, ranging from the 1939 World's Fair, where a selection of "Masterpieces" was featured, to summer loan exhibitions held at The Met (1958–60).[23] Time and again critics took note of Seurat's "often seen" and "unforgettable" painting as it succeeded to hold its own in the best of company and make its presence felt on the New York art scene.[24] As early as 1933, on its first return to the Modern, a writer for *Art News* was quick to name the "patterned finality of Seurat's 'Sideshow'. . . among the works on view which have entered most deeply into our treasure house of mental images."[25] Such was the indelible impression made by Clark's "touchstone pictures" in general, as a *New York Times* critic observed twenty years later, struck by the number of his paintings that "both by virtue of excellence and familiarity, become touchstones against which we try the quality of the rest of [an artist's] work." The fact is, she remarked, "you can hardly think of Van Gogh without remembering his 'Night Café'" (purchased by Clark in 1933, now, Yale University Art Gallery) or "Seurat without the dual view of his work in the black-and-white, magically created form in the 'Portrait of Aman-Jean' and the total vision expressed in 'La Parade.'"[26]

The impact of seeing Clark's pictures *ensemble* in their "native habitat"—the Jacobean-style town house at 46 East 70th Street (built for him by Frederick Sterner in 1911)—proved dazzling, as an *Art Digest* critic advised his readers at mid-century: "The Alice-in-Wonderland sensation that this collection evokes is particularly noticeable when you get to the library on the second floor. The large, familiar *La Parade* by Seurat does its best to dominate the room [see fig. 113]. It would, too, except that the adjoining walls are occupied by Cézanne's *Card Players* and his *Mme. Cézanne in the Greenhouse* [The Metropolitan Museum of Art, 61.101.2], two paintings, which play second fiddle to none." Perhaps what was most compelling about his through-the-looking-glass tour was the "feeling of having seen it before, so well-known are most of the paintings," as they had been frequently lent to exhibitions and reproduced.[27]

Clark's unerring sensibility as a collector and his generosity as a lender and donor conspired to place him in the same "superlative" class as his prized possessions, which enjoy the same "air of familiarity" as they did during his lifetime, even if their shared heritage is less well known.[28]

This was much as he intended when he dispersed the contents of his collection among institutions where a single work or stellar group would make the most fitting contribution (insisting on anonymity early on, and no fanfare later). When he died in September 1960, having long supported public institutions, large and small, he split what remained of the "pictures and other works of art [bought] for his own personal enjoyment and not for the sake of forming a noted collection"[29] in a similar fashion, between The Metropolitan Museum of Art and Yale.[30]

The following spring Seurat's *Circus Sideshow* left Clark's library for The Met, with instructions that it should "always be hung 'mantelpiece high'" (the vantage point from which he had enjoyed it for years) accompanied by a full complement of pictures by Cézanne, Renoir, and Degas of like monumentality, classical directness, and evocative power.[31] Carrying in tow a past that spanned its rise from neglect to its emergence as a towering example of the artist's genius and primed to make good on a mother's wishful thinking, Seurat's scene of circus performers—as if on cue—claimed what had become its rightful place in the installation of the Clark bequest that fall: standing heads and tails above the crowd, front and center, not unlike the trombonist who anchors the painting (fig. 114).

ONCE AGAIN, exactly 130 years since this scene from modern life captivated the artist's attention and long after it first captivated New York's museum-going public, Seurat's *Circus Sideshow* takes center stage. In the present exhibition its heritage and legacy are reconsidered, and fittingly, in the context of a museum that affords a wide-enough lens on the history of art to retrace the lines of descent—from the ancients, old masters, and French Neoclassicists forward to the Cubists, Bauhaus artists, and Purists—that have variously secured its place within a time-honored chain. A prominent fixture in The Met's nineteenth-century galleries, it is notable—within a collection of twenty-four works by Seurat—as his most ambitious painting, by virtue of its scale and intention.[32] This same distinction applies to the drawing of Aman-Jean from the Clark bequest; both were exhibition pictures destined to make their mark. In keeping with the sensibility of a collector celebrated in "Impressionist and Early Modern Paintings: The Clark Brothers Collect" (2007), two of the Cézannes from Clark's bequest have likewise encouraged focused exhibitions at The Met: witness "Cézanne's *Card Players*" (2011) and "Madame Cézanne" (2015).

SEURAT'S CIRCUS SIDESHOW: MATERIALS, TECHNIQUE, EVOLUTION

CHARLOTTE HALE AND SILVIA A. CENTENO

Circus Sideshow (*Parade de cirque*), painted by Georges Seurat in 1887–88, has reached the present day in exceptional condition, its canvas never lined and its surface never varnished (see fig. 1). It thus allows unusually direct access to the artist's working process, as well as a vivid sense of his intentions in this nocturnal fairground scene, which depicts performers outside the Corvi Circus, his first in a series of paintings of popular entertainments. The current exhibition, "Seurat's Circus Sideshow," offered the occasion for an in-depth technical study of this jewel of The Metropolitan Museum of Art's collection, normally on permanent view. In February 2016 the painting was brought to the Museum's Sherman Fairchild Paintings Conservation Center for four weeks of examination and analysis. This essay presents the key findings of the study.[1]

Seurat's creative process depended on extensive research and meticulous planning. His major figure paintings were preceded by studies that signify his preoccupations for each. In keeping with the reduced scale of extant preparatory work for his mature production, for *Circus Sideshow* there are three drawings in conté crayon corresponding to the left, middle, and right of the painting (see figs. 56–58) and two compositional studies, one in ink dots on paper (see fig. 61), the other in oil paint on panel (see fig. 62), respectively establishing the painting's tonal range and palette. Another conté crayon drawing and two further studies in oil on panel (or *croquetons*, as the artist called them) are recorded in the posthumous inventory of Seurat's studio, but are now missing.[2] Seurat also made two notational sketches that include the Corvi Circus's box office window (see figs. 39, 72).

The composition of *Circus Sideshow* appears boldly abstracted, but comparing it with contemporary photographs of the Corvi Circus (see figs. 5, 40), it is striking how faithfully the artist recorded the scene while simultaneously imposing order and grandeur, both by adopting a severely frontal viewpoint and by following the template of his geometrical plan. At almost exactly 100 x 150 centimeters, the canvas he selected has a height-to-width ratio of 2:3. Within this format, Seurat used a grid of vertical and horizontal lines, forming 25 x 25 centimeter squares, four down and six across, to organize his composition (fig. 115).[3] While this grid is clearly visible on the ink-dot and oil studies (figs. 61, 62), its presence on the painting itself had not been confirmed until now, with the use of macro-X-ray fluorescence (MA-XRF) imaging.[4] The map showing the distribution of calcium acquired using this technique features sections of the same grid that underlies the ink-dot and oil studies (fig. 116).[5]

Although the grid would have facilitated the accurate transfer of his design from the much smaller studies to his large canvas, it served primarily as Seurat's framework for structuring his painting's composition. The central vertical grid line provides the axis for the placement of the trombonist, and the central horizontal bisects him at his cinched waist and further runs along the tops of the shoulders of the two musicians to his immediate left (the shorter clarinet player and the cornet player), as well as those of the woman buying tickets at the far right. The leftmost edges of the circus proprietor (Ferdinand Corvi) and of the shorter clarinet player and the rightmost edge of the taller clarinet player are aligned with vertical grid lines, as is the stripe on the side of the trousers of the boyish buffoon. More broadly, the exterior gas jets and the interior globe lights lie within the top horizontal quadrant, while the darkened members of the crowd lie within the bottom quadrant. Seurat's adoption of a geometric grid to guide placement of figures and other elements of his painting recalls the theories of Charles Blanc, whose writings had a significant influence on the artist. As Robert L. Herbert observed, "According to Blanc, rules of proportion, like other rules of art, are not straitjackets but foundations on which the artist, freed from uncertainty and the anarchy of isolated observations, can build his own structures."[6]

The canvas used for *Circus Sideshow*, which is still on its original stretcher, is not of a standard size, and so was probably a special order by the artist. It was prepared by

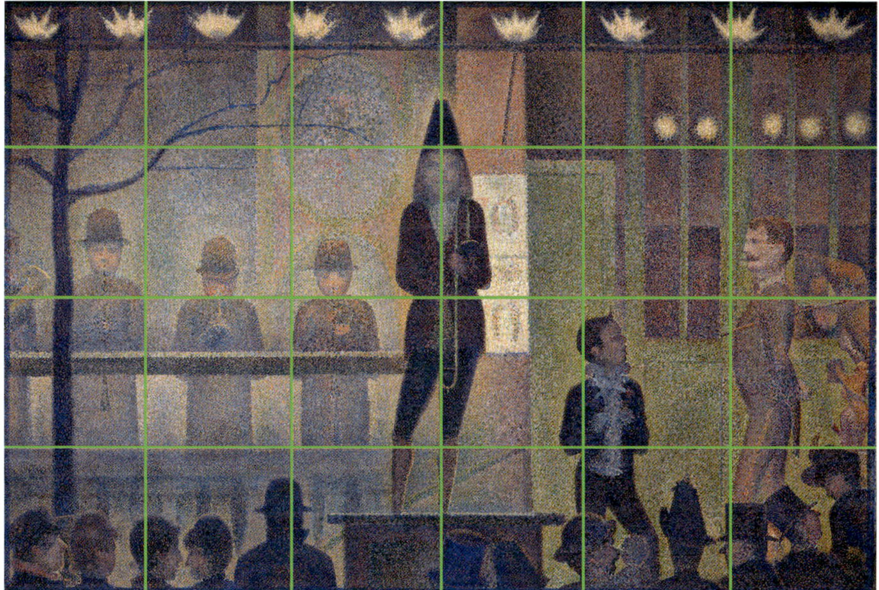

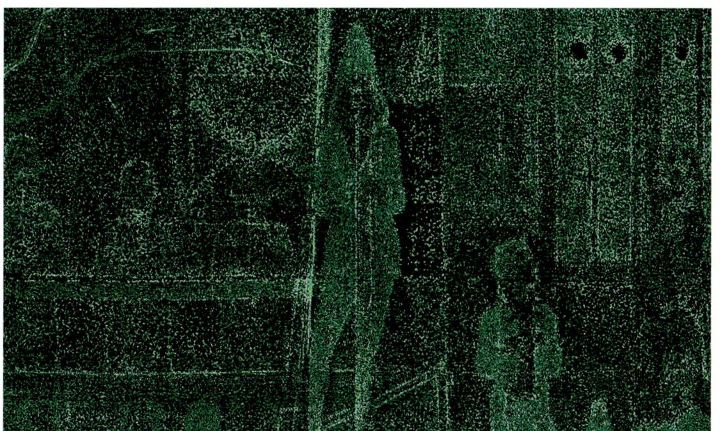

the Paris color merchant Chabod, whose stamp is seen on the reverse. Exceptionally finely woven and pre-primed with pale gray, it would have provided a smooth support for Seurat's intricate painting technique.[7] After laying in the grid, Seurat seems to have transferred at least some of his design to the canvas using colored chalk; while they cannot be seen under the microscope, contour lines show up on the same MA-XRF calcium map as the grid, for example, under the slanted banister behind the trombonist (fig. 116). The calcium map also shows an initial sweeping edge in the painted backdrop that extends to the left of the trombonist, behind the other musicians, concealing the circus's main tent. Such draping is characteristic of fabric stretched between rails, as can be seen in historic photographs of the Corvi Circus (see fig. 5), but was not recorded by Seurat in his studies. Evidently the artist thought better of this naturalistic detail, opting instead for a more geometric rendering of the backdrop. In addition to the chalk lines, Seurat used thinned Prussian blue paint to lay in the contours of some of the figures. These strokes can be glimpsed through the web of overlying paint in a few areas—the brim of the top hat in the bottom right, for example — but in general they are hidden by Seurat's later applications of paint, as he seems to have wanted to cover his initial tracks.

Although a wide range of pigments, many of them recent inventions, was available to artists in the 1880s, the palette that Seurat used to realize his vision in *Circus Sideshow* was quite limited. The following pigments were identified in the recent study: zinc yellow, chrome yellow, cadmium yellow, vermilion, red madder lake, manganese violet, cobalt blue, French ultramarine, Prussian blue, a chrome-based green (viridian or opaque oxide of chromium), and emerald green, together with lead white and carbon black.[8] The artist's earlier paintings included ocher pigments, but in the middle of the 1880s he narrowed his selection to pigments of strong spectral purity that had the best potential for the practical application of color theory, which he is known to have studied.[9] So it is all the more surprising that some of the colors comprise multiple pigments, thereby complicating the spectral purity of the hues.[10] Perhaps this practice reflects the challenges of painting a nocturnal, gaslit scene, which ultimately called for a great variety of tone, hue, and effect, achieved by carefully mixing, layering, and varying his application of these colors. Brushstrokes that appear black are in fact made of extremely finely divided cobalt blue, sometimes with the addition of red lake or emerald green. Mauves and violets were made with various combinations of French ultramarine, vermilion, red lake, and lead white. Manganese violet, introduced in 1868, was used for the feather in the hat of the woman mounting the stairs in the bottom right.[11]

Some indication of Seurat's advance thinking about the palette he would use for the painting may be gathered from notations made, likely from the motif, on the reverse of his conté crayon drawing of the trombonist (fig. 57). He followed these color notes in paint. The trombonist's "red-violet" coat, for example, was realized with red lake underpaint, overlaid with cobalt blue, orange (a mixture of zinc yellow and vermilion), and further touches of red lake.[12]

Viewed from a distance the painting gives the impression of a constellation of tiny painted dots. On closer inspection it becomes apparent that it was constructed with brushstrokes whose size, shape, and function vary considerably. Seurat initially applied very large, widely spaced dots and dashes of paint in what would be the dominant color of a given area and then continued with a progression of dots and dashes of diminishing size.

This was an efficient and effective way of building up the composition, but it also emphasizes the artist's intellectual processes of concentration and distillation. A sense of what the painting looked like in its early stages can be gleaned from the MA-XRF maps, which, in combination with results from other methods of examination, allow us to "unpack" the buildup. In the bottom right corner, for example, over a loosely brushed underpaint of thinned Prussian blue, large dots of very dark blue paint — a mixture of cobalt blue and emerald green — were used in the early stages of the foreground figures (fig. 117). Smaller dots of red lake and a cobalt blue of a different composition (characterized by its higher nickel content) followed.[13] And finally Seurat applied tiny orange dots and dashes — mixtures of vermilion and chrome yellow — mimicking the gaslight falling on the figures. On the collar of the top-hatted gent, the strokes run parallel to the contour. Here and elsewhere, the size and orientation of dots and dashes create varied degrees of definition, ranging from the large strokes and ambiguous content of the oval on the painted backdrop to the left of the trombonist's head (perhaps a figure on horseback?), to the fine blue "running stitch" strokes that define the bottom edge of the placard listing prices.[14] Boundaries are the most highly worked areas because it was here that contrasting zones of tone and color created shading and form; paraphrasing Blanc, Seurat defined painting as "the art of hollowing out a surface."[15] But the contours in *Circus Sideshow* are in general diffuse, as the particular effects of gaslight and backlighting are integral to the painting.

While *Circus Sideshow* attracted very little attention when it was first shown in spring 1888 at the Salon des Indépendants, what did receive comment was the nocturnal lighting.[16] Seurat's pointillist technique, with its distinct dots of paint representing both local and illuminating color, theoretically formed an "optical mixture" in the eyes of the beholder.[17] However, in practical terms the paintings have a slightly foggy appearance, which in the case of *Circus Sideshow* was particularly well suited to evoking the soft edges of night vision. To quote Herbert: "The light everywhere has the hazy indistinctness of gaslight, and acquires a kind of powdery substance of its own."[18] The pastel quality of the picture surface would also have contributed to the effect. We cannot know the full impact of the painting's original appearance, as the oil paint has become less saturated over time, but certainly the matte effect — originally and still today unobstructed by the "horror of varnish" — was deliberate.[19]

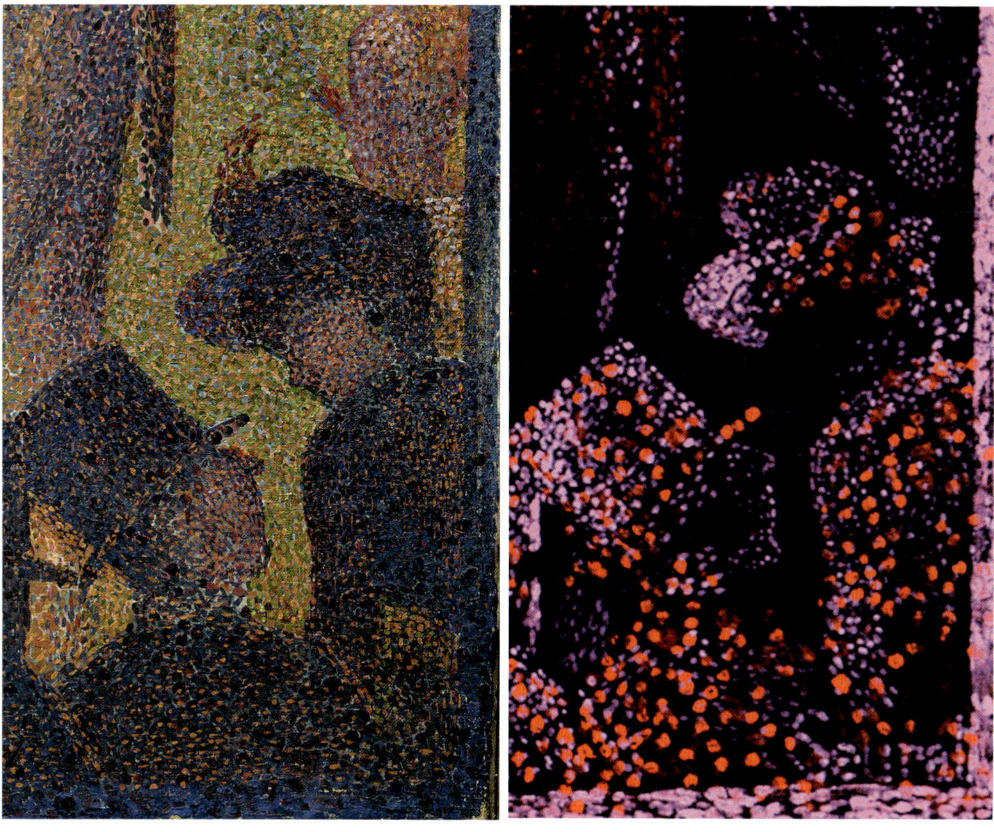

The painting's few deviations from the ink-dot drawing and the oil study, or *croqueton*, are further evidence of Seurat's methodical approach (figs. 61, 62). The most obvious of these are the addition of the tree and four figures at the sides: the cropped player of the ophicleide or saxhorn at far left and the woman, her small daughter, and the ticket seller at far right. Some of these elements are present in the conté drawings: the sheet with the tree includes a musician on the far left (fig. 56), and the sheet with the buffoon and proprietor has the suggestion of a form behind an open ticket window (fig. 58). (This drawing also includes a miniature pony that Seurat omitted from the compositional studies and was never a part of the painting.)

Early additions, as indicated by patches of pale-gray priming visible through the paint buildup that show the background was not finished before they were put in, include the cropped musician, the head and shoulder of the woman buying tickets, and the ticket seller. The ticket window was originally painted closed; the decision to depict it open was probably made in conjunction with the insertion of the two women selling and buying tickets, and perhaps the musician at far left was then put in place to balance the composition. At an intermediate stage—over existing paint layers—Seurat added the little girl and the forearm of her mother above her, creating a rhythm of three upward-moving diagonal forms: the girl's arm and umbrella, the brim of her hat, and the woman's forearm.[20] The tree, added over the background, initially resembled its predecessor in the drawing (fig. 56), but Seurat made alterations to some of the branches, resulting in a more stylized form.[21] He also painted the small conical hat over the right side of the base of the trombonist's dais, whereas in the ink-dot and oil studies a similar hat is seen on the left side of the dais, and he added the feathered hat on the head of the woman mounting the stairs at lower right—initially she was hatless, with a topknot (fig. 117).[22]

The final stage in the making of *Circus Sideshow* was applying the painted border; Seurat added this feature on top of the composition, which extends beneath it all the way to the edges. Painted almost entirely in cobalt blue, the border takes on a multicolored appearance due to the sporadic application of the cobalt in medium-sized dots and dashes, which allows the variously colored dots of the composition to show through from below. The only dots applied to the border in colors other than blue are to be found below the left side of the trombonist's dais, painted in a brilliant mixture of red lake and vermilion, and adjacent to the little girl, in pure red lake.[23]

Throughout his short career Seurat was deeply preoccupied by the integral relationship between framing and the work of art.[24] Initially using white or off-white wood frames, like other avant-garde artists, he began experimenting with colored framing in 1887 as he worked on *Models* (*Poseuses*) (fig. 48). Shown alongside *Circus Sideshow* at the Salon des Indépendants in 1888, this large canvas drew considerable attention, in part for the novelty of its polychrome inner frame — its colors contrasting with those adjacent in the painting — which was in turn surrounded by a white frame.[25] In advance Seurat had prepared a smaller study, a *croqueton* (private collection), his first work with borders painted on the picture panel or canvas itself: present only on the left and right edges, the borders may have been a method of resolving the problem of unpainted margins that resulted from imposing the geometric scheme of his painting (in this case, based on a 3:4 ratio) on a wider, standard-sized support — that is, the composition filled the full height but not the full width.[26] In landscapes painted in the summer of 1889 the artist anticipated the inclusion of painted borders by leaving blank space at the perimeter of his compositions, as in *View of Le Crotoy from Upstream* (Detroit Institute of Arts). But otherwise it has proved extremely hard to determine the date of borders on pictures painted between 1887 and 1889 because Seurat added them retrospectively to many completed works, either painting them on top of the outer edges of the compositions, as in *Circus Sideshow*, or remounting the canvases on larger stretchers to create room for them.[27]

The most unexpected find of the present technical examination — one that raises a series of questions — is the large signature in the bottom right corner of the painting, hidden below the paint, and revealed using infrared and MA-XRF imaging: *Seurat* (fig. 117). Painted in sizable, distinct dots and dashes, in form and placement it resembles the signature on the *croqueton* (fig. 62). Given its prominence there, it is plausible that the signature was in place the only time that Seurat exhibited *Circus*

Sideshow, at the 1888 Salon des Indépendants, and was later painted over. But what about the painted border? Unlike *Models*, *Circus Sideshow* attracted no mention of its framing in the reviews that followed the Salon. This might suggest that its presentation was unremarkable, but it could also be that all aspects of the painting were overshadowed by its larger companion, *Models*. While we may wonder at *Circus Sideshow*'s lukewarm reception, its effect would certainly have been subdued without the blue border, or if surrounded only by a white frame.[28] Was this the reason for the reworking of the painting?

Technical examination cannot pinpoint when the blue border was added, but the timing is, in any case, limited by Seurat's death in March 1891. Two factors suggest that the reworking was done relatively soon after the composition was completed: tiny paint samples viewed in cross section show no buildup of dirt between the original paint and that of the border; and the nickel-rich cobalt blue used for the border is similar to that used in the later stages of the painting (fig. 117). Unlike Seurat's multicolored borders, which contrast with each area of the adjacent picture, the dark blue border recalls those on the figure paintings from the last two years of his life: *Young Woman Powdering Herself* (1889–90; The Courtauld Gallery, London), *Chahut* (fig. 6), and *Circus* (fig. 7). In such works Seurat created an analogy to composer Richard Wagner's Bayreuth stage, where the brilliant lighting was accentuated by the innovation of a darkened auditorium, something the painter had read about.[29] In *Circus Sideshow*, Seurat heightened the contrast between border and painting by adding orange dots to the composition adjacent to the blue edging. In reworking the painting he camouflaged his signature completely. This correlates to his practice in *Chahut* and *Circus*, neither of which is signed, and also in a way to *Young Woman Powdering Herself*, where, as a recent technical study found, Seurat painted over a self-portrait in the background, thus effacing his presence.[30] The latter work is signed, but as in some other late works conceived with a border, the signature is placed on the border itself and is barely visible. Perhaps it was purely an aesthetic decision on Seurat's part not to have signatures interfere with the effect of his borders. But it is intriguing to consider whether Seurat came to view his innovative painted borders, or his style in a broader sense, as signifying his authorship. The complex interrelationship between format, composition, framing, and signature — all highly considered aspects of the presentation of his work — is certainly one that invites further study.[31]

NOTES

SEURAT'S CIRCUS SIDESHOW:
A PARADE OF PARADOXES

1. Robert L. Herbert, *Seurat: Drawings and Paintings* (New Haven and London: Yale University Press, 2001), p. 144. My thanks to E. Bradley Strauchen-Scherer, Department of Musical Instruments, The Metropolitan Museum of Art, for identifying the musicians' instruments in light of contemporary band instrumentation.

2. Gustave Kahn, "Peinture: Exposition des indépendants," *La Revue indépendante* 7, no. 18 (April 1888), p. 161; Herbert, "*Parade de cirque* de Seurat et l'esthétique de Charles Henry," *Revue de l'art* 50 (1981), p. 10. The Heidbrinck was first published by Herbert in his 1981 article; hereafter references are to the revised 2001 text: Herbert, *Seurat: Drawings and Paintings*.

3. For evidence of sagging canvas in the underdrawing, see Charlotte Hale and Silvia A. Centeno, "Seurat's *Circus Sideshow*: Materials, Technique, Evolution," in this volume, p. 113.

4. Michelle Foa, *Georges Seurat: The Art of Vision* (New Haven and London: Yale University Press, 2015), p. 131.

5. Ségolène Le Men, *Seurat et Chéret: Le Peintre, le cirque et l'affiche*, 2nd ed. (Paris: CNRS Editions, 2003), p. 23.

6. *Catalogue des oeuvres exposées, 1888: 4ᵉ exposition*, exh. cat., Pavillon de la Ville de Paris (Paris: Société des Artistes Indépendants, 1888), no. 614 (painting), nos. 615–18 (drawings).

7. Richard Thomson, *Seurat* (Oxford: Phaidon, 1985), p. 153; Jonathan Crary, *Suspensions of Perception: Attention, Spectacle, and Modern Culture* (Cambridge, Mass., and London: MIT Press, 1999), pp. 150, 278; Herbert, *Seurat: Drawings and Paintings*, p. 156; Robyn Roslak, *Neo-Impressionism and Anarchism in Fin-de-siècle France: Painting, Politics and Landscape* (Aldershot, U.K., and Burlington, Vt.: Ashgate, 2007), p. 86; Jonathan Crary, "Illuminations of Disenchantment: Seurat's *Parade de cirque*," in *Seurat Re-viewed*, edited by Paul Smith (University Park: Pennsylvania State University Press, 2009), p. 88; Joan Ungersma Halperin, "The Ironic Eye/I in Jules Laforgue and Georges Seurat," in *Seurat Re-viewed*, p. 115.

8. Paul Alexis, "Visite à *La Revue indépendante*," *Le Cri du peuple*, April 14, 1888, in *"Naturalisme pas mort": Lettres inédites de Paul Alexis à Emile Zola, 1871–1900*, edited by Bard H. Bakker (Toronto: University of Toronto Press, 1971), p. 514, no. A:59; Camille Pissaro, letter to Paul Signac, February 24, 1888, in *Correspondance de Camille Pissarro*, edited by Janine Bailly-Herzberg (Paris: Presses Universitaires de France, 1980–86), vol. 2, p. 218, no. 472.

9. Richard Thomson, "The Imperatives of Style: Seurat's Drawings, 1886–1891," in Jodi Hauptman, *Georges Seurat: The Drawings*, exh. cat., 2007–8 (New York: Museum of Modern Art, 2007), p. 176.

10. For example, the Foire Saint-Lazare is traceable to 1131, and the Foire du Lendit, held in mid-June on the Plaine Saint-Denis to the north of Paris, ran at least from the twelfth century onward. See E. Foussier, *Rapport présenté par M. Foussier, au nom de la 2ᵉ commission, au sujet du roulement des fêtes foraines dans Paris*, Conseil Municipal de Paris 108 (Paris: Conseil Municipal de Paris, 1895), pp. 5–7.

11. Robert M. Isherwood, *Farce and Fantasy: Popular Entertainment in Eighteenth-Century Paris* (New York and Oxford: Oxford University Press, 1986), pp. 30–35.

12. Hugues Le Roux, *Les Jeux du cirque et la vie foraine* (Paris: E. Plon, Nourrit, 1889), p. i.

13. A. Beaujean and Emile Littré, *Dictionnaire de la langue française abrégé du dictionnaire de E. Littré*, 7th ed. (Paris: Hachette, 1883), p. 806; Le Men, *Seurat et Chéret*, p. 114.

14. Jean Starobinski, *Portrait de l'artiste en saltimbanque*, Les Sentiers de la Création 7 (Paris: Julliard, 1970); Francis Haskell, "The Sad Clown: Some Notes on a 19th Century Myth," in *French 19th Century Painting and Literature: With Special Reference to the Relevance of Literary Subject-Matter to French Painting*, edited by Ulrich Finke, Manchester Studies in the History of Art 1 (Manchester, U.K.: Manchester University Press, 1972), pp. 2–16.

15. Maurice Denis, August 24, 1884, in *Journal* (Paris: La Colombe, 1957), vol. 1, p. 19; Jules Vallès, "Les Fausses accusations," in *Le Tableau de Paris*, edited by Maxime Jourdan (Paris: Berg International, 2007), pp. 68–71.

16. See Dieter Noack and Lilian Noack, *The Daumier Register*, www.daumier-register.org (accessed May 15, 2016), which lists fifty-five works on the theme of *saltimbanques*.

17. Haskell, "The Sad Clown," pp. 12–13; T. J. Clark, *The Absolute Bourgeois: Artists and Politics in France,*

1848–1851 (London: Thames and Hudson, 1973), pp. 120, 122–23.

18. Figure 8 was number 203 in the exhibition catalogue, figure 9 was number 104, and figure 11 was number 127. Figure 10 is a study for the most finished drawing of the series, *La Parade foraine* (Musée d'Orsay, Paris, RF 4164), which was no. 196; see *Exposition des peintures et dessins de H. Daumier*, exh. cat., Galeries Durand-Ruel (Paris: Gauthier-Villars, 1878). See also Arsène Alexandre, *Honoré Daumier: L'Homme et l'oeuvre* (Paris: H. Laurens, 1888), p. 169, ill.

19. Edmond Duranty, "Daumier, I," *Gazette des beaux-arts*, year 20, ser. 2, 17, no. 5 (May 1, 1878), p. 435. See also Paul Mantz, "La Caricature moderne," *Gazette des beaux-arts*, year 30, ser. 2, 37, no. 4 (April 1, 1888), p. 310; and Louis Gonse, "Bibliographie: II [Review of Alexandre, *Honoré Daumier*]," *Gazette des beaux-arts*, year 30, ser. 2, 38, no. 2 (August 1, 1888), p. 176.

20. Richard Thomson, "Theo van Gogh: An Honest Broker," in Chris Stolwijk and Richard Thomson, *Theo Van Gogh, 1857–1891: Art Dealer, Collector, and Brother of Vincent*, exh. cat., Van Gogh Museum, Amsterdam, and Musée d'Orsay, Paris, 1999–2000 (Amsterdam: Van Gogh Museum; Zwolle: Waanders, 1999), p. 90.

21. Arsène Alexandre, *Honoré Daumier; Exposition des peintres, aquarelles, dessins et lithographies des maîtres français de la caricature et de la peinture de moeurs au XIX siècle*, with preface by Paul Mantz, exh. cat., Ecole des Beaux-Arts (Paris: Maison Quantin, 1888).

22. Félix Fénéon, "Calendrier d'avril, VI: Oeuvres des maîtres français de la caricature et de la peinture de moeurs au XIXe siècle, Ecole des Beaux-Arts," *La Revue indépendante* 7, no. 19 (May 1888), in *Oeuvres plus que complètes*, edited by Joan Ungersma Halperin, Histoire des Idées et Critique Littéraire 107 (Geneva: Droz, 1970), vol. 1, p. 110.

23. Louis Hayet, letter to Lucien Pissarro, September 16, 1886, Department of Western Art, Ashmolean Museum of Art and Archaeology, University of Oxford.

24. Beaujean and Littré, *Dictionnaire de la langue française*, p. 806.

25. John Grand-Carteret, *Les Moeurs et la caricature en France* (Paris: Librairie Illustrée, 1888), p. 187.

26. Bruce Laughton, *Honoré Daumier* (New Haven and London: Yale University Press, 1996), p. 13.

27. Charles Baudelaire, "Salon de 1846," in *Curiosités esthétiques: L'Art romantique, et autres oeuvres critiques*, edited by Henri Lemaître, Classiques Garnier (Paris: Editions Garnier Frères, 1962), p. 142.

28. Philippe Durey, "Nouvelles acquisitions des musées de province, 1977–1979; XIX siècle: Peintures et dessins de 1800 à 1870," *La Revue du Louvre et des musées de France* 5–6 (1980), p. 309.

29. Robin Ptacek in *The Cult of Images: Baudelaire and the 19th-Century Media Explosion / Le Culte des images: Baudelaire and the 19th-Century Media Explosion*, exh. cat. (Santa Barbara: University of California, Santa Barbara, Art Museum, 1977), p. 45, no. 34.

30. James Jackson Jarves, *Parisian Sights and French Principles: Seen through American Spectacles* (New York: Harper and Bros., 1852), p. 101.

31. Edouard Ourliac, "Essai sur les moeurs des saltimbanques," in *Le Diable à Paris: Paris et les parisiens; Mœurs et coutumes, caractères et portraits des habitants de Paris, tableau complet de leur vie privée, publique, politique, artistique, littéraire, industrielle* (Paris: Hetzel, 1846), vol. 2, pp. 163–65.

32. For Hadol, see Bertrand Tillier, "Paul Hadol et sa ménagerie! Ou Le Cirque d'un caricaturiste antibonapartiste," *Gavroche: Revue d'histoire populaire* 14, no. 80 (March–April 1995), pp. 1–8.

33. Jules Vallès, "Le Tableau de Paris: Les Foires, I," *Gil Blas* 4, no. 870 (April 6, 1882), in *Le Tableau de Paris*, p. 65.

34. Richard Thomson, *Art of the Actual: Naturalism and Style in Early Third Republic France, 1880–1900* (New Haven and London: Yale University Press, 2012).

35. Louis de Fourcaud, "Le Salon de 1884: Deuxième article," *Gazette des beaux-arts*, year 26, ser. 2, 29, no. 6 (June 1, 1884), pp. 465–66.

36. Gaston Escudier, *Les Saltimbanques: Leur vie, leurs moeurs* (Paris: Michel Lévy, 1875), pp. 239–58; Raoul Ponchon, "La Foire au pain d'épices," *Le Courrier français* 5, no. 16 (April 15, 1888), p. 3.

37. Th. Véron, *Dictionnaire Véron, ou organe de l'Institut universel des sciences, des lettres et des arts du XIXe siècle (Section des beaux-arts): Salon de 1885* (Poitiers: Th. Véron, 1885), p. 80.

38. *Catalogue illustré des oeuvres de Jean-François Raffaëlli: Exposées 28 bis, avenue de l'Opera suivi d'une étude des mouvements de l'art moderne et du beau caractériste*, exh. cat., 28 bis, Avenue de l'Opera, Paris (Paris: [s.n.], 1884), nos. 78, 79.

39. Jean-François Raffaëlli (artist), "Les Saltimbanques—L'Orchestre en parade," *Paris illustré*, July 1, 1884, pp. 88–89, ill.

40. Isabelle Collet, "'Grimaces et misère': Le Retour des peintures de Fernand Pelez au Petit Palais, Musée des Beaux-Arts de la Ville de Paris," *La Revue des musées de France: Revue du Louvre* 55, no. 5 (December 2005), p. 72.

41. André Michel, "Salon de 1888: Troisième et dernier article," *Gazette des beaux-arts*, year 30, ser. 2, 38, no. 2 (August 1, 1888), p. 139; Georges Lafenestre, "Le Salon de 1888: I.—La Peinture," *Revue des deux mondes*, ser. 3, 58, no. 87 (June 1, 1888), p. 663.

42. Louis-Ariste [Passerieu], *Causeries sur le salon de 1888* (Paris: Grand Imprimerie, 1888), p. 82; Léonce Bénédite, "Salon de 1888, VI," *Paris illustré*, ser. 3, 6, no. 22 (June 2, 1888), p. 350.

43. Henry Houssaye, *Le Salon de 1888* (Paris: Boussod, Valadon et Cie, 1888), p. 61; Bénédite, "Salon de 1888, VI," p. 350; Gabriel Séailles,

"Salon de 1888," *L'Illustration*, no. 2357 (April 28, 1888), unpag.

44. Robert Rosenblum, "Fernand Pelez, or the Other Side of the Post-Impressionist Coin," in *Art, the Ape of Nature: Studies in Honor of H. W. Janson*, edited by Moshe Barasch and Lucy Freeman Sandler (New York: H. N. Abrams; Englewood Cliffs, N.J.: Prentice-Hall, 1981), pp. 707–18.

45. Séailles, "Salon de 1888."

46. Hippolyte Gautier (artist), Ch. Delagrave (editor), "Gravures extraites de 'L'an 1789,'" *Le Courrier français* 5, no. 23 (June 3, 1888), p. 12, ill.; de Saint-Aubin, *A Street Show in Paris* (National Gallery, London).

47. Edmond de Goncourt, *Les Frères Zemganno*, 2nd ed. (Paris: Charpentier, 1879), p. 89.

48. *Monticelli et le baroque provençal*, exh. cat., Orangerie des Tuileries, Paris (Paris: Editions des Musées Nationaux, 1953), p. 42.

49. Etienne Gervais, *La Foire aux pains d'épice* (Tours: A. Mame et fils, 1866), p. 8.

50. Robert Tombs, *The War against Paris, 1871* (Cambridge, U.K., and New York: Cambridge University Press, 1981), p. 159.

51. Gervais, *La Foire aux pains d'épice*, p. 9; George Augustus Sala, *Paris Herself Again in 1878-9* (London: Remington and Co., 1879), p. 497.

52. Gervais, *La Foire aux pains d'épice*, pp. 10–11. Edmond Texier, in contrast, describes the fair as "this rendezvous of working-class Paris"; see Texier, *Tableau de Paris* (Paris: Paulin et Le Chevalier, 1852–53), vol. 1, p. 328.

53. Texier, *Tableau de Paris*, vol. 1, p. 329.

54. Sala, *Paris Herself Again in 1878-9*, pp. 499–501.

55. Le Roux, *Les Jeux du cirque et la vie foraine* (see note 12), pp. 43–45, 51, 56, 69, 73.

56. Bruno Béguet, "La Vulgarisation scientifique au XIXe siècle," in Bruno Béguet, Maryline Cantor, and Ségolène Le Men, *La Science pour tous*, Les Dossiers du Musée d'Orsay 52, exh. cat., Musée d'Orsay, Paris (Paris: Réunion des Musées Nationaux, 1994), pp. 44–46. I am grateful to Isolde Pludermacher for this reference.

57. Karl Baedeker, *Paris and Environs with Routes from London to Paris and from Paris to the Rhine and Switzerland: Handbook for Travellers* (Leipzig: Karl Baedeker; London: Dulau and Co., 1881), p. 208.

58. Pierre Véron, "Courrier de Paris," *Le Monde illustré* 32, no. 1618 (March 31, 1888), p. 198; Pierre Véron, "Courrier de Paris," *Le Monde illustré* 32, no. 1619 (April 7, 1888), p. 214.

59. Des Réaux, "La Foire au pain d'épice," *La Vie moderne* 2, no. 16 (April 17, 1880), p. 245.

60. Escudier, *Les Saltimbanques* (see note 36), p. 263.

61. Charles Dickens, *Dickens's Dictionary of Paris, 1882: An Unconventional Handbook* (London: Macmillan, 1882), p. 97.

62. Foussier, *Rapport présenté par M. Foussier* (see note 10), p. 5.

63. Ibid., pp. 19–21.

64. Sala, *Paris Herself Again in 1878-9*, p. 497.

65. Le Roux, *Les Jeux du cirque et la vie foraine*, pp. 8–9; Le Men, *Seurat et Chéret*, p. 69.

66. Le Roux, *Les Jeux du cirque et la vie foraine*, p. 19; Foussier, *Rapport présenté par M. Foussier*, p. 43.

67. Vallès, "Célébrités d'antan," in *Le Tableau de Paris* (see note 15), pp. 65–90.

68. Dr. Fourès, "Le Vieux Montmartre [manuscript]," in Foussier, *Rapport présenté par M. Foussier*, p. 18.

69. Herbert, *Seurat: Drawings and Paintings*, p. 138.

70. Escudier, *Les Saltimbanques*, p. 389. Rossi was popular in the 1870s.

71. Des Réaux, "La Foire au pain d'épice," p. 245.

72. Le Roux, *Les Jeux du cirque et la vie foraine*, pp. 86–87.

73. Ibid., p. 88.

74. J. Hoche, "Les Forains," *Paris illustré*, September 3, 1887, cited in Paul Smith, *Seurat and the Avant-Garde* (New Haven and London: Yale University Press, 1997), p. 191n3.

75. Joris-Karl Huysmans, "Pierre Wagner," *La Cravache parisienne*, August 4, 1888; see Huysmans, *Certains: G. Moreau–Degas–Chéret–Wisthler*[sic]*–Rops–Le Monstre–Le Fer, etc.* (Paris: Tresses & Stock, 1889), pp. 40–41, and Huysmans, *Ecrits sur l'art, 1867–1905*, edited by Patrice Locmant (Paris: Bartillat, 2006), pp. 358–59.

76. Paul Signac, "Lettre," *La Cravache parisienne*, September 22, 1888, p. 2.

77. Gilles Caillaud with Hélène Bailly-Marcilhac and Charles Bailly, *Léon Pourtau: Vie et oeuvre d'un pionnier du pointillisme; Essai de catalogue raisonné* (Milan: Skira, 2014), pp. 20–24.

78. For Seurat's career, see Anne Distel, "Chronology," in Robert L. Herbert with Françoise Cachin, Anne Distel, Susan Alyson Stein, and Gary Tinterow, *Georges Seurat, 1859–1891*, exh. cat., Grand Palais, Paris, and The Metropolitan Museum of Art, New York, 1991–92 (New York: The Metropolitan Museum of Art, 1991), pp. 399–412.

79. Based on recent archival discoveries, Nancy Ireson ("Seurat and the 'Cours de M. Yvon,'" *Burlington Magazine* 153, no. 1296 [March 2011], pp. 174–80) puts Seurat's time at the Ecole des Beaux-Arts at three years at least.

80. Ogden N. Rood, *Modern Chromatics, with Applications to Art and Industry*, International Scientific Series 26 (New York: D. Appleton and Company, 1879); French ed., *Théorie scientifique des couleurs et leurs applications à l'art et à l'industrie*, Bibliothèque Scientifique Internationale 38 (Paris: G. Baillière et Cie, 1881).

81. For *Bathers*, see John Leighton and Richard Thomson with David Bomford, Jo Kirby, and Ashok Roy, *Seurat and the Bathers*, exh. cat. (London: National Gallery, 1997).

82. For *La Grande Jatte*, see Robert L. Herbert, *Seurat and the Making of La Grande Jatte*, exh. cat. (Chicago: Art Institute of Chicago in association with the University of California Press, Berkeley, 2004).

83. Jean Le Fustec, "Exposition de la

société des artistes indépendants," *Le Journal des artistes*, no. 34 (August 22, 1886), p. 282. I am grateful to Emmelyn Butterfield-Rosen and Susan Alyson Stein for drawing this to my attention.

84. For *Models*, see Françoise Cachin, "*Poseuses*, 1886–1888," in Herbert, *Georges Seurat, 1859–1891*, pp. 273–95, nos. 183–92, which leaves open the question of whether the small oil was a study for, or a replica made after, *Models*.

85. Camille Pissarro, letter to Paul Signac, June 16, 1887, in *Correspondance de Camille Pissarro*, vol. 2, pp. 187–88, no. 441.

86. Vincent van Gogh, letter to Paul Gauguin, October 3, 1888, in *Vincent van Gogh: The Letters; The Complete Illustrated and Annotated Edition*, edited by Leo Jansen, Hans Luijten, and Nienke Bakker (London and New York: Thames and Hudson in association with the Van Gogh Museum, Amsterdam, and Huygens Institute, The Hague, 2009), vol. 4, pp. 304–5, no. 695. The letter records the visit but does not name any of the paintings seen. Vincent refers to *Models*, writing to Theo (October 22, 1888, in ibid., vol. 4, pp. 340–41, no. 710), and Theo refers to *Circus Sideshow* in a letter to Vincent (September 5, 1889, in ibid., vol. 5, pp. 77–78, no. 799), making it probable that they saw both works in Seurat's studio, as the editors of the Van Gogh Letters Project contend.

87. Seurat gives the dimensions of *Bathers* and *La Grande Jatte* as 2 x 3 meters, and of *Models* as 2 x 2.5 meters, while *Circus Sideshow* measures 1 x 1.5 meters; Robert L. Herbert, "Appendix E: Seurat's *Esthétique*," in *Georges Seurat, 1859–1891*, p. 382. The confined space of Seurat's studio and its effect on his large-scale works was noted by Paul Signac in his journal on December 29, 1894; see Signac, "Extraits du journal inédit de Paul Signac: I, 1894–1895," edited by John Rewald, *Gazette des beaux-arts*, year 91, ser. 6, 36, nos. 989–91 (July–September 1949), p. 114.

88. Herbert in *Georges Seurat, 1859–1891*, p. 37, no. 19 (now in the André Bromberg Collection). Fénéon was responsible, along with Maximilien Luce and Paul Signac, for drawing up an inventory of Seurat's work after his death in 1891 and could have made the annotation then. See Robert Rey, "Inventaire de l'atelier de Seurat, en 1891," in Rey, *La Peinture française à la fin du XIXe siècle: La Renaissance du sentiment classique; Degas, Renoir, Gauguin, Cézanne, Seurat* (Paris: G. van Oest, 1931), p. 144.

89. Herbert in *Georges Seurat, 1859–1891*, pp. 66, 68, nos. 44 (private collection), 45.

90. Labruyère, "Les Impressionnistes, II," *Le Cri du peuple*, May 28, 1886, pp. 1–2, in *The New Painting: Impressionism, 1874–1886: Documentation*, edited by Ruth Berson (San Francisco: Fine Arts Museums, 1996), vol. 1, pp. 460–61.

91. Thomson, "The Imperatives of Style," p. 173. De Hauke identified the proprietorial man in the drawing as "Monsieur Loyal," the name of a famous ringmaster and his various descendants, some active in Seurat's day; see Gary Tinterow in Herbert, *Georges Seurat, 1859–1891*, p. 314–16, no. 203; César M. de Hauke, *Seurat et son oeuvre*, vol. 2 (Paris: Gründ, 1961) p. 246, no. 669.

92. William I. Homer, "The Literature of Art: Seurat's Paintings and Drawings [Review of *Seurat et son oeuvre* by C. M. de Hauke (1961)]," *Burlington Magazine* 105, no. 723 (June 1963), pp. 282–84.

93. Tinterow in Herbert, *Georges Seurat, 1859–1891*, p. 316, no. 204.

94. Rey, "Inventaire de l'atelier de Seurat, en 1891," p. 144; see also Henri Dorra and John Rewald, *Seurat: L'Oeuvre peint; Biographie et catalogue critique* (Paris: Les Beaux-Arts, 1959), lxxv–lxxvi. Gary Tinterow (in Herbert, *Georges Seurat, 1859–1891*, p. 312, no. 201) suggests that the fourth drawing might be *Sidewalk Show* (fig. 51); he incorrectly notes that the inventory included four, as opposed to three, small oil panels.

95. Herbert, "Appendix C: Seurat's Collection of Prints, Reproductions, and Photographs," in *Georges Seurat, 1859–1891*, pp. 378–80.

96. Charles Blanc, *Grammaire des arts du dessin: Architecture, sculpture, peinture*, 4th ed. (Paris: Renouard, 1882; first pub. 1867), p. 636; Thomson, *Seurat*, pp. 155–56.

97. I am grateful to Susan Alyson Stein for this suggestion, February 2016.

98. C. Blanc, *Grammaire des arts du dessin*, pp. 503, 556.

99. Henri Dorra, "Japanese Sources for Two Paintings by Seurat," *Gazette des beaux-arts*, year 131, ser. 6, 114, no. 1448 (September 1989), pp. 95–96.

100. Charles Virmaître, *Paris-palette* (Paris: A. Savine, 1888), p. 64.

101. Thomson, *Art of the Actual*, p. 259.

102. Observation by Charlotte Hale, conservator, Paintings Conservation, The Metropolitan Museum of Art, New York, July, 17, 2015; see also Hale and Centeno, "Seurat's *Circus Sideshow*: Materials, Technique, Evolution," in this volume, p. 112.

103. Tinterow, "*Parade de cirque*, 1887–1888," in Herbert, *Georges Seurat, 1859–1891*, p. 308.

104. Gary Tinterow reports that when viewed in The Metropolitan Museum's conservation laboratory as if under gaslight, the whole painting glowed as if lit from behind; see ibid., pp. 306–8.

105. Herbert, *Seurat: Drawings and Paintings*, p. 143.

106. Crary, *Suspensions of Perception* (see note 7), pp. 195–96.

107. Michael F. Zimmermann, *Seurat and the Art Theory of His Time*, translated by Patricia Crampton (Antwerp: Fonds Mercator, 1991), p. 346.

108. Herbert, "Appendix E," p. 382. The final draft of Seurat's letter to Beaubourg is in a private collection; it was first published by Fénéon ("De Seurat," *Bulletin*, no. 9 [June 17, 1914], in *Oeuvres plus que complètes*, vol. 1, pp. 300–302). For an English translation, see Herbert, "Appendix E," pp. 381–83.

109. Zimmermann, *Seurat and the Art Theory of His Time*, p. 346.

110. See, for example, Crary, *Suspensions of Perception*, pp. 188–89; Herbert, *Seurat: Drawings and Paintings*, p. 149; and Foa, *Seurat*, p. 118.

111. *Les Dessins de Georges Seurat (1859–1891)*, 2 vols. (Paris: Bernheim-Jeune, 1928); Herbert, "Appendix E," p. 383. Seurat's letter to Fénéon of June 20, 1890, is held in the Département de Manuscrits, Bibliothèque Nationale de France, Paris; for an English translation, see Herbert, "Appendix F: Seurat's Letter to Fénéon, June 20, 1890," in *Georges Seurat, 1859–1891*, pp. 383–84. See also Herbert, "Appendix G: Charles Blanc," in ibid., pp. 384–86.

112. C. Blanc, *Grammaire des arts du dessin*, pp. 25–26.

113. David Pierre Giottino Humbert de Superville, *Essai sur les signes inconditionnels de l'art* (Leiden: C. C. Van der Hoek, 1827); C. Blanc, *Grammaire des arts du dessin*, p. 34.

114. C. Blanc, *Grammaire des arts du dessin*, pp. 145, 500.

115. Ibid., p. 510.

116. Ibid., p. 42.

117. Ibid., p. 440.

118. Ibid., pp. 145–46.

119. Ibid., pp. 561–62.

120. Herbert, "Appendix F," p. 383; Herbert, "Appendix K: Ogden Rood," in *Georges Seurat, 1859–1891*, pp. 390–91.

121. Herbert, "Appendix F," p. 383. Given Seurat's unsystematic study of theory, he should not be considered an expert in the color science of his period; see John Gage, *Colour and Meaning: Art, Science and Symbolism* (London: Thames and Hudson, 1999), pp. 212, 218.

122. Jules Laforgue, letter to Gustave Kahn, August 13, 1886, in *Lettres à un ami: 1880–1886*, edited by G. Jean-Aubry (Paris: Mercure de France, 1941), pp. 206–7, letter L; Herbert, "Appendix F," p. 383.

123. For Henry, see, for example, José A. Argüelles, *Charles Henry and the Formation of a Psychophysical Aesthetic* (Chicago and London: University of Chicago Press, 1972);

124. Fénéon, "Signac," *Les Hommes d'aujourd'hui* 8, no. 373 (1890), in *Oeuvres plus que complètes*, vol. 1, pp. 177–78.

125. Thomson, *Seurat*, p. 152.

126. Jean Moréas, "Un Manifeste littéraire: Le Symbolisme," *Le Figaro: Supplément littéraire*, September 18, 1886, p. 1.

127. Tinterow, "*Parade de cirque, 1887–1888*," p. 308.

128. Herbert, *Seurat: Drawings and Paintings*, p. 145.

129. Herbert, "Appendix L," p. 393; Herbert, *Seurat: Drawings and Paintings*, pp. 146–47.

130. Charles Henry, *Cercle chromatique: Présentant tous les compléments et toutes les harmonies de couleurs avec une introduction sur la théorie générale de contraste, du rythme et de la mesure* (Paris: Charles Verdin, 1888), p. 81.

131. Herbert, *Seurat: Drawings and Paintings*, p. 148.

132. Félix Fénéon, "'Une Esthétique scientifique," *La Cravache* [*parisienne*], May 18, 1889, in *Oeuvres plus que complètes*, vol. 1, pp. 145–48; Joan Ungersma Halperin, *Félix Fénéon: Aesthete and Anarchist in Fin-de-Siècle Paris* (New Haven: Yale University Press, 1988), p. 124.

133. I am grateful to Charlotte Hale for this observation, July 2015.

134. For the identification of cobalt blue as the color used here by Seurat, see Hale and Centeno, "Seurat's *Circus Sideshow*: Materials, Technique, Evolution," in this volume, p. 114.

135. Zimmermann, *Seurat and the Art Theory of His Time*, p. 354.

136. On the late addition of the girl and of her mother's arm, also at a "happy" angle, see Hale and Centeno, "Seurat's *Circus Sideshow*: Materials, Technique, Evolution," in this volume, p. 115.

137. Gustave Coquiot, *Seurat* (Paris: A. Michel, 1924), p. 43.

138. Louis Hayet, letter to Lucien Pissarro, March 5, 1887, Department of Western Art, Ashmolean Museum

of Art and Archaeology, University of Oxford.

139. Jean Moréas, letter to Léon Vanier, 1889, in *Cent-soixante treize lettres de Jean Moréas à Raymond de La Tailhède et à divers correspondants*, edited by Robert A. Jouanny, Avant-Siècle 4 (Paris: Lettres Modernes, 1968), pp. 138–39; quoted in Christophe Charle, *La Crise littéraire à l'époque de naturalisme: Roman, théâtre et politique; Essai d'histoire sociale des groupes et des genres littéraires* (Paris: Presses de l'Ecole Normale Supérieure, 1979), p. 20.

140. Emile Verhaeren, "Georges Seurat," *La Sociêté nouvelle* 7, no. 1 (April 1891), in *Sensations* (Paris: Bibliothèque Dionysienne; G. Crès, 1927), p. 199; *Les Dessins de Georges Seurat*.

141. Smith, *Seurat and the Avant-Garde* (see note 74), p. 124. See also Crary, *Suspensions of Perception* (see note 7), pp. 249, 251, 255.

142. On the addition of the border, see Hale and Centeno, "Seurat's *Circus Sideshow*: Materials, Technique, Evolution," in this volume, p. 116.

143. Jean Ajalbert, "Le Salon des impressionnistes," *La Revue moderne: Littéraire, politique et artistique* 3, no. 30 (June 20, 1886), p. 392; Octave Mirbeau, "Exposition de peinture: 1, rue Lafitte," *La France*, May 21, 1886, pp. 1–2.

144. Camille Pissarro, letter to Paul Durand-Ruel, November 6, 1886, in *Correspondance de Camille Pissarro*, vol. 2, p. 75, no. 368.

145. C. Blanc, *Grammaire des arts du dessin*, p. 540.

146. Camille Pissarro, letter to Lucien Pissarro, July 8(?) 1883, in *Correspondance de Camille Pissarro*, vol. 1, p. 229, no. 167.

147. See, for example, Robert L. Herbert, *Seurat's Drawings* (New York: Shorewood, 1962), p. 127; and Herbert, *Seurat: Drawings and Paintings*, pp. 149–50.

148. C. Blanc, *Grammaire des arts du dessin*, pp. 486, 526.

149. Armand Dayot, *Salon de 1884* (Paris: L. Baschet, 1884), p. 35.

150. C. Blanc, *Grammaire des arts du dessin*, p. 532.

151. Jules Claretie, *La Vie à Paris, 1883* (Paris: V. Havard, 1883), p. 39.

152. Gustave Kahn, "Réponse des symbolistes," *L'Evènement*, September 28, 1886, unpag.; Le Men, *Seurat et Chéret*, p. 24.

153. For the Indépendants and *Bathers*, see Richard Thomson, "1884: Rejection and Response," in Leighton and Thomson, *Seurat and the Bathers*, pp. 120–25.

154. Ernest Hoschedé, "Préface," in *Catalogue des oeuvres exposées, 1888: 4e exposition, pavillon de la ville de Paris—Champs-Elysées* (Paris: Société des Artistes Indépendants, 1888), pp. 6–7.

155. Arsène Alexandre, "La Semaine artistique: Une Exposition peu convenable," *Paris*, March 26, 1888.

156. For the full list, see Distel, "Chronology," p. 408.

157. For the *café-concert* drawings, see, for example, Herbert, *Seurat's Drawings*, pp. 136–50; James H. Rubin, "Seurat and Theory: The Near-Identical Drawings of the Café-Concert," *Gazette des beaux-arts*, year 112, ser. 6, 76, no. 1221 (October 1970), pp. 242–43; Gary Tinterow, "The Café-Concert, 1886–1888," in Herbert, *Georges Seurat, 1859–1891*, pp. 296–302, nos. 193–97; Zimmermann, *Seurat and the Art Theory of His Time*, pp. 364–70; Thomson, "The Imperatives of Style," pp. 169–83; Cornelia Homburg, *Neo-Impressionism and the Dream of Realities: Painting, Poetry, Music*, exh. cat., Phillips Collection, Washington, D.C., 2014–15 (New Haven: Yale University Press, 2014), pp. 28–29.

158. Tinterow, "The Café-Concert, 1886–1888," pp. 297–98, no. 193.

159. Seurat made two almost identical versions of *At the Gaîté Rochechouart*. The one that was shown in 1888 is held by the Fogg Museum, Harvard Art Museums (Bequest of Grenville L. Winthrop [1943.918]). On the two versions, see Rubin, "Seurat and Theory," pp. 242–43; Tinterow, "The Café-Concert, 1886–1888," p. 301, no. 196; and Susan Alyson Stein in *A Private Passion: 19th-Century Paintings and Drawings from the Grenville L. Winthrop Collection, Harvard University*, edited by Stephan Wolohojian with Anna Tahinci, exh. cat., Musée des Beaux-Arts, Lyon, National Gallery, London, and The Metropolitan Museum of Art, New York, 2003–4 (New York: The Metropolitan Museum of Art; New Haven: Yale University Press, 2003), pp. 307–8, no. 129.

160. For contemporary images of *café-concert* subjects in the popular press, see Herbert, *Seurat's Drawings*, p. 147; and Thomson, "The Imperatives of Style," (see note 9) p. 180.

161. Henri Somm, "Exposition des artistes indépendants," *Le Chat noir* 7, no. 326 (April 7, 1888), p. 1098.

162. Maurice de Faramond, "Les Artistes indépendants," *La Vie franco-russe*, no. 6 (March 24, 1888), p. 114; Gustave Geffroy, "Chronique: Pointillé-cloisonisme," *La Justice*, no. 3010 (April 11, 1888), p. 1.

163. Paul Adam, "Les Impressionnistes à l'exposition des indépendants," *La Vie moderne* 10 (April 15, 1888), p. 229; Jules Christophe, "Le Néo-impressionnisme au pavillon de la ville de Paris," *Le Journal des artistes*, no. 19 (May 6, 1888), pp. 147–48.

164. Félix Fénéon, "Le Néo-impressionnisme: A la IVe exposition des artistes indépendants," *L'Art moderne* (Brussels) 8, no. 16 (April 15, 1888), in *Oeuvres plus que complètes*, vol. 1, p. 84.

165. Néo [Paul Signac], "Quatrième exposition des artistes indépendants," *Le Cri du peuple*, March 29, 1888; Fénéon, "Le Néo-impressionnisme: A la IVe exposition des artistes indépendants," in *Oeuvres plus que complètes*, vol. 1, p. 84.

166. Rodolphe Darzens, "L'Exposition des indépendants," *La Revue moderne*, no. 57 (May 10, 1888), p. 446.

167. Kahn, "Peinture," p. 161.

168. Faramond, "Les Artistes indépendants," p. 114.

169. "Lettre de Paris," *L'Echo du Nord*, March 29, 1888; Geffroy, "Chronique," p. 1.

170. Seurat's letters to Beaubourg and Fénéon list what the artist considered his major paintings. Herbert, "Appendix E," pp. 381–83; Herbert, "Appendix F," pp. 383–84. See also Hale and Centeno, "Seurat's *Circus Sideshow*: Materials, Technique, Evolution," in this volume, p. 116, for evidence that Seurat painted over his signature on *Circus Sideshow*.

171. [Paul Adam, Jean Moréas, and Félix Fénéon,] *Petit bottin des lettres et des arts* (Paris: E. Giraud, 1886), p. 144.

172. For the translation, see James McNeill Whistler, *Le "Ten O'Clock" de M. Whistler*, translated by Stéphane Mallarmé (Paris: Librairie de la Revue Indépendante, 1888); and Gustave Kahn, "Au temps du pointillisme," *Mercure de France* 171, no. 619 (April 1–May 1, 1924), p. 14.

173. Néo [Paul Signac], "Les XX," *Le Cri du peuple*, February 9, 1888.

174. Camille Pissarro, letter to Lucien Pissarro, March 13(?), 1887, in *Correspondance de Camille Pissarro*, vol. 2, p. 140, no. 403.

175. For the drawings, see Jean-Marie Cusinberche, "Pont-Aven," in *Gauguin e i suoi amici pittori in Bretagna / Gauguin et ses amis peintres en Bretagne / Gauguin and His Painter Friends in Brittany: Pont-Aven et le Pouldu*, edited by Jean-Marie Cusinberche, exh. cat., Centro Saint-Benin / Antico Convento San-Benin, Museo Archeologico Regionale, Aosta (Milan: Fabbri, 1993), vol. 2, pp. 19–21; and Dorothée Hansen, "*L'Enfance d'un peintre*—Ein Album mit frühen Zeichnungen von Emile Bernard," in *Emile Bernard: Am Puls der Moderne*, edited by Dorothée Hansen, exh. cat. (Bremen: Kunsthalle; Cologne: Wienand, 2015), pp. 18–19, figs. 38–40, 43. Van Gogh mentioned Bernard's painting in a letter to his brother, Theo (June 23, 1888, in *Vincent van Gogh: The Letters*, vol. 4, pp. 150–51, no. 630).

176. Emile Verhaeren, "Chronique bruxelloise: L'Exposition des XX à Bruxelles (1), 1888," *La Revue*

indépendante 6, no. 17 (March 1888), p. 456.

177. Néo [Signac], "Les XX."

178. Geffroy, "Chronique," p. 1.

179. Kahn, "Peinture," (see note 2) p. 164.

180. Fénéon, "L'Impressionnisme," *L'Emancipation sociale* (Narbonne), April 3, 1887, in *Oeuvres plus que complètes*, vol. 1, p. 64.

181. Edouard Dujardin, "Aux XX et aux indépendants: Le Cloisonisme (1)," *La Revue indépendante* 6, no. 17 (March 1888), pp. 489–90.

182. Charles Angrand, letter to Charles Frechon, mid-December 1887, in Angrand, *Correspondances, 1883–1926*, edited by François Lespinasse (Rouen: [François Lespinasse], 1988), p. 23.

183. Fénéon, "Le Néo-impressionnisme," *L'Art moderne* (Brussels), May 1, 1887, in *Oeuvres plus que complètes*, vol. 1, p. 75. For the lighting in Angrand's *An Accident*, see Andreas Blühm and Louise Lippincott, *Light! The Industrial Age, 1750–1900; Art and Science, Technology and Society*, exh. cat., Van Gogh Museum, Amsterdam, and Carnegie Museum of Art, Pittsburgh, 2000–2001 (London: Thames and Hudson, 2000), p. 196.

184. Guy Dulon and Christophe Duvivier, *Louis Hayet, 1864–1940: Peintre et théoricien du néo-impressionnisme*, exh. cat., Musée Tavet, Pontoise (Pontoise: Musée de Pontoise, 1991), p. 87.

185. Néo [Signac], "Quatrième exposition des artistes indépendants."

186. Dulon and Duvivier, *Louis Hayet, 1864–1940*, p. 62. See also Gage, *Colour and Meaning* (see note 121), p. 223.

187. Louis Hayet, letter to Lucien Pissarro, March 5, 1887, Department of Western Art, Ashmolean Museum of Art and Archaeology, University of Oxford.

188. Dulon and Duvivier, *Louis Hayet, 1864–1940*, p. 62.

189. Fénéon, "Tableaux: Exposition de M. Claude Monet . . . ; 5ᵉ exposition de la société des artistes indépendants . . .," *La Vogue*, September 1889, in *Oeuvres plus que complètes*,

vol. 1, p. 163. Theo van Gogh likewise compared Hayet's *La Place de la Concorde*, also called *Five O'clock* (see Dulon and Duvivier, *Louis Hayet, 1864–1940*, p. 18, ill.), to *Circus Sideshow*. He felt the Hayet was a "little like" Seurat's painting "but more harmonious." See Theo van Gogh, letter to Vincent van Gogh, September 5, 1889, in *Vincent van Gogh: The Letters*, vol. 5, pp. 77–78, no. 799.

190. Emile Zola, *Nana* (Paris, 1880), in *Oeuvres complètes*, edited by Henri Mitterand (Paris: Cercle du Livre Précieux, 1967), vol. 4, p. 24.

191. Edouard Dujardin, *Les Lauriers sont coupés*, edited by Jean-Pierre Bertrand, GF 1092 (Paris: Flammarion, 2001; first pub. 1887), p. 39.

192. Ibid., p. 48.

193. John Russell, *Seurat* (London: Thames and Hudson, 1965), pp. 218–19; Tinterow, "*Parade de cirque*, 1887–1888," pp. 309–10; Herbert, *Seurat: Drawings and Paintings*, p. 153.

194. Maurice Vaucaire, *Effets de théâtre*, Poètes Contemporains (Paris: A. Lemerre, 1886), pp. 121–22; Zimmermann, *Seurat and the Art Theory of His Time*, p. 355.

195. Jean Lorrain, *Modernités*, 2nd ed. (Paris: E. Giraud & Cie, 1885), p. 3.

196. Albert Samain, *Carnets intimes*, 2nd ed. (Paris: Mercure de France, 1939), pp. 56–58.

197. Jules Christophe, "Notices sur Georges Seurat: Le Peintre," *Les Hommes d'aujourd'hui* 8, no. 368 (April 1890).

198. Seurat died during an epidemic of virulent diphtheria. See Jules Christophe, "Chromo-luminaristes: Georges Seurat," *La Plume* 3, no. 57 (September 1, 1891), p. 292; [Fénéon,] [Untitled obituary for Georges Seurat], *Entretiens politiques et littéraires*, April 1891, in Fenéon, *Oeuvres plus que complètes*, vol. 1, p. 183. In effect, the critics were following Seurat's lead, as he did not list *Circus Sideshow* among his major canvases; see Herbert, "Appendix E," p. 382.

199. Gustave Kahn, "Seurat," *L'Art*

moderne (Brussels) 11, no. 14 (April 5, 1891), p. 110; Téodor de Wyzewa, "Georges Seurat," *L'Art dans les deux mondes*, ser. 1, 2, no. 22 (April 18, 1891), p. 263.

200. Pierre Louis [Maurice Denis], "Notes sur l'exposition des indépendants," *La Revue blanche* 2, no. 1 (April 1892), pp. 232–34; Charles Saunier, "L'Art nouveau: I, Camille Pissarro; II, les indépendants," *La Revue indépendante* 23, no. 66 (April 1892), pp. 30–48; [Remy de Gourmont,] "Les Premiers Salons: Indépendants — Rose Croix — Exposition de Mme Jeanne Jacquemin," *Mercure de France* 5, no. 29 (May 1892), pp. 60–66; Fénéon, "Au pavillon de la ville de Paris: Société des artistes indépendants," *Le Chat noir*, April 2, 1892, in *Oeuvres plus que complètes*, vol. 1, pp. 212–13.

201. Emile Verhaeren, "Beaux-arts: Exposition des XX," *Art et critique* 4, no. 89 (February 13, 1892), p. 75; Albert Arnay, "Chronique artistique: L'Annuel des XX," *Floréal* 1, no. 3 (March 1892), pp. 84–87; Eugène Demolder, "Chronique artistique: L'Exposition des XX à Bruxelles," *La Société nouvelle*, year 8, 1, no. 87 (March 1892), p. 349; Pierre-M. Olin, "Les XX," *Mercure de France* 4, no. 28 (April 1892), p. 341.

202. Henri-Gabriel Ibels (artist), "Modestie foraine," *L'Echo de Paris* 10, no. 3367 (August 6, 1893), cover ill. See Georges d'Esparbès, André Ibels, Maurice Lefèvre, and Georges Montorgueil, *Les Demi-cabots; Dessins de H.-G. Ibels: Le Café-concert, Le cirque, les forains* (Paris: G. Charpentier et E. Fasquelle, 1896), p. 219; and Patricia Eckert Boyer, *Artists and the Avant-Garde Theater in Paris, 1887–1900: The Martin and Liane W. Atlas Collection*, exh. cat., National Gallery of Art, Washington, D.C., and National Academy Museum, New York, 1998–99 (Washington, D.C.: National Gallery of Art, 1998), p. 50.

203. Esparbès et al., *Les Demi-cabots*, p. 226.

204. Ibid., pp. 202, 207.

205. Carol Clark, Nancy Mowll

Mathews, and Gwendolyn Owens, *Maurice Brazil Prendergast, Charles Prendergast: A Catalogue Raisonné* (Williamstown, Mass.: Williams College Museum of Art; Munich: Prestel, 1990), nos. 1599, 1600.

206. *Circus Sideshow* was purchased from the *Revue blanche* exhibition by the dealers Josse and Gaston Bernheim-Jeune; see Susan Alyson Stein, "*Circus Sideshow* Comes to Town," p. 107, and "Provenance and Exhibition History," p. 139, in this volume.

207. Georges Rouault, letter to Edouard Schuré, 1905, in *Sur l'art et sur la vie*, Bibliothèque Médiations 80 (Paris: Denoël/Gonthier, 1971), p. 171.

208. C. Blanc, *Grammaire des arts du dessin*, p. 484.

209. Christophe, "Notices sur Georges Seurat."

CIRCUS SIDESHOW COMES TO TOWN

<hr>

I am grateful to Laura Corey for her brilliant research assistance.

1. Paul Signac, journal entries of September 15, 1894, April 3, 1900, and March 12, 1898, respectively, as cited in translation in Anne Distel, "Chronology," in Robert L. Herbert with Françoise Cachin, Anne Distel, Susan Alyson Stein, and Gary Tinterow, *Georges Seurat, 1859–1891*, exh. cat., Grand Palais, Paris, and The Metropolitan Museum of Art, New York, 1991–92 (New York: The Metropolitan Museum of Art, 1991), p. 412; originals in Signac Archives, Paris.

2. For complete provenance and exhibition history, see p. 139 in this volume.

3. Seurat's "Side Show (La Parade)," was number 55 in a catalogue that lists one hundred works (inclusive of 34a and 72a), although the count is usually given as ninety-eight; see *First Loan Exhibition: Cézanne, Gauguin, Seurat, Van Gogh*, exh. cat. (New York: Trustees of the Museum of Modern Art, 1929).

4. Alfred H. Barr Jr., "Foreword," ibid., pp. 25–26; and Alfred H. Barr Jr., "An American Museum of Modern Art," *Vanity Fair* (November 1929), p. 136.

5. "Shows Modern Art Here Tomorrow: New Museum in the Heckscher Building to Hold Private Exhibition Today; Work of Pioneers on View; Cezanne, Gauguin, Seurat and Van Gogh Represented by 98 Canvases Lent for Opening Exhibit," *New York Times*, November 7, 1929, p. 26.

6. Per the Museum of Modern Art attendance ledger, reproduced in Harriet S. Bee and Michelle Elligott, *Art in Our Time: A Chronicle of the Museum of Modern Art* (New York: Museum of Modern Art; Distributed Art Publishers, 2004), p. 31.

7. Alfred H. Barr Jr., "Modern Museum," *Charm*, November 1929, p. 84.

8. Alfred H. Barr Jr., "A New Museum Which Will Devote Itself to the Masters of Modern Art," *Vogue* 74, no. 9 (October 26, 1929), p. 85; and Barr, "Modern Museum," p. 17.

9. Earlier in the year there had been a flurry of reporting on the well-advertised—and very ambitious—price tag of £60,000 ($290,000) placed on the picture when it was showcased at the Glasgow branch of Reid & Lefevre among the "Ten Masterpieces of French Art: Worth a Quarter of a Million," as one headline (W. J. W., *Glasgow Evening Times*, April 16, 1929), of many, noted. The asking price would drop to $100,000 in January 1930—presumably in response to the plummeting global economy—yet that same month the Art Institute of Chicago's trustees turned down successive offers from the French government of $250,000 and $400,000 for *La Grande Jatte* (or eight times its 1924 purchase price), as was widely reported in the national press in early March–May. See Neil Harris, "The Park in the Museum: The Making of an Icon," in Robert L. Herbert, *Seurat and the Making of La Grande Jatte*, exh. cat. (Chicago: Art Institute of Chicago in association with the University of California Press, Berkeley, 2004), pp. 238, 257n16, 258n29.

10. Roger Fry, "Seurat's *La Parade*," *Burlington Magazine* 55, no. 321 (December 1929), pp. 290–91, 293.

11. By the mid-1920s, when Seurat's posthumous fame seemed assured, many formalist critics took up the subject of the recognition that had been slow in coming to him. See, for example, Thomas Craven, "A Neglected Master," *The Dial*, September 1924, p. 260; Henry McBride, "Modern Art," *The Dial*, February 1925, p. 167. Barr and Fry voiced similar sentiments in the writings cited above.

12. Walter Pach, *Georges Seurat* (New York: Duffield and Company; Arts, 1923), pp. 27–29, in which "La Parade" is discussed and illustrated. The thirty-one-work Seurat solo exhibition was held at Joseph Brummer, New York, December 4–27, 1924; see *Paintings and Drawings by Georges Seurat*, with introduction by Walter Pach, exh. cat. (New York: Joseph Brummer, 1924).

13. See Russell Lynes, *Good Old Modern: An Intimate Portrait of the Museum of Modern Art* (New York: Atheneum, 1973), p. 3.

14. Alfred H. Barr Jr., "Modern Art in London Museums," *Arts* 14 (October 1928), p. 187, cited in Sybil Gordon Kantor, *Alfred H. Barr, Jr. and the Intellectual Origins of the Museum of Modern Art* (Cambridge, Mass.: MIT Press, 2002), pp. 149–50. Kantor relays that Barr was surprised to find "no Seurats in Moscow," and adds that "Seurat was assuredly on the top of Barr's list of impressionists and postimpressionists and Monet at the bottom"; see p. 164.

15. See the well-documented account published by Gilbert T. Vincent and Sarah Lees in "A Life with Art: Stephen Carlton Clark as Collector and Philanthropist," in *The Clark Brothers Collect: Impressionist and Early Modern Paintings*, exh. cat., Sterling and Francine Clark Art Institute, Williamstown, Mass., and The Metropolitan Museum of Art, New York, 2006–7 (Williamstown, Mass.: Sterling and Francine Clark Art Institute, 2006), pp. 150,

156nn80–82. Sarah Lees generously allowed me to consult her research notes.

16. Stephen C. Clark, letter to Charles Henschel of M. Knoedler and Co., October 28, 1932, Knoedler Gallery Archives (courtesy of Sarah Lees); copy in the object files of the Department of European Paintings, The Metropolitan Museum of Art, New York. As documented in Sarah Lees, "List of Works Owned by Stephen Carlton Clark," in *The Clark Brothers Collect*, pp. 321, 344, Clark purchased the Seurat drawing in February 1931 and Cézanne's *The Card Players* in August, and returned the small Seurat *Bathers* to Knoedler that September (having owned it since March 1929).

17. Etienne Bignou, "Foreword," in *Masterpieces by Nineteenth Century French Painters*, exh. cat. (New York: Knoedler Galleries, 1930), unpag. Clark's purchase is recorded in Knoedler's sales book 15, p. 153 (A610), Knoedler Gallery Archives, Getty Research Institute, Los Angeles, which indicates that he returned two paintings by André-Dunoyer de Segonzac for a credit of $4,000. Apparently the dealer, as he claimed, took a loss on *Circus Sideshow*, having bought it for roughly $78,000 (£16,097) jointly with Reid & Lefevre, London and Glasgow, in January 1929.

18. During his tenure as president, Clark was responsible for firing Barr (October 1943). Clark may also be credited as the anonymous donor to the Museum of Modern Art of at least twenty-two works between 1930 and 1951.

19. Clark, letter to Charles Henschel, October 28, 1932, Knoedler Gallery Archives (courtesy of Sarah Lees); copy in the object files of the Department of European Paintings, The Metropolitan Museum of Art, New York.

20. Clark, letter to the dealer Martin Birnbaum, March 8, 1930, cited in Vincent and Lees, "A Life with Art," p. 144; see also ibid., pp. 144–60, more generally, for Clark's activities as a collector and donor during this period.

21. For details of these first donations, see ibid, pp. 150–51; Daniel Cohen-McFall, Mari Yoko Hara, and Sarah Lees, "Chronology," pp. 306–7; and Sarah Lees, "Stephen C. and Susan V. Clark's Gifts and Bequests to Public Institutions," in *The Clark Brothers Collect*, pp. 314–16, which discusses them in the context of Clark's patronage of fifteen American institutions, including the museums he founded to revitalize the economy of his hometown of Cooperstown, namely, the Fenimore Art Museum and National Baseball Hall of Fame and Museum.

22. Clark was a long-standing trustee of the Metropolitan Museum (1932–46, 1950–60) and served as vice president of the board (1941–44); his lifetime gifts to the Museum include three Trie Cloister capitals (36.94.1–.3) and a Millet painting (38.75).

23. For these exhibitions, see p. 139 in this volume. The "Masterpieces of Art" exhibition was held at the World's Fair in May–October 1940; see *Masterpieces of Art: Catalogue of European and American Paintings, 1500–1900*, introduction and descriptions by Walter Pach, biographies and notes compiled by Christopher Lazare with Anne A. Wallis, Marion Haviland, and Simonetta de Vries, exh. cat., World's Fair, New York (New York: Art Aid Corporation, 1940).

24. Jerome Klein, "Museum of Modern Art Celebrates Anniversary; Finest Exhibition Since Opening Five Years Ago Is Arranged—More than 1,000,000 Visitors Have Seen 'At Home' Shows," *Baltimore Sun*, December 30, 1934; Alfred M. Frankfurter, ". . . And the Modern Masters," *Art News* 38, no. 17 (January 27, 1940), p. 30.

25. Mary Morsell, "The Modern Museum Extends Loan Show to Usher in Season," *Art News* 32 no. 1 (October 7, 1933), p. 9.

26. Aline B. Louchheim, "Rare Art Works on View Tonight: Masterpieces from Louvre, Clark Collection Shown at Galleries Here," *New York Times*, January 11, 1954, p. 19.

27. Alonzo Lansford, "Clark Collection Shown for Charity," *Art Digest* 22, no. 12 (March 15, 1948), p. 9.

28. Ibid.

29. Clark, letter to Martin Birnbaum, August 9, 1930, cited in Vincent and Lees "A Life with Art," p. 144.

30. For the complete contents of each bequest, which were extended by his widow, Susan V. Clark, in 1967, see Lees, "Stephen C. and Susan V. Clark's Gifts and Bequests to Public Institutions," pp. 315–16.

31. Met director James Rorimer's secretary, memorandum to curator Theodore Rousseau Jr., May 2, 1961, in the object files of the Department of European Paintings, The Metropolitan Museum of Art, New York.

32. See summary, "Seurat in The Met," in this volume, p. 129.

SEURAT'S CIRCUS SIDESHOW: MATERIALS, TECHNIQUE, EVOLUTION

1. The following methods of examination were used: surface examination in ordinary light and using an Olympus SZX9 microscope; X-radiography; infrared reflectography using a FLIR Merlin Near Infrared indium gallium arsenide camera with a spectral range of 900–1700 nanometers, with a StingRay Optics macro lens optimized for this range; infrared photography using a modified Canon EOS with internal 850-nanometer filter; ultraviolet photography; transmitted light photography from front and reverse, in both ordinary and infrared light; macro-X-ray fluorescence (MA-XRF) imaging using a Bruker M6 JETSTREAM; limited pigment and cross-section analysis with Raman spectroscopy using a Renishaw Raman 1000 Microscope System, surface-enhanced Raman scattering (SERS), and scanning electron microscopy–energy dispersive X-ray spectroscopy (SEM-EDS) using a Zeiss Sigma HD field emission scanning electron

microscope, equipped with an Oxford Instruments X-Max^N 80 silicon drift detector.

The authors would like to thank Federico Carò, Associate Research Scientist, Department of Scientific Research, The Metropolitan Museum of Art, New York, for the SEM-EDS analyses; Evan Read, Associate Manager of Technical Documentation, Department of Paintings Conservation, The Metropolitan Museum of Art, New York, for the infrared and X-ray imaging; and Federica Pozzi, Conservation Scientist, Solomon R. Guggenheim Museum, New York, for helpful discussions about SERS.

2. For a full transcription of the inventory, see Robert Rey, "Inventaire de l'atelier de Seurat, en 1891," in Rey, *La Peinture française à la fin du XIXe siècle: La Renaissance du sentiment classique; Degas, Renoir, Gauguin, Cézanne, Seurat* (Paris: G. van Oest, 1931), p. 144. The fourth conté drawing listed may be *Sidewalk Show* (see fig. 51); see Gary Tinterow in Robert L. Herbert with Françoise Cachin, Anne Distel, Susan Alyson Stein, and Gary Tinterow, *Georges Seurat, 1859–1891*, exh. cat., Grand Palais, Paris, and The Metropolitan Museum of Art, New York (New York: The Metropolitan Museum of Art, 1991), p. 312, no. 201. *Croqueton* is a diminutive of *croquis* (sketch).

3. Seurat used similar grids for *A Sunday on La Grande Jatte (1884)* (fig. 47)—both in the final study for the work (The Metropolitan Museum of Art, 51.112.6) and in the finished painting. See Frank Zuccari and Allison Langley, "Seurat's Working Process: The Compositional Evolution of *La Grande Jatte*," in Robert L. Herbert, *Seurat and the Making of La Grande Jatte*, exh. cat. (Chicago: Art Institute of Chicago in association with the University of California Press, Berkeley, 2004), pp. 179–80.

4. Macro-X-ray fluorescence (MA-XRF) imaging, developed at the University of Antwerp and the Delft University of Technology, maps the distribution of elements present in pigments and other materials; see Matthias Alfeld, Koen Janssens, Joris Dik, Wout De Nolf, and Geert van der Snickt, "Optimization of Mobile Scanning Macro-XRF Systems for the *In Situ* Investigation of Historical Paintings," *Journal of Analytical Atomic Spectrometry* 26, no. 5 (May 2011), pp. 899–909; and Matthias Alfeld, Joana Vaz Pedroso, Margriet van Eikema Hommes, Geert Van der Snickt, Gwen Tauber, Jorik Blaas, Michael Haschke, Klaus Erler, Joris Dik, and Koen Janssens, "A Mobile Instrument for *In Situ* Scanning Macro-XRF Investigation of Historical Paintings," *Journal of Analytical Atomic Spectrometry* 28, no. 5 (May 2013), pp. 760–67.

The MA-XRF maps of *Circus Sideshow* were acquired using a Bruker M6 instrument with the X-ray source operated at 50 kilovolts and 500 milliamps. Maps of four quadrants were obtained by scanning at 80-millisecond/pixel with a 500-micron spot size and a 600-micron step size. A smaller area along the bottom of the right edge was scanned at 90-millisecond/pixel with a 700-micron spot size and a 600-micron step size.

5. Based on its presence in the MA-XRF map for calcium, the material used for the grid and underdrawing is probably a colored chalk. Infrared reflectography, an analytical technique that images carbon-based materials, revealed only the intersection of two grid lines within the oval form to the left of the head of the trombonist, the central figure. Additionally, two faint, dark marks at the turnover edge, where the canvas bends over the stretcher, on the middle right and the lower left, are visible under magnification. Snap lines (made with chalked string) appear to have been used for the grid on the much larger *La Grande Jatte*; see Zuccari and Langley, "Seurat's Working Process," p. 180. In that painting, tack holes thought to relate to snap lines are seen on the top and right edges; no tack holes were observed in the canvas of *Circus Sideshow*.

6. Robert L. Herbert, "Appendix G: Charles Blanc," in Herbert, *Georges Seurat, 1859–1891*, p. 384. For Blanc's influence on Seurat, see Richard Thomson "Seurat's *Circus Sideshow*: A *Parade* of Paradoxes," in this volume, pp. 70–73, 76, 104–5.

7. The oval stamp reads: *M. CHABOD / Md de COULEURS / TOILES à TABLEAUX / RUE JACOB, 20.* Chabod stamps have also been found on the reverse of Seurat's *Young Woman Powdering Herself* (1889–90; The Courtauld Gallery, London) and *Le Bec du Hoc, Grandcamp* (1885/88; National Gallery, London, on loan from Tate Britain, London); see Jo Kirby, Kate Stonor, Ashok Roy, Aviva Burnstock, Rachel Grout, and Raymond White, "Seurat's Painting Practice: Theory, Development and Technology," *National Gallery Technical Bulletin* 24 (2003), p. 34n60. The stamp is also present on the reverse of *Chahut* (fig. 6), as illustrated in a wall text of the exhibition "Seurat: Master of Pointillism," Kröller-Müller Museum, Otterlo, May 23–September 7, 2014. The plainly woven canvas of *Circus Sideshow* has an average weave count of 31.6 horizontal threads per square centimeter and 36 vertical; see Thread Count Automation Project [C. Richard Johnson Jr., Don H. Johnson, and Robert G. Erdmann], "Thread Count Report," prepared by Don H. Johnson, June 2016, departmental files, Department of Paintings Conservation, The Metropolitan Museum of Art, New York. Similarly fine canvases were used for the *Study for "A Sunday on La Grande Jatte"* (The Metropolitan Museum of Art, 51.112.6) and *Le Bec du Hoc, Grandcamp*; see Kirby et al., "Seurat's Painting Practice," p. 19.

The pale-gray priming is seen on the top, left, and bottom tacking margins. The right tacking edge—the only one to show cusping (distortions from initial stretching)—is unprimed, and must have come from one side of a large, industrially primed canvas. The priming was found to comprise a very thin fossiliferous calcite layer followed by a much thicker lead white and fossiliferous calcite layer with some carbon-based black particles (analyzed using SEM-EDS and Raman spectroscopy).

8. Zinc yellow, chrome yellow, vermilion, French ultramarine, emerald green, lead white, and carbon-based black were identified by Raman spectroscopy in selected sample scrapings and in paint cross sections. The madder lake was identified in two sample scrapings by SERS analysis using a silver colloid prepared following the procedure reported in P. C. Lee and D. Meisel, "Adsorption and Surface-Enhanced Raman of Dyes on Silver and Gold Sols," *Journal of Physical Chemistry* 86, no. 17 (August 1982), pp. 3391–95. The samples were first hydrolyzed by exposing them to hydrogen fluoride vapors as described in Marco Leona, Jens Stenger, and Elena Ferloni, "Application of Surface-Enhanced Raman Scattering Techniques to the Ultrasensitive Identification of Natural Dyes in Works of Art," in "Raman Spectroscopy in Art and Archaeology II," special issue, *Journal of Raman Spectroscopy* 37, no. 10 (October 2006), pp. 981–92. After this step, the samples were removed from the microchamber, a drop of the colloid was added, and the analyses were carried out using a Renishaw Raman 1000 Microscope System. The chrome-based green pigment, cadmium yellow, cobalt blue, Prussian blue, and manganese violet were identified by MA-XRF mapping and by light microscopy. Detailed elemental-composition data on the different cobalt-based blue pigments were obtained by SEM-EDS analysis of sample scrapings and paint cross sections.

9. See Thomson, "Seurat's *Circus Sideshow*: A *Parade* of Paradoxes," in this volume, pp. 52, 73–74. On the development of Seurat's palette and his engagement with color theory, see Kirby et al., "Seurat's Painting Practice," pp. 4–27. See also Paul

Smith, *Seurat and the Avant-Garde* (New Haven and London: Yale University Press, 1997), pp. 23–48; and Inge Fiedler, "*La Grande Jatte*: A Study of the Materials and Painting Technique," in Herbert, *Seurat and the Making of La Grande Jatte*, pp. 206–8.

10. For example, a dark green in the window mullion of the ticket booth was made of the following pigments: emerald green, zinc yellow, some vermilion and carbon-based black pigments, and a little lead white (all identified using Raman spectroscopy).

11. Manganese violet pigment was first prepared by E. Leykhauf in 1868; see Rutherford J. Gettens and George L. Stout, *Painting Materials: A Short Encyclopaedia* (New York: Dover Publications, 1966), pp. 128–29, and references.

12. A full transcription of Seurat's notes is included in Gary Tinterow in *Georges Seurat, 1859–1891*, p. 313, no. 202. Seurat described the trombonist's coat "Habit rouge violet."

13. Compositional analysis with SEM-EDS of the nickel-containing cobalt blue pigment in sample scrapings and in paint cross sections showed that the nickel-to-cobalt ratios are between 0.1 and 0.17. Research on cobalt blues used by Vincent van Gogh shows that these ratios are comparatively high. See Muriel Geldof and Lise Steyn, "Van Gogh's Cobalt Blue," in *Van Gogh's Studio Practice*, edited by Marije Vellekoop et al. (Brussels: Mercantorfonds; Amsterdam: Van Gogh Museum, 2013), pp. 256–67. In *Circus Sideshow* it is not clear how the presence of nickel affects the hue of the cobalt blue.

14. See Thomson, "Seurat's *Circus Sideshow*: A *Parade* of Paradoxes, in this volume, pp. 48–50, 65.

15. Quoted in Herbert, "Appendix G," p. 384.

16. See Thomson, "Seurat's *Circus Sideshow*: A *Parade* of Paradoxes," in this volume, p. 82–83.

17. "Optical mixture" ("mélange optique") was a term used by Blanc in his *Grammaire des arts du dessin:*

Architecture, sculpture, peinture, (Paris: Renouard, 1867); as quoted in Herbert, "Appendix G," p. 384. See also Seurat's letter of August 28, 1890, to Maurice Beaubourg: "The means of expression is the optical mixture of tones, of tints (of local color and the illuminating color: sun, oil lamp, gas, etc.)"; as quoted in Herbert, "Appendix E: Seurat's *Esthétique*," in *Georges Seurat, 1859–1891*, p. 382.

18. Robert L. Herbert, *Seurat: Drawings and Paintings* (New Haven and London: Yale University Press, 2001), p. 144.

19. In a letter of January 19, 1887, to Octave Maus, the secretary of Les XX in Brussels, Seurat wrote: "It is appropriate that I tell you of my horror of varnish. Often some paint-shop proprietor will apply varnish without being told to, thinking he's doing the right thing and then sending in his little bill. VETO. I'm against any varnishing of my canvases, either free or for a fee"; as quoted in Anne Distel, "Chronology," in *Georges Seurat, 1859–1891*, p. 405. Changes in the surface gloss of oil paints are of critical importance, particularly for artists and conservators, but hard to quantify. Many factors—relating both to the internal composition of the paint and to external variables like light exposure, environmental conditions, and human intervention—are involved. But the impact of these is subtle in comparison to the potentially saturating and homogenizing surface effects of an inappropriate varnish.

20. On upward diagonals in Seurat and the artist's engagement with the theories of Charles Henry, see Thomson, "Seurat's *Circus Sideshow*: A *Parade* of Paradoxes," in this volume, p. 73.

21. Analysis using MA-XRF imaging revealed that the adjustments to some of the branches were made using a cobalt blue containing nickel, whereas the tree was first painted with a cobalt blue without a detectable nickel content. See note 13.

22. The hatless woman was laid in with

large dots of cobalt blue with no detectable nickel content, while the hat (along with the upper layers of the dress) was painted with cobalt blue containing nickel; these pigments are differentiated in the MA-XRF cobalt and nickel maps; see note 13. During painting, Seurat also added a raised brim to the conical hat of the woman standing between the buffoon and Corvi and a cap to the man on the far left, previously hatless.

23. In a paint cross section of a sample taken from the border below the left side of the trombonist's dais, a layer structure of red lake and vermilion laid over exceptionally finely divided cobalt blue, laid over a layer of ultramarine and lead white was observed; pigments were identified with Raman spectroscopy. Within the painting madder lake was identified using SERS; based on a visual comparison under ordinary and ultraviolet lights, it is possible that the red lake dots in the border sample areas are also madder lake (all fluoresce bright orange).

24. On Seurat's painted borders and frames, see Didier Semin, "Note sur Seurat et le cadre," *Avant-guerre: Sur l'art, etc.* 2 (1980), pp. 53–59; Robert L. Herbert, "Appendix A: Seurat's Painted Borders and Frames," in *Georges Seurat, 1859–1891*, pp. 376–77; and Michelle Foa, *Georges Seurat: The Art of Vision* (New Haven and London: Yale University Press, 2015), pp. 101–11. See also Matthias Waschek, "Georges Seurat: The Frame as Boundary and Extension of the Artwork," in Eva Mendgen, *In Perfect Harmony: Picture + Frame, 1850–1920*, exh. cat., Van Gogh Museum, Amsterdam, and Kunstforum, Vienna (Amsterdam: Van Gogh Museum; Zwolle: Waanders, 1995), pp. 149–62.

25. See Henri Dorra and John Rewald, *Seurat: L'Oeuvre peint; Biographie et catalogue critique* (Paris: Les Beaux-Arts, 1959), p. xxii; and Foa, *Seurat*, p. 217n48. After seeing the large *Models* in Seurat's studio on June 16, 1887, Camille Pissarro wrote to Paul Signac: "His big picture . . . will evidently be a very beautiful thing, but what will be surprising will be the execution of the frame. . . . Positively one only gets an idea of sunshine or gray weather thanks to this indispensable complement"; as quoted in Herbert, "Appendix A," p. 377n3. Neither interior nor outer frame remains on the large *Models*. Polychrome borders are visible on the top, right, and bottom of the painting. The authors would like to thank Sylvie Patry, Barbara Buckley, and Anya Shutov for facilitating a close look at the painting at the Barnes Foundation, Philadelphia.

26. *Models, Small Sketch* is painted on a number 1 *figure* panel, with the standard size of 16 x 22 centimeters (the actual dimensions, listed in Françoise Cachin in *Georges Seurat, 1859–1891*, p. 289, no. 188, are 15.8 x 22 cm); illustrated in ibid., p. 288, no. 188. *Moored Boats and Trees* (1890; Philadelphia Museum of Art), also painted on a number 1 panel, has borders at top and bottom (in addition to a painted inner border around all sides of the composition), which in this case may have been inspired by the use of a shorter geometrical format, leaving unpainted space above and below.

27. For example, Seurat restretched the canvases for *La Grande Jatte* and the final sketch for it (The Metropolitan Museum of Art, 51.112.6). See, respectively, Fiedler, "*La Grande Jatte*," p. 202; and Zuccari and Langley, "Seurat's Working Process," p. 195n17. There is a range of opinion on the dating of Seurat's addition of painted borders to his works; see Semin, "Note sur Seurat et le cadre," p. 55, translated by Charlotte Hale: "Taking into account the borders on the right and left of *Poseuses* [the sketch] one could propose 1887 as the date when picture and border were conceived simultaneously"; see Herbert, "Appendix A," p. 376: "In 1888 Seurat began painting borders directly on his canvases rather than on an interior wood member, as he had done for *Poseuses* [the large painting], and in the final three years of his life he displayed his pictures with these borders as well as with frames." But in the catalogue entry for *The Eiffel Tower*, painted in January 1889, Herbert (in *Georges Seurat, 1859–1891*, p. 328, no. 210) remarks, "It may be the first border to have been conceived as part of a work from the beginning; the borders on paintings before 1889 were all added after the fact (except for the panel for *Poseuses* . . . , which has crude borders on two sides)." Dorra and Rewald (*Seurat: L'Oeuvre peint*, p. xvi) date the retrospective addition of borders to the time when Seurat's friend Félix Fénéon noted this innovation: autumn 1889. Clearly, this is an area that needs further study, one that would benefit particularly from technical examination.

28. On the lukewarm reception of the painting, see Thomson, "Seurat's *Circus Sideshow*: A *Parade* of Paradoxes," in this volume, pp. 82–84.

29. On the influence of Wagner's ideas on Seurat, see ibid., p. 75; see also Smith, *Seurat and the Avant-Garde*, pp. 105–56.

30. Aviva Burnstock and Karen Serres, "Seurat's Hidden Self-Portrait," in "Art in France," special issue, *Burlington Magazine* 156, no. 1333 (April 2014), pp. 240–42. Our thanks to Emmelyn Butterfield-Rosen for making this connection.

31. Michelle Foa (*Seurat*, pp. 110–11) discusses the relationship between frames and signatures.

Seurat is handsomely represented in The Met's collection by two dozen works, thanks to the generosity of ten donors and six curatorial purchases. Fifty years in the making, these holdings were initiated in 1951, with the artist's final *Study for "A Sunday on La Grande Jatte"* from the bequest of Sam A. Lewisohn (51.112.6), and most recently extended with a landscape painting of the same site, *Gray Weather, Grande Jatte*, from the 2002 bequest of Walter H. Annenberg (2002.62.3). The contents comprise a total of nine paintings (four easel-size and five small oils on panel, or *croquetons*, to use Seurat's term) and fifteen drawings (twelve in conté crayon from his maturity and three graphite studies dating to his youth).

Of admirable quality and unrivaled breadth, the collection affords a vivid sense of the pace of Seurat's accomplishment. Drawings take us from the mid-1870s, when the classically trained teenage student challenged his pencil to meet Ingres's pure line, to his authoritative mastery of conté crayon in richly tonal works of the 1880s that are more heir to Rembrandt's wizardry in their magical sleight of hand. Paintings span nearly the same range. Anchored by his first plein-air studies on both canvas and panel, they chart his sure-footed path from forests redolent of Barbizon and riverbanks on the fringes of Impressionist Paris to urban scenes that distill the pulse of modern life into timeless freeze-frame images. — SAS

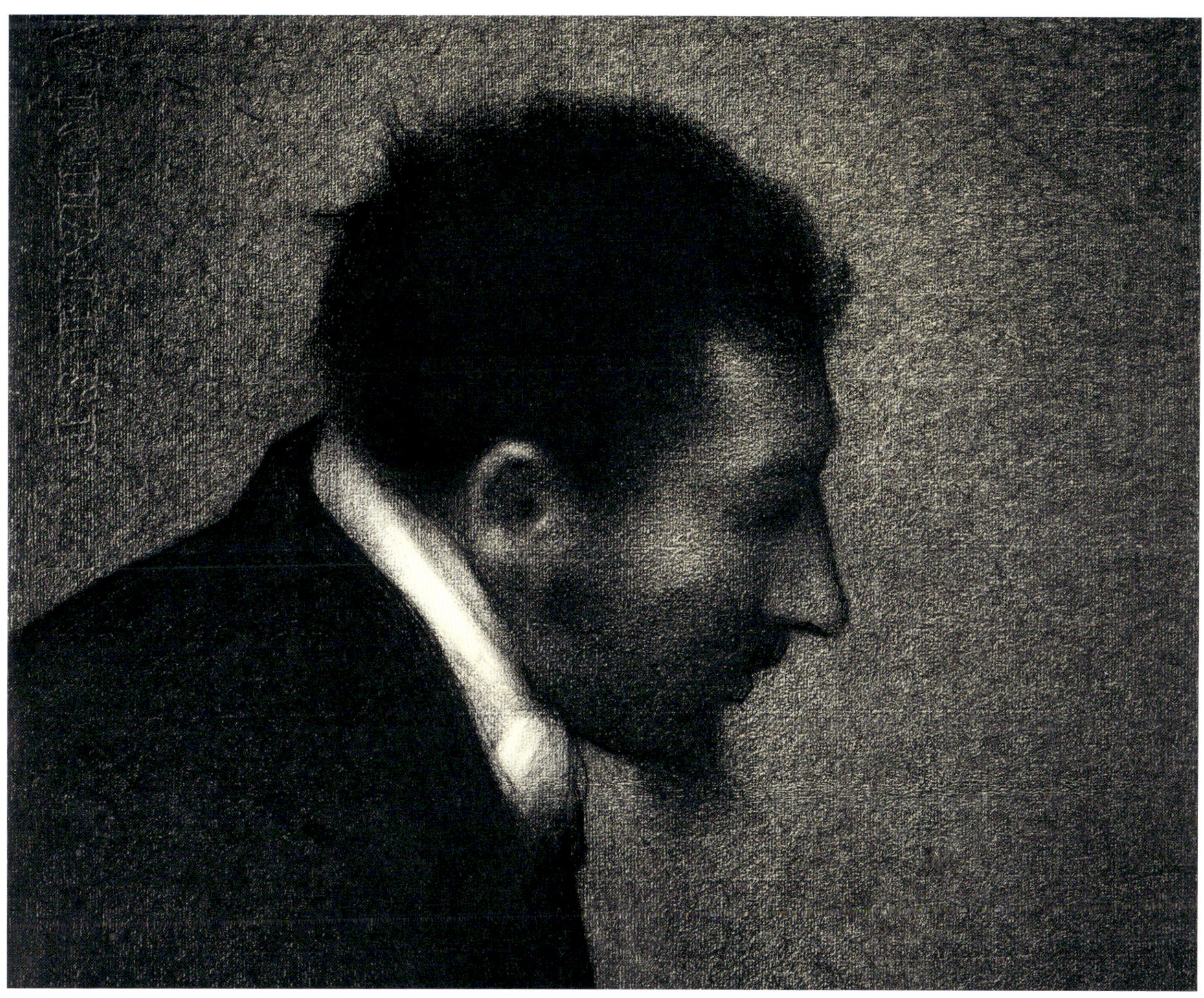

CHECKLIST

GEORGES SEURAT

Georges Seurat (French, 1859–1891)
Circus Sideshow (*Parade de cirque*),
1887–88
Oil on canvas
39 ¼ x 59 in. (99.7 x 149.9 cm)
The Metropolitan Museum of Art,
New York
Bequest of Stephen C. Clark, 1960
(61.101.17)
Fig. 1

Models (*Poseuses*), small version, 1887–88
Oil on canvas
15 ½ x 19 ¼ in. (39.5 x 49 cm)
Private collection
Fig. 49

Study for "Models," 1886–87
Conté crayon on paper
11 ¾ x 8 ⅞ in. (29.7 x 22.5 cm)
The Metropolitan Museum of Art,
New York
Robert Lehman Collection, 1975
(1975.1.704)
Fig. 50

Sidewalk Show (*Une Parade*), ca. 1883–84
Conté crayon on paper
12 ⅝ x 9 ⅝ in. (32.1 x 24.5 cm)
The Phillips Collection, Washington, D.C.
Fig. 51

The Saltimbanques, ca. 1886
Conté crayon on paper
9 ½ x 12 ¼ in. (24.1 x 31.1 cm)
Private collection, New York
Fig. 52

Pierrot and Colombine, ca. 1886–88
Conté crayon on paper
9 ¾ x 12 ⅜ in. (24.8 x 31.2 cm)
Kasama Nichido Museum of Art
Fig. 53

Two Clowns (*Une Parade*), ca. 1886–88
Conté crayon on paper
9 ¼ x 12 ⅛ in. (23.3 x 30.8 cm)
Fine Arts Museums of San Francisco
Museum purchase, Archer M. Huntington
Fund
Fig. 54

Dancer with a Cane, ca. 1888–90
Conté crayon on paper
12 ⅛ x 9 ⅛ in. (30.7 x 23.2 cm)
Private collection
Fig. 55

The Tree, 1887–88
Conté crayon on paper
11 ⅞ x 9 ½ in. (30 x 24 cm)
Private collection
Fig. 56

Trombonist, 1887–88
Conté crayon with white chalk on paper
12 ¼ x 9 ⅜ in. (31.1 x 23.8 cm)
Philadelphia Museum of Art
The Henry P. McIlhenny Collection in
memory of Frances P. McIlhenny, 1986
Fig. 57

Ferdinand Corvi and Pony, 1887–88
Conté crayon on paper
11 ⅝ x 8 ⅝ in. (29.5 x 22 cm)
Private collection
Fig. 58

A Shop and Two Figures, ca. 1882
Colored crayon on paper
5 ⅞ x 9 ¼ in. (14.9 x 23.5 cm)
Solomon R. Guggenheim Museum,
New York
The Hilla Rebay Collection
Fig. 68

Eden Concert, ca. 1886–87
Conté crayon, gouache, chalk, and ink on
paper
11 ⅝ x 8 ⅞ in. (29.5 x 22.5 cm).
Van Gogh Museum, Amsterdam (Vincent
van Gogh Foundation)
Fig. 74

At the Gaîté Rochechouart, ca. 1887–88
Conté crayon with gouache on paper
12 x 9 ¼ in. (30.5 x 23.5 cm)
Museum of Art, Rhode Island School of
Design
Gift of Mrs. Murray S. Danforth
Fig. 75

At the Divan Japonais, ca. 1887–88
Conté crayon on paper
12 ⅜ x 9 ¼ in. (31.5 x 23.5 cm)
Private collection
Fig. 76

High C (*Forte Chanteuse*), ca. 1887–88
Conté crayon and white gouache on paper
11 ⅞ x 9 ⅛ in. (30 x 23 cm)
Private collection
Fig. 77

At the Concert Européen, ca. 1887–88
Conté crayon and gouache on paper
12 ¼ x 9 ⅜ in. (31.1 x 23.8 cm)
The Museum of Modern Art, New York
Lillie P. Bliss Collection, 1934
Fig. 78

At the Concert Parisien, ca. 1887–88
Conté crayon and white chalk on paper
12 ⅜ x 9 ¼ in. (31.4 x 23.6 cm)
The Cleveland Museum of Art
Leonard C. Hanna, Jr. Fund
Fig. 79

Louis Anquetin (French, 1861–1932)
Avenue de Clichy (Street — Five O'clock in the Evening), 1887
Oil on paper, laid down on canvas
27 ⅛ x 21 in. (69.2 x 53.5 cm)
Wadsworth Atheneum Museum of Art,
Hartford, Connecticut
The Ella Gallup Sumner and Mary Catlin
Sumner Collection Fund
Fig. 83

Emile Bernard (French, 1868–1941)
Saltimbanques, 1887
Oil on canvas
25 ⅝ x 19 ⅜ in. (65 x 49 cm)
Museo de Bellas Artes Juan Manuel
Blanes, Montevideo
Fig. 82

Emile Bernard
At Le Tabarin, 1888–89
Oil on canvas
10 ⅝ x 24 ½ in. (27 x 62.2 cm)
Mr. and Mrs. Barron U. Kidd
Fig. 92

Charles-Albert Arnoux Bertall (French,
1820–1882)
Saltimbanques, from *Le Diable à Paris*,
vol. II (Paris, 1846), p. 161
Wood engraving
The Metropolitan Museum of Art,
New York
Gift of Mrs. Edwin De T. Bechtel, 1961
(61.538.4.2)
Fig. 20

Charles-Albert Arnoux Bertall
The Fair of Ideas, from *Le Journal pour
rire*, October 14, 1848
Lithograph
The Morgan Library and Museum,
New York
Purchased on the Gordon N. Ray Fund,
2007
Fig. 21

Pierre Bonnard (French, 1867–1947)
Fairground Sideshow (Parade), ca. 1892
Oil on cardboard, laid down on parquet
board
14 ⅜ x 11 in. (36.5 x 28 cm)
Private collection, courtesy Luc Bellier
Fig. 100

Pierre Bonnard
Illustration for *Fairground Stall (La
Baraque)*, from Claude Terrasse, *Petites
scènes familières* (musical compositions),
1895, p. 41
Lithograph
Image: 4 ⅛ x 8 ½ in. (10.6 x 21.7 cm)
The Museum of Modern Art, New York
Gift of Abby Aldrich Rockefeller, 1948
Fig. 101

Gabriel Boutet (French, 1848–1900)
The Fair at Montrouge, 1885
Oil on canvas
31 ½ x 23 ¾ in. (80 x 60.3 cm)
Scott and Nicole Mather
Fig. 26

Jules Chéret (French, 1836–1933)
Folies-Bergère: Corvi Circus, 1881
Color lithograph
22 ⅞ x 16 ⅞ in. (58 x 43 cm)
Bibliothèque Nationale de France, Paris
Fig. 41

Honoré Daumier (French, 1808–1879)
Saltimbanques, ca. 1866–67
Charcoal, pen and ink, wash, watercolor,
and conté crayon on paper
13 ¼ x 15 ⅝ in. (33.7 x 39.7 cm)
Victoria and Albert Museum, London
Bequeathed by C. A. Ionides
Fig. 8

Honoré Daumier
The Sideshow (La Parade), ca. 1865–66
Charcoal, pen and ink, gray wash,
watercolor, gouache, and conté crayon on
paper
17 ¼ x 13 ¼ in. (43.8 x 33.7 cm)
Private collection
Fig. 9

Honoré Daumier
*The Sideshow (La Parade de
saltimbanques)*, ca. 1865
Watercolor, charcoal, pen and ink, and
chalk on paper
10 ¼ x 13 ⅝ in. (26 x 34.6 cm)
Hammer Museum, Los Angeles
The Armand Hammer Daumier and
Contemporaries Collection, Gift of the
Armand Hammer Foundation
Fig. 10

Honoré Daumier
The Saltimbanques Changing Place,
ca. 1866–67
Charcoal, gray wash, watercolor, and
conté crayon on paper
15 ⅞ x 12 ½ in. (40.3 x 31.9 cm)
Wadsworth Atheneum Museum of Art,
Hartford, Connecticut
The Ella Gallup Sumner and Mary Catlin
Sumner Collection Fund
Fig. 11

Honoré Daumier
The Strong Man, ca. 1865
Oil on wood
10 ⅝ x 13 ⅞ in. (27 x 35.2 cm)
The Phillips Collection, Washington, D.C.
Fig. 12

Honoré Daumier
Sideshow (Parade de saltimbanques),
ca. 1860–64
Oil on wood
9 ⅞ x 13 in. (25 x 33 cm)
Private collection
Fig. 13

Honoré Daumier
*Bring Down the Curtain; the Farce Is Over
(Baissez le rideau, la farce est jouée)*, from
La Caricature, September 11, 1834
Lithograph
10 ⅛ x 13 ¼ in. (25.8 x 33.8 cm)
The Metropolitan Museum of Art,
New York
Gift of Louise S. Bechtel, 1958
(58.580.38)
Fig. 14

Honoré Daumier
*Here You See the Great Celebrities of
Literary, Musical, and Artistic France;
They Are Thirty-Six Feet Tall — Measured
below Sea Level (Vous voyez ici les grandes
célébrités de la France littéraire, musicale et
artistique, ils ont tous 36 pieds au dessous
du niveau de la mer)*, from *La Caricature*,
April 28, 1839
Lithograph, second state of four
12 ½ x 9 ⅞ in. (31.8 x 25 cm)
The Metropolitan Museum of Art,
New York
The Elisha Whittelsey Collection,
The Elisha Whittelsey Fund, 1962
(62.650.476)
Fig. 15

Honoré Daumier
Sideshow (Parade) of "Le Charivari,"
from *Le Charivari*, January 6, 1839
Lithograph, second state of three
14 ⅝ x 10 ⅛ in. (37.1 x 25.6 cm)
The Metropolitan Museum of Art,
New York
The Elisha Whittelsey Collection,
The Elisha Whittelsey Fund, 1962
(62.650.243)
Fig. 16

Louis Philibert Debucourt (French,
1755–1832)
*Drum-Major and Sapper from the Parisian
National Guard*, after Carle Vernet, 1814
Hand-colored aquatint
Image: 13 ⅞ x 9 ⅝ in. (35.1 x 24.4 cm)
Bibliothèque Nationale de France, Paris
Fig. 64

Léon Dehesghues (French, 1852–1910)
*The Fair at Neuilly — "Let's go and see
Marseille" ("Allons chez Marseille")*, 1884
Oil on canvas
50 x 80 in. (127 x 203.2 cm)
Allan Charles, Baltimore
Fig. 25

Georges de Feure (French, 1868–1943)
The Corvi Circus (Le Cirque Corvi),
ca. 1893
Gouache, watercolor, and pencil on paper
15 ⅝ x 16 in. (39.5 x 40.5 cm)
Sterling and Francine Clark Art Institute,
Williamstown, Massachusetts
Fig. 99

Jean-Louis Forain (French, 1852–1931)
Tight-Rope Walker, ca. 1885
Oil on canvas
18 ⅛ x 15 in. (46.2 x 38.2 cm)
The Art Institute of Chicago
Gift of Mrs. Emily Crane Chadbourne
Fig. 27

J. J. Grandville (French, 1803–1847) and
Auguste Desperret (French, 1804–1865)
*Zing! Zing! Boom_Boom_Boom!!! The
Show of the Grrrreat Political Tumblers
(Zin ! zin ! baoun_baoun_baoun !! _zin
! baoun ! zin ! baoun ! zin_zin_zin ! . . .
. . . . Entrrrrrrrrrrrrez, messieurrrrs
et dames ! venez, venez, venez voirrrr ici
dedans les grrrands sauteurrrs politiques
qui font l'admirrration de tous les
souverrrains de l'eurrrope, c'est l'instant,
c'est la minute, ça va finirrrr !)*, from
L'Association mensuelle, August 1833
Lithograph
14 ¼ x 21 ⅝ in. (36.2 x 54.9 cm)
The Metropolitan Museum of Art,
New York
Bequest of Edwin De T. Bechtel, 1957
(57.650.623[14])
Fig. 19

Eugène Grasset (Swiss, 1845–1917)
The Sideshow (La Parade), from *Paris
illustré*, February 1, 1887
Chromotypogravure
17 ¼ x 12 ¾ in. (43.8 x 32.4 cm)
The Metropolitan Museum of Art, New
York, Thomas J. Watson Library
Gift of Friends of Watson Library
Fig. 29

Henri Gray (French, 1858–1924)
The Saltimbanques, Cirque d'Hiver, 1892
Color lithograph
50 x 36 in. (127 x 91.5 cm)
Zimmerli Art Museum at Rutgers
University
Museum Purchase
Fig. 93

Paul Hadol (attributed) (French,
1835–1875)
*The Sideshow (La Parade: Théâtre
Badinguet)*, 1871
Hand-colored lithograph
22 ⅛ x 31 ⅛ in. (56.1 x 79.1 cm)
Musée Carnavalet — Histoire de Paris
Fig. 22

Louis Hayet (French, 1864–1940)
At the Café-Concert, 1888
Gouache over pencil on paper
6 ⅜ x 8 in. (16.2 x 20.3 cm)
Private collection
Fig. 87

Louis Hayet
Color Wheel, 1886
Watercolor and gouache on paper, laid
down on board
Diam. 10 ¼ in. (26 cm)
The Ashmolean Museum, Oxford
Presented by John Rewald, 1979
Fig. 88

Louis Hayet
Fair at Night (Fête foraine la nuit),
1888–89
Oil on cardboard, laid down on wood
7 ⅝ x 10 ⅝ in. (19.5 x 27 cm)
Musée Camille Pissarro, Pontoise
Fig. 89

Louis Hayet
*Fair at Night, the Sideshow (Fête foraine
la nuit, la parade)*, 1888
Oil on canvas
28 ¾ x 36 ¼ in. (73 x 92 cm)
Association des Amis du Petit Palais,
Geneva
Fig. 90

Oswald Heidbrinck (French, 1860–1914)
At the Gingerbread Fair, from *Le Courrier
français*, May 1, 1887
Photomechanical print
15 ⅞ x 22 ¼ in. (40.2 x 56.6 cm)
Zimmerli Art Museum at Rutgers
University
Museum Purchase
Fig. 4

Oswald Heidbrinck
The Three Fat Men (Les Trois Gras), from
Le Courrier français, July 1, 1888
Photomechanical print
16 x 11 ¼ in. (40.5 x 28.5 cm)
Zimmerli Art Museum at Rutgers
University
Museum Purchase
Fig. 30

Henri-Gabriel Ibels (French, 1867–1936)
Program for *The Grapnel (Le Grappin)*
and *The Emancipated (L'Affranchie)* at
the Théâtre Libre, 1892
Color lithograph
9 ½ x 12 ⅝ in. (24 x 32 cm)
Zimmerli Art Museum at Rutgers
University
Museum Purchase
Fig. 95

Henri-Gabriel Ibels
Mademoiselle Olympe, 1893
Pastel over charcoal on paper
21 x 6 ¾ in. (53.3 x 17 cm)
Zimmerli Art Museum at Rutgers
University
Museum Purchase, Lillian Lilien
Memorial Art Acquisition Fund
Fig. 96

Henri-Gabriel Ibels
*Mademoiselle Olympe from the
Folies-Bergère in Paris! in other words,
from the Alcazar in Bordeaux!!!*
(*Mademoiselle Olympe de Folies-Bergère
de Paris! en un mot, de l'alcazar de
Bordeaux!!!*), from *Les Demi-cabots*
(Paris, 1896), p. 226
Lithograph
Zimmerli Art Museum at Rutgers
University
Museum Purchase, Norma B. Bartman
Research Library Fund
Fig. 97

Henri-Gabriel Ibels
Four Strong Men, from the portfolio
Les Forains, ca. 1894
Etching
Image: 4 ½ x 5 ⅜ in. (11.4 x 13.5 cm)
Zimmerli Art Museum at Rutgers
University
Museum Purchase, David A. and Mildred
H. Morse Acquisition Fund

Henri-Gabriel Ibels
Sideshow (*Parade*) from the portfolio
Les Forains, ca. 1894
Etching
Image: 5 ⅜ x 4 ¾ in. (13.5 x 12.1 cm)
Zimmerli Art Museum at Rutgers
University
Museum Purchase, David A. and Mildred
H. Morse Art Acquisition Fund

Henri-Gabriel Ibels
Pierrefort, 1897
Color lithograph
24 ¼ x 31 ⅝ in. (61.6 x 80.3 cm)
Mr. and Mrs. Jack Rennert, New York
Fig. 98

Kobayashi Kiyochika (Japanese, 1847–
1915)
Fireworks at Ikenohata, 1881
Polychrome woodblock print; ink and
color on paper
9 ¼ x 13 ½ in. (23.5 x 34.3 cm)
The Metropolitan Museum of Art,
New York
Gift of Miki and Sebastian Izzard, 2016
(2016.577)
Fig. 66

Maximilien Luce (French, 1858–1941)
Paris: Boulevard at Night, ca. 1893
Oil on paper, laid down on canvas
17 ¾ x 13 ⅛ in. (45.1 x 33.2 cm)
Museo Soumaya. Fundación Carlos Slim,
Mexico City
Fig. 91

Adolphe Monticelli (French, 1824–1886)
Sideshow (*La Parade des saltimbanques*),
ca. 1877
Oil on wood
14 ⅝ x 19 in. (37 x 48.1 cm)
Musée Grobet-Labadié, Marseille
Fig. 33

Felicien Myrbach (Austrian, 1853–1940)
The Gingerbread Fair, from *Paris illustré*,
July 1, 1884
Gillotage
17 ¼ x 12 ¾ in. (43.8 x 32.4 cm)
The Metropolitan Museum of Art, New
York, Thomas J. Watson Library
Gift of Friends of Watson Library
Fig. 34

Fernand Pelez (French, 1848–1913)
*Grimaces and Misery — The
Saltimbanques*, 1888
Oil on canvas, in five sections
87 ⅜ in. x 20 ft. 6 ⅞ in. (222 x 627 cm)
Petit Palais, Musée des Beaux-Arts de la
Ville de Paris
Collection Dutuit
Fig. 31

Octave Penguilly-L'Haridon (French,
1811–1870)
*Sideshow (Parade): Pierrot Presents His
Companions Harlequin and Polichinelle to
the Crowd*, 1846
Oil on wood
10 ⅝ x 18 in. (27 x 45.8 cm)
Musées de Poitiers
Fig. 17

Edouard Pépin (pseudonym of Claude
Guillaumin) (French, 1842–1927)
The Troupe's Last Shows (*Les Dernières
Représentations de la troupe*), from
Le Grelot, August 19, 1888
Color lithograph
19 ⅛ x 25 ¾ in. (48.5 x 65.5 cm)
New York State Library, Albany
Fig. 24

Pablo Picasso (Spanish, 1881–1973)
Fairground Stall, 1900
Oil on canvas
15 x 18 ¼ in. (38.1 x 46.3 cm)
Museu Picasso, Barcelona
Barcelona Culture Foundation acquisition,
2005
Fig. 106

Lucien Pissarro (French, 1863–1944)
At the Café-Concert, 1888
Watercolor and gouache on silk
7 ¼ x 8 ⅞ in. (18.4 x 22.5 cm)
The British Museum, London
Fig. 86

Charles Simon Pradier (French, 1783–
1847)
Tu Marcellus Eris, after Jean Auguste
Dominique Ingres, 1832
Etching and engraving
30 ⅛ x 22 ⅝ in. (76.5 x 57.4 cm)
The Metropolitan Museum of Art,
New York
Gift of Joseph Verner Reed, 1950
(50.576.5)
Fig. 65

Maurice Prendergast (American,
1858–1924)
Circus Band, ca. 1895
Color monotype with pencil additions
12 ⅜ x 9 ½ in. (31.4 x 23.9 cm)
Max N. Berry
Fig. 102

Maurice Prendergast
Girl with Drum, ca. 1895
Color monotype with pencil additions
10 ⅜ x 9 ⅛ in. (26.4 x 23.1 cm)
Max N. Berry
Fig. 103

Jean-François Raffaëlli (French, 1850–1924)
Saltimbanques — The Sideshow Orchestra (*Les Saltimbanques — L'Orchestre en parade*), ca. 1884
Oil on paper, laid down on canvas
15 x 21 ⅝ in. (38 x 55 cm)
Private collection
Fig. 28

Auguste Raffet (French, 1804–1860)
Title page, *Album lithographique*, 1835
Lithograph
10 ¾ x 15 ⅛ in. (27.3 x 38.5 cm)
The Metropolitan Museum of Art, New York
Gift of Mrs. Edwin De T. Bechtel, 1961 (61.538.2)
Fig. 18

Georges Redon (French, 1869–1943)
Champ de Foire: 25, rue Fontaine, 1897
Color lithograph
25 ⅝ x 33 ⅞ in. (65 x 86 cm)
Bibliothèque Nationale de France, Paris
Fig. 94

Rembrandt (Rembrandt van Rijn) (Dutch, 1606–1669)
Christ Presented to the People, 1655
Drypoint, fourth state of eight
14 ⅜ x 17 ⅞ in. (36.4 x 45.4 cm)
The Metropolitan Museum of Art, New York
Gift of Felix M. Warburg and his family, 1941 (41.1.35)
Fig. 63

Henri Rivière (French, 1864–1951)
Illustration for *Pride* (*L'Orgueil*), from *La Tentation de Saint-Antoine* (Paris, 1888), p. 25
Stencil-colored photorelief
9 ⅞ x 12 ⅝ in. (25 x 32 cm)
Charles Deering McCormick Library of Special Collections, Northwestern University Libraries
Fig. 67

Albert Robida (French, 1848–1926)
1879! Grand Sideshow with Beating Tom-Toms, Animals' Screeches, and Various Music (*1879! Grande Parade avec coups de tam-tam, cris d'animaux, et musiques variées*), supplement to *La Caricature*, January 3, 1880
Color lithograph
12 x 44 ⅜ in. (30.3 x 112.5 cm)
Charles Deering McCormick Library of Special Collections, Northwestern University Libraries
Fig. 23

Georges Rouault (French, 1871–1958)
Sideshow (*Parade*), 1907–10
Watercolor, oil, ink, and pastel on paper, laid down on canvas
25 ⅝ x 38 ⅛ in. (65 x 100 cm)
Centre Pompidou, Paris, Musée National d'Art Moderne/Centre de Création Industrielle
Gift of Mme Rouault and her children, 1959
Fig. 107

Marcel Roux (French, 1878–1922)
The Fair: Those Death Takes by Surprise (*La Fête: Ceux qu'elle surprend*), from *Danse macabre*, 1905
Intaglio and etching
17 ¾ x 22 ⅞ in. (45 x 58.2 cm)
Bibliothèque Municipale de Lyon
Fig. 104

Marcel Roux
The Fair: Those Death Takes by Surprise (*La Fête: Ceux qu'elle surprend*), 1905
Charcoal and chalk on paper
8 ¼ x 11 ⅛ in. (20.8 x 28.1 cm)
Bibliothèque Municipale de Lyon
Fig. 105

Paul Signac (French, 1863–1935)
Place de Clichy, 1887
Oil on wood
10 ¾ x 14 in. (27.3 x 35.6 cm)
The Metropolitan Museum of Art, New York
Robert Lehman Collection, 1975 (1975.1.210)
Fig. 84

Paul Signac
Application of Charles Henry's Chromatic Circle
Théâtre-Libre playbill of January 31, 1889
Color lithograph
6 ⅛ x 7 ⅛ in. (15.5 x 18 cm)
The Metropolitan Museum of Art, New York
Purchase, Reba and Dave Williams Gift, 1990 (1990.1056)

ADDITIONAL CONTEXTUAL MATERIAL

Geoffroy et Cie, Gien
The Open-Air Sideshow (*La Parade en plein-vent*)
Child's plate, ca. 1850
Transfer-printed earthenware
Diam. 7 ⅞ in. (20 cm)
The Metropolitan Museum of Art, New York
Funds from various donors, 2016 (2016.564)
Fig. 36a

Ernest Buval
Cover for *Les Saltimbanques: Opéra comique* (musical score), ca. 1899
The Metropolitan Museum of Art, New York
Fig. 36c

ILLUSTRATED BOOKS AND JOURNALS

Arsène Alexandre
Honoré Daumier: L'Homme et l'oeuvre (Paris, 1888)
The Metropolitan Museum of Art, New York, Thomas J. Watson Library
Jacob S. Rogers Fund

Clement-August Andrieux
The Gingerbread Fair (*La Foire au pain d'épice — Une Baraque de saltimbanque à la Barrière du Trône*), from *Le Journal illustré*, April 15–22, 1866
Wood engraving
14 ⅞ x 11 in. (37.8 x 28 cm)
The Metropolitan Museum of Art, New York

Paul Avril
Illustration of sunshades at the
Gingerbread Fair, from Octave Uzanne,
The Sunshade, the Glove, the Muff
(London, 1884), p. 61
Tinted photogravure
The Metropolitan Museum of Art,
New York, Thomas J. Watson Library
Gift of Sophie B. Steel

Charles Blanc
*Grammaire des arts du dessin: Architecture,
sculpture, peinture* (Paris, 1876)
The Metropolitan Museum of Art,
New York, Thomas J. Watson Library
Jacob S. Rogers Fund
Fig. 71

Eugène Courboin
*Fair at the Tuileries — Clowns and
Saltimbanques*, from *Paris illustré,*
August 26, 1883
Gillotage
17 ¼ x 25 ½ in. (43.8 x 64.8 cm)
The Metropolitan Museum of Art,
New York, Thomas J. Watson Library
Gift of Friends of Watson Library

Gaston Escudier
Les Saltimbanques: Leur Vie, leurs moeurs
(Paris, 1875)
Zimmerli Art Museum at Rutgers
University
Museum Purchase, Norma B. Bartman
Research Library Fund
Fig. 38

Alexandre Ferdinandus (pseudonym)
*Paris — The Gingerbread Fair (La Foire
aux pains d'épice)*, from *Le Journal
illustré*, April 8, 1877
Wood engraving
14 ⅞ x 11 in. (37.7 x 28 cm)
The Metropolitan Museum of Art,
New York
Fig. 36b

Edmond-Emile Gotorbe
Recollections of Bastille Day Fairs, from
L'Univers illustré, July 31, 1880
Wood engraving
15 ¾ x 11 ⅛ in. (40 x 28.2 cm)
The Metropolitan Museum of Art,
New York
Fig. 37

John Grand-Carteret
Les Moeurs et la caricature en France
(Paris, 1888)
The Metropolitan Museum of Art, New
York, Thomas J. Watson Library
Gift of Jane E. Andrews

Frédéric de Haenen
*At the Gingerbread Fair — The Athletic
Arena (À la Foire au pain d'épice —
L'Arène athlétique)*, from *Le Monde
illustré*, April 21, 1883
Wood engraving
14 ⅝ x 10 ½ in. (37 x 26.5 cm)
The Metropolitan Museum of Art,
New York

Hugues Le Roux
Les Jeux du cirque et la vie foraine
(Paris, 1889)
The Metropolitan Museum of Art, New
York, Irene Lewisohn Costume Reference
Library
Gift of The New York City Ballet from
the Library of Barbara Karinska
Fig. 3

Daniel Vierge
*Paris — The Gingerbread Fair (La Foire
au pain d'épice)*, from *Le Monde illustré*,
April 19, 1873
Wood engraving
14 ⅝ x 10 ½ in. (37 x 26.5 cm)
The Metropolitan Museum of Art,
New York

Hermann Vogel
*At the Gingerbread Fair (A la foire au pain
d'épice)*, from *Revue illustrée*, 1889/90
Wood engraving
9 ¼ x 12 ½ in. (23.4 x 31.8 cm)
The Metropolitan Museum of Art,
New York

Paris illustré, No. 15, "Les Fêtes foraines"
("Traveling Fairs"), July 1, 1884
The Metropolitan Museum of Art,
New York, Thomas J. Watson Library
Gift of Friends of Watson Library

*The University Taking Advantage of
the Gingerbread Fair to Display the
Results of Its Physical Education System
(L'Université profitant de la Foire au pain
d'épices pour y exhiber les résultats de son
système d'éducation physique)*, from *Le
Charivari*, April 4, 1890
Lithograph
16 ⅛ x 11 ⅝ in. (40.9 x 29.3 cm)
The Metropolitan Museum of Art,
New York

PRINTS, POSTERS, AND POSTCARDS

L. Isoré
Ferdinand Corvi, Jr. (M. Fd Corvi Fils),
ca. 1882
Lithograph
9 ⅝ x 9 in. (24.5 x 22.7 cm)
Musée Carnavalet — Histoire de Paris
Fig. 42

Affiches Américaines, Charles Lévy
(printer)
*Fair at the Tuileries: F. Corvi's Miniature
Theater-Circus*, ca. 1882–88
Color lithograph
43 ⅛ x 33 ⅛ in. (109.5 x 84 cm)
Musée Carnavalet — Histoire de Paris
Fig. 43

Affiches Américaines, Charles Lévy
(printer)
*Fair at the Tuileries: F. Corvi's Miniature
Theater-Circus*, ca. 1882–88
Color lithograph
22 ¾ x 16 ½ in. (57.9 x 42 cm)
Musée Carnavalet — Histoire de Paris
Fig. 44

Affiches Américaines, Charles Lévy
(printer)
Corvi: We're Here!, ca. 1882–88
Color lithograph
15 ½ x 21 ¾ in. (39.4 x 55.2 cm)
Musée Carnavalet — Histoire de Paris
Fig. 45

The Corvi Circus at the fair at Neuilly,
ca. 1900
Postcard
The Metropolitan Museum of Art,
New York
Fig. 40

Sideshow at the Gingerbread Fair, Paris
(*Parade à la Foire au pain d'épices*),
ca. 1900
Stereoscopic postcard
The Metropolitan Museum of Art,
New York

Traveling fair: sideshow musicians (*Fête
foraine: Musiciens à la parade*), ca. 1900
Postcard
The Metropolitan Museum of Art,
New York

Traveling fair: sideshow (*Fête foraine:
La Parade*), ca. 1900
Postcard
The Metropolitan Museum of Art,
New York

Traveling fair: sideshow wrestlers (*Fête
foraine: Parade des lutteurs*), ca. 1900
Postcard
The Metropolitan Museum of Art,
New York

MUSICAL INSTRUMENTS

F. Besson, Paris
Cornet in B-Flat, Three Périnet Valves,
ca. 1915
Silver-plated brass
The Metropolitan Museum of Art,
New York
Promised gift of David Lessen from
the collection developed by Dr. Martin
Lessen, 2016

Buffet Crampon et Cie, Paris
Clarinet in A, Boehm System, ca. 1860–65
Stained-boxwood body with brass keys
The Metropolitan Museum of Art,
New York
Purchase, Robert Alonzo Lehman
Bequest, 2002 (2002.343)

Gautrot aîné, Paris
Clarinet in B-Flat, Thirteen-Key Müller
System, ca. 1900–1915
Cocus-wood body with nickel-silver keys
and ferrules
The Metropolitan Museum of Art,
New York
The Crosby Brown Collection of Musical
Instruments, 1889 (89.4.2349)

Charles Joseph Sax, Brussels
Alto Ophicleide in E-Flat, Nine Keys,
ca. 1845
Brass
The Metropolitan Museum of Art,
New York
The Crosby Brown Collection of Musical
Instruments, 1889 (89.4.2719)

Jérôme Thibouville-Lamy, Paris
Clarinet in C, ca. 1866–88
Boxwood body with nickel-silver keywork
and ivory ferrules
The Metropolitan Museum of Art,
New York
Gift of William J. Maynard, 1997
(1997.219.1)

Jérôme Thibouville-Lamy, Paris
Contrabass Trombone, ca. 1880
Brass
The Metropolitan Museum of Art,
New York
The Crosby Brown Collection of Musical
Instruments, 1889 (89.4.2071)

Alto Saxhorn, Three Berlin Valves,
probably French, ca. 1860
Brass
The Metropolitan Museum of Art,
New York
The Crosby Brown Collection of Musical
Instruments, 1889 (89.4.2177)

Adam, Paul. "Les Impressionnistes à l'exposition des indépendants." *La Vie moderne* 10 (April 15, 1888), pp. 228–29.

Becker, Christoph, and Julia Burckhardt Bild. *Georges Seurat: Figure in Space.* With contributions by Gottfried Boehm, Michelle Foa, and Wilhelm Genazino. Exh. cat., Kunsthaus, Zurich; and Schirn Kunsthalle Frankfurt, 2009–10. Ostfildern: Hatje Cantz, 2009.

Blanc, Charles. *Grammaire des arts du dessin: Architecture, sculpture, peinture.* 4th ed. Paris: Renouard, 1882. First published 1867.

Boime, Albert. *Revelation of Modernism: Responses to Cultural Crises in Fin-de-Siècle Painting.* Columbia: University of Missouri Press, 2008.

Christophe, Jules. "Le Néo-impressionnisme au pavillon de la ville de Paris." *Le Journal des artistes*, no. 19 (May 6, 1888), pp. 147–48.

Christophe, Jules. "Notices sur Georges Seurat: Le Peinture." *Les Hommes d'aujourd'hui* 8, no. 368 (April 1890).

Christophe, Jules. "Chromo-luminaristes: Georges Seurat." *La Plume* 3, no. 57 (September 1, 1891), p. 292.

Collet, Isabelle. "*Grimaces et misère*: Le Retour des peintures de Fernand Pelez au Petit Palais, Musée des Beaux-Arts de la Ville de Paris." *La Revue des musées de France: Revue du Louvre* 55, no. 5 (December 2005), pp. 70–77.

Collet, Isabelle, ed. *Fernand Pelez, 1848–1913: La Parade des humbles.* Exh. cat., 2009–10. Paris: Paris Musées; Petit Palais, 2009.

Conforti, Michael, James A. Ganz, Neil Harris, Sarah Lees, and Gilbert T. Vincent. *The Clark Brothers Collect: Impressionist and Early Modern Paintings.* With additional contributions by Daniel Cohen-McFall, Mari Yoko Hara, Susannah Maurer, Kathleen M. Morris, Kathryn Price, Richard Rand, and Marc Simpson. Exh. cat., Sterling and Francine Clark Art Institute, Williamstown, Mass., and The Metropolitan Museum of Art, New York, 2006–7. Williamstown, Mass.: Sterling and Francine Clark Art Institute, 2006.

Coquiot, Gustave. *Seurat.* Paris: A. Michel, 1924.

Crary, Jonathan. *Suspensions of Perception: Attention, Spectacle, and Modern Culture.* Cambridge, Mass., and London: MIT Press, 1999.

Crary, Jonathan. "Illuminations of Disenchantment: Seurat's *Parade de cirque.*" In *Seurat Re-viewed*, edited by Paul Smith, pp. 83–96. University Park: Pennsylvania State University Press, 2009.

Darzens, Rodolphe. "L'Exposition des indépendants." *La Revue moderne*, no. 57 (May 10, 1888), pp. 445–48.

Les Dessins de Georges Seurat (1859–1891). With an introduction by Gustave Kahn. 2 vols. Paris: Bernheim-Jeune, 1928. English ed.: *The Drawings of Georges Seurat.* With an introduction by Gustave Kahn. Translated by Stanley Appelbaum. New York: Dover Publications, 1971.

Dorra, Henri. "Japanese Sources for Two Paintings by Seurat." *Gazette des beaux-arts*, year 131, ser. 6, 114, no. 1448 (September 1989), pp. 95–99.

Dorra, Henri, and John Rewald. *Seurat: L'Oeuvre peint; Biographie et catalogue critique.* Paris: Les Beaux-Arts, 1959.

Dujardin, Edouard. "Aux XX et aux indépendants: Le Cloisonisme (1)." *La Revue indépendante* 6, no. 17 (March 1888), pp. 487–92.

Dulon, Guy, and Christophe Duvivier. *Louis Hayet, 1864–1940: Peintre et théoricien du néo-impressionnisme.* Exh. cat., Musée Tavet, Pontoise. Pontoise: Musée de Pontoise, 1991.

Faramond, Maurice de. "Les Artistes indépendants." *La Vie franco-russe*, no. 6 (March 24, 1888), p. 114.

Fénéon, Félix. *Oeuvres plus que complètes.* Edited by Joan Ungersma Halperin. Histoire des Idées et Critique Littéraire 107. Geneva: Droz, 1970.

First Loan Exhibition: Cézanne, Gauguin, Seurat, Van Gogh. With foreword by Alfred H. Barr Jr. Exh. cat. New York: Museum of Modern Art, 1929.

Foa, Michelle. *Georges Seurat: The Art of Vision.* New Haven and London: Yale University Press, 2015.

Foussier, E. *Rapport présenté par M. Foussier, au nom de la 2ᵉ commission, au sujet du roulement des fêtes foraines dans Paris.* Conseil Municipal de Paris 108. Paris: Conseil Municipal de Paris, 1895.

Fry, Roger. "Seurat's *La Parade.*" *Burlington Magazine* 55, no. 321 (December 1929), pp. 290–91, 293.

Gage, John. *Colour and Meaning: Art, Science and Symbolism.* London: Thames and Hudson, 1999.

Geffroy, Gustave. "Chronique: Pointillé-cloisonisme." *La Justice*, no. 3010 (April 11, 1888), p. 1.

Goldwater, Robert J. "Some Aspects of the Development of Seurat's Style." *Art Bulletin* 23, no. 2 (June 1941), pp. 117–30.

Halperin, Joan Ungersma. *Félix Fénéon: Aesthete and Anarchist in Fin-de-Siècle Paris.* With foreword by Germaine Brée. New Haven: Yale University Press, 1988.

Hauke, César M. de. *Seurat et son oeuvre.* 2 vols. Paris: Gründ, 1961.

Hauptman, Jodi. *Georges Seurat: The Drawings.* With essays by Karl Buchberg, Hubert Damisch, Bridget Riley, and Richard Thomson. Exh.

cat., 2007–8. New York: Museum of Modern Art, 2007.

Henry, Charles. *Cercle chromatique: Présentant tous les compléments et toutes les harmonies de couleurs avec une introduction sur la théorie générale de contraste, du rythme et de la mesure.* Paris: Charles Verdin, 1888.

Herbert, Robert L. *Seurat's Drawings.* New York: Shorewood, 1962.

Herbert, Robert L. "*Parade de cirque* de Seurat et l'esthétique de Charles Henry." *Revue de l'art* 50 (1981), pp. 9–23.

Herbert, Robert L., with Françoise Cachin, Anne Distel, Susan Alyson Stein, and Gary Tinterow. *Georges Seurat, 1859–1891.* Exh. cat., Grand Palais, Paris; and The Metropolitan Museum of Art, New York, 1991–92. New York: The Metropolitan Museum of Art, 1991.

Herbert, Robert L. *Seurat: Drawings and Paintings.* New Haven and London: Yale University Press, 2001.

Herbert, Robert L. *Seurat and the Making of La Grande Jatte.* With essay by Neil Harris. Exh. cat. Chicago: Art Institute of Chicago in association with the University of California Press, Berkeley, 2004.

Homburg, Cornelia. *Neo-Impressionism and the Dream of Realities: Painting, Poetry, Music.* With contributions by Laura D. Corey, Simon Kelly, Noelle C. Paulson, Christopher Riopelle, and Paul Smith. Exh. cat., Phillips Collection, Washington, D.C., 2014–15. New Haven: Yale University Press, 2014.

Hoschedé, Ernest. "Préface." In *Catalogue des oeuvres exposées, 1888: 4ᵉ exposition, pavillon de la ville de Paris — Champs-Elysées,* pp. 5–10. Paris: Société des Artistes Indépendants, 1888.

House, John. "Meaning in Seurat's Figure Paintings." *Art History* 3, no. 3 (September 1980), pp. 345–56.

Hutton, John Gary. *Neo-Impressionism and the Search for Solid Ground: Art, Science, and Anarchism in Fin-de-Siècle France.* Baton Rouge: Louisiana State University Press, 1994.

Jooren, Marieke, Suzanne Veldink, and Helewise Berger. *Seurat.* Exh. cat. Otterlo: Kröller-Müller Museum, 2014.

Kahn, Gustave. "Peinture: Exposition des indépendants." *La Revue indépendante* 7, no. 18 (April 1888), pp. 160–64.

Kahn, Gustave. "Seurat." *L'Art moderne* (Brussels) 11, no. 14 (April 5, 1891), pp. 107–10.

Lebensztejn, Jean-Claude. *Chahut.* Paris: Hazan, 1989.

Leighton, John, and Richard Thomson, with David Bomford, Jo Kirby, and Ashok Roy. *Seurat and the Bathers.* Exh. cat. London: National Gallery, 1997.

Le Men, Ségolène. *Seurat et Chéret: Le Peintre, le cirque et l'affiche.* 2nd ed. Paris: CNRS Editions, 2003.

Le Roux, Hugues. *Les Jeux du cirque et la vie foraine.* Paris: E. Plon, Nourrit, 1889.

Néo [Paul Signac]. "Quatrième exposition des artistes indépendants." *Le Cri du peuple,* March 29, 1888.

Pissarro, Camille. *Correspondance de Camille Pissarro.* Edited by Janine Bailly-Herzberg. With preface by Bernard Dorival. 2 vols. Paris: Presses Universitaires de France, 1980–86.

Ponchon, Raoul. "La Foire au pain d'épices." *Le Courrier français* 5, no. 16 (April 15, 1888), p. 3.

Rey, Robert. "Inventaire de l'atelier de Seurat, en 1891." In Robert Rey, *La Peinture française à la fin du XIXe siècle: La Renaissance du sentiment classique; Degas, Renoir, Gauguin, Cézanne, Seurat,* p. 144. Paris; G. van Oest, 1931.

Rosenblum, Robert. "Fernand Pelez, or the Other Side of the Post-Impressionist Coin." In *Art, the Ape of Nature: Studies in Honor of H. W. Janson,* edited by Moshe Barasch and Lucy Freeman Sandler, pp. 707–18. New York: H. N. Abrams; Englewood Cliffs, N.J.: Prentice-Hall, 1981.

Russell, John. *Seurat.* London: Thames and Hudson, 1965.

Smith, Paul. *Seurat and the Avant-Garde.* New Haven and London: Yale University Press, 1997.

Smith, Paul, ed. *Seurat Re-viewed.* University Park: Pennsylvania State University Press, 2009.

Sterling, Charles, and Margaretta M. Salinger. *French Paintings: A Catalogue of the Collection of The Metropolitan Museum of Art.* Vol. 3, *XIX–XX Centuries.* New York: The Metropolitan Museum of Art, 1967.

Thomson, Richard. *Seurat.* Oxford: Phaidon, 1985.

Thomson, Richard. "Seurat et la IIIe République: Opposant, caricaturiste ou supporter?" *48/14: La Revue du Musée d'Orsay,* no. 21 (Fall 2005), pp. 6–19.

Thomson, Richard. "The Imperatives of Style: Seurat's Drawings, 1886–1891." In Jodi Hauptman, *Georges Seurat: The Drawings,* pp. 169–83. Exh. cat., 2007–8. New York: Museum of Modern Art, 2007.

Thomson, Richard. *Art of the Actual: Naturalism and Style in Early Third Republic France, 1880–1900.* New Haven and London: Yale University Press, 2012.

Vallès, Jules. *Le Tableau de Paris.* Edited by Maxime Jourdan. Paris: Berg International, 2007.

Zimmermann, Michael F. *Seurat and the Art Theory of His Time.* Translated by Patricia Crampton. Antwerp: Fonds Mercator, 1991.

Selected Bibliography

Georges Seurat
Circus Sideshow (*Parade de cirque*)
1887–88
Oil on canvas
39 ¼ x 59 in. (99.7 x 149.9 cm)
The Metropolitan Museum of Art, New
York, Bequest of Stephen C. Clark, 1960
61.101.17

PROVENANCE

The artist, Paris (until d. 1891); his
mother, Mme Ernestine Seurat, Paris
(1891–at least 1892, and presumably until
her death in 1898); the artist's brother
and brother-in-law, Emile Seurat and
Léon Appert, Paris (until 1900; sold with
another work for Fr 1,000 through Félix
Fénéon to Bernheim-Jeune); Josse and
Gaston Bernheim-Jeune, Paris (1900–
1929; sold on January 1, 1929, for £16,097
to Reid & Lefevre and Knoedler); [Reid
& Lefevre, Glasgow and London, and
M. Knoedler and Co., New York, jointly
owned in half-shares, 1929–32; sold by
Knoedler, stock no. A610, in November
1932 for $47,000 to Clark]; Stephen C.
Clark, New York (1932–d. 1960)

EXHIBITION HISTORY

"Salon des Indépendants (4ᵉ exposition),"
Pavillon de la Ville de Paris, March
22–May 3, 1888, no. 614 (as "Parade
de cirque," marked for sale)
"Neuvième exposition annuelle des XX,"
Musée d'Art Moderne, Brussels,
February 6–March 6, 1892, no. 10
(lent by Mme Seurat)

"Salon des Indépendants (8ᵉ exposition),"
Pavillon de la Ville de Paris,
March 19–April 27 1892, no. 1084
(lent by Mme Seurat)
"Georges Seurat (1860[*sic*]–1891):
Oeuvres peintes et dessinées," Revue
Blanche, Paris, March 19–April 5,
1900, no. 32
"Georges Seurat (1859–1891)," Bern-
heim-Jeune, Paris, December 14,
1908–January 9, 1909, no. 69 (lent
by MM. J[osse]. and G[aston].
B[ernheim].-J[eune].)
"Exposition de peinture moderne,"
Bernheim-Jeune, Paris, June 14–23,
1917, no. 30
"Georges Seurat (1859–1891)," Bernheim-
Jeune, Paris, January 15–31, 1920,
no. 28
"Soirée de Paris: Exposition l'art au
théâtre, au music-hall, et au cirque,"
Théâtre de la Cigale, Paris, May 17–
June 30, 1924, no. 38 (lent by MM.
Bernheim)
"Exposition d'oeuvres des XIXe et XXe
siècles," Bernheim-Jeune, Paris, June–
July 1925, no. 116
"Trente ans d'art indépendant: 1884–
1914," Grand Palais des Champs-
Elysées, Paris, February 20–March 21,
1926, no. 3216 (lent by MM. Bernheim-Jeune et cie.)
"Peintures des écoles impressionniste et
néo-impressionniste," Lucerne (location unknown), February 1929, no. 20
[per César M. de Hauke, *Seurat et
son oeuvre*, vol. 1 (Paris: Gründ, 1961),
p. 151]
"Ten Masterpieces by Nineteenth Century French Painters," Alex. Reid &
Lefevre, Ltd., Glasgow, April 1929,
no. 8
"Ten Masterpieces by Nineteenth Century French Painters," Alex. Reid
& Lefevre, Ltd., London, June–July
1929, no. 7

"First Loan Exhibition: Cézanne,
Gauguin, Seurat, Van Gogh," The
Museum of Modern Art, New York,
November 7–December 7, 1929, no. 55
(lent by M. Knoedler and Company,
New York, London, and Paris)
"Modern French Art," Rhode Island
School of Design, Providence,
March 11–31, 1930, no. 36 (lent by
M. Knoedler & Co., New York)
"Cent ans de peinture française," Galerie
Georges Petit, Paris, June 15–30, 1930,
no. 31
"Masterpieces by Nineteenth Century
French Painters," Knoedler Galleries,
New York, October–November 1930,
no. 11
"French Art: 1200–1900," Royal Academy
of Arts, London, January 4–March 12,
1932, no. 552 (lent by Roland F.
Knoedler) [commemorative catalogue,
no. 509]
"Exhibition of Modern European Art,"
The Museum of Modern Art, New
York, October 4–25, 1933, unnum-
bered cat. (lent from a private
collection)
"French Painting from the Fifteenth
Century to the Present Day," Califor-
nia Palace of the Legion of Honor, San
Francisco, June 8–July 8, 1934, no. 148
(lent by Mr. Stephen C. Clark, New
York)
"Modern Works of Art," The Museum of
Modern Art, New York, November 20,
1934–January 20, 1935, no. 29 (lent
from a private collection)
"Twentieth Anniversary Exhibition,"
Cleveland Museum of Art, June 26–
October 4, 1936, no. 313 (lent by Mr.
Stephen C. Clark, New York)
"Art in Our Time," The Museum of Mod-
ern Art, New York, May 10–Septem-
ber 30, 1939, no. 76 (lent by Stephen
C. Clark, New York)

"Modern Masters from European and American Collections," The Museum of Modern Art, New York, January 26–March 24, 1940, no. 13 (lent by Stephen C. Clark, New York)

"Masterpieces of Art: European and American Paintings, 1500–1900," World's Fair, New York, May–October 1940, no. 366 (lent by Mr. Stephen C. Clark, New York)

"Art in Progress," The Museum of Modern Art, New York, May 24–October 15, 1944, unnumbered catalogue (lent by Stephen C. Clark)

"Paintings from the Stephen C. Clark Collection," Century Association, New York, June 6–September 28, 1946, unnumbered checklist

"Trends in European Painting, 1880–1930," Century Association, New York, February 2–March 31, 1949, no. 3 (lent by Stephen C. Clark, New York)

"Seurat, 1859–1891: Paintings and Drawings," Knoedler Galleries, New York, April 19–May 7, 1949, no. 22 (lent by Stephen C. Clark, Esq.)

"A Collector's Taste: Selections from the Collection of Mr. and Mrs. Stephen C. Clark," M. Knoedler & Co., New York, January 12–30, 1954, no. 20

"Paintings from Private Collections," The Museum of Modern Art, New York, May 31–September 5, 1955, no. 139 (lent by Stephen C. Clark)

"Paintings from Private Collections: Summer Loan Exhibition," The Metropolitan Museum of Art, New York, July 1–September 1, 1958, no. 124 (lent by Stephen C. Clark)

"Paintings from Private Collections: Summer Loan Exhibition," The Metropolitan Museum of Art, New York, July 7–September 7, 1959, no. 101 (lent by Stephen C. Clark)

"Paintings from Private Collections: Summer Loan Exhibition," The Metropolitan Museum of Art, New York, July 6–September 4, 1960, no. 112 (lent by Stephen C. Clark)

"French Paintings from the Bequest of Stephen Clark," The Metropolitan Museum of Art, New York, October 17, 1961–January 7, 1962, no catalogue

"Neo-Impressionism," Solomon R. Guggenheim Museum, New York, February 9–April 7, 1968, no. 82

"Masterpieces of Fifty Centuries," The Metropolitan Museum of Art, New York, November 15, 1970–February 15, 1971, no. 387

"Impressionism: A Centenary Exhibition," The Metropolitan Museum of Art, New York, December 12, 1974–February 10, 1975, not in catalogue

"Seurat, 1859–1891," Galeries Nationales du Grand Palais, Paris, April 9–August 12, 1991, no. 198

"Georges Seurat, 1859–1891," The Metropolitan Museum of Art, New York, September 24, 1991–January 12, 1992, no. 200

"Neo-Impressionism: The Circle of Paul Signac," The Metropolitan Museum of Art, New York, October 1–December 31, 2001, no catalogue

"Impressionist and Early Modern Paintings: The Clark Brothers Collect," Sterling and Francine Clark Art Institute, Williamstown, Mass., June 4–September 4, 2006, and The Metropolitan Museum of Art, New York, May 22–August 19, 2007, (no. 378 in the accompanying catalogue, *The Clark Brothers Collect: Impressionist and Early Modern Paintings*)